The Child

A
unique,
curious,
human being
is the child
who arrives at kindergarten.

This child's
personal background is
distinct and special,
as is the individuality
of each child.

This young learner
is active,
growing,
changing,
playing,
an explorer and a discoverer
who displays
a sense of wonder
about
the changing world.

Viewing this world
through personal experience only,
this egocentric child
is advancing through
a unique stage of development.

For this,
the young learner requires
a variety
of new experiences
in order to build
and extend concepts
about
the natural and social world.

Each child
then learns ways
of representing
the knowledge
that is being gathered.

The kindergarten child
requires an environment
that provides
warmth,
care,
guidance,
and the encouragement
necessary to nurture and sustain
growth and development
in the complex world
of childhood.

Joyce Mahy and Pam Turner

KINDERGARTEN CURRICULUM GUIDE and RESOURCE BOOK

Ministry of Education
Schools Department
Curriculum Development Branch
Parliament Buildings
Victoria, British Columbia
(Revised 1985)

Canadian Cataloguing in Publication Data
Main entry under title:
Kindergarten curriculum guide and resource book

 Cover title.
 Bibliography: p.
 ISBN 0-7726-0085-6

 1. Kindergarten - Curricula. 2. Kindergarten -
Methods and manuals. 3. Kindergartens - British
Columbia. I. British Columbia. Schools Dept.
Curriculum Development Branch.

LB1242.B7K56 1984 372'.218'09711 C84-092154-3

Contents

Preface

The 1980 Kindergarten Needs Assessment was conducted by the Learning Assessment Branch, Ministry of Education in order to gather a broad base of information on a number of topics relating to kindergarten and to identify needs as perceived by teachers, administrators, and parents. This information was then made available to the Kindergarten Curriculum Committee, which was charged with reviewing the current kindergarten program and making recommendations to the Ministry regarding necessary revisions to the curriculum.

The Kindergarten Curriculum Committee then received approval to write a new curriculum guide and revise the *Resource Book for Kindergartens* (1973). The starting point for this project was the kindergarten child. The committee studied the characteristics of children at this level to determine the many needs to be met through the kindergarten program as outlined in the curriculum guide. A philosophy was written and seven goals for the kindergarten program were identified.

Philosophically, the kindergarten curriculum continues to emphasize the need for children to learn by being actively involved with people and things in their environment. Because of their stage of development, kindergarten children continue to learn best through "hands-on" and "minds-on" experiences. A comprehensive, well-balanced program will include experiences that lead to growth and development in each of seven goal areas. While these goals are identified separately for the purpose of this document, they are inter-related; and growth in several areas may occur simultaneously, depending on the experience the child is involved in.

Two of the seven goals identified in the guide — intellectual and language development — have received greater emphasis. This should not suggest that development in these areas is more important than development in the other five goal areas. Rather, it reflects the fact that much research has been done in these areas in the years since the last guide was written, and it was the aim of the Curriculum Committee to reflect this research in the guide. The Committee recognizes that this current guide does reflect much of the good teaching practice that already occurs in classrooms all over this province.

Acknowledgments

The Ministry of Education appreciates the work and advice of the Kindergarten Curriculum Committee in preparing the *Kindergarten Curriculum Guide/Resource Book.*

Elizabeth Balla	School District No. 59 (Peace River South)
Rosemary Bradford	School District No. 4 (Windermere)
Lilian Corriveau	School District No. 3 (Kimberley)
David Greenberg	School District No. 57 (Prince George)
Joyce Mahy	School District No. 38 (Richmond)
Shirley Meister	School District No. 22 (Vernon)
Colleen Politano	School District No. 62 (Sooke)
Hannah Polowy	University of British Columbia
Nora Szaka	School District No. 65 (Cowichan)

The involvement of the following teachers who served on the Kindergarten Project Team and assisted with the writing of both documents is also appreciated.

Linda Cook	School District No. 65 (Cowichan)
Liz Gowan	School District No. 62 (Sooke)
Daphne Morris	School District No. 62 (Sooke)
Pam Turner	School District No. 70 (Alberni)

The valuable efforts of the following teachers for whom the writing of the resource book was a major responsibility are greatly appreciated.

Sheila Campbell	School District No. 38 (Richmond)
Daphne Morris	School District No. 62 (Sooke)
Colleen Politano	School District No. 62 (Sooke)
Gina Rae	School District No. 38 (Richmond)

The contribution of Janis Cleugh, Curriculum Co-ordinator, Ministry of Education, who co-ordinated the revision of the Curriculum Guide and the work of the committees, is gratefully acknowledged.

Thanks is also given to Daphne Morris, Curriculum Co-ordinator, Ministry of Education, for co-ordinating the writing of the resource book section of this document.

Thanks is also given to Gordon Thorne, publishing consultant, for his help in producing this document.

The committee would like to thank the teachers throughout the province who contributed to district projects and to Resource Books for Kindergarten. The following materials were borrowed from the Provincial Resource Centre and have been used as references.

Kindergarten Handbook, School District No. 22 (Vernon)
The Primary Development Project, School District No. 33 (Chilliwack)
Kindergarten Manual, School District No. 41 (Burnaby)
Kindergarten Resource Book, School District No. 68 (Nanaimo)
Teaching Science: A Learning Experience, School District No. 39 (Vancouver)
Nifty Nibbles: An Ideas Book for Kindergarten Snack Program, School District No. 57 (Prince George)
Kindergarten Integrated Cooking Program Developed for Special Little People, School District No. 69 (Qualicum)
Resource Book for K-1 Teachers, School District No. 43 (Coquitlam)
Kindergarten Parents' Handbook, School District No. 24 (Kamloops)
Making The Most of Your Child's Skills and Abilities, School District No. 31 (Merritt)
. . . and Soon, I'll Go to School, School District No. 38 (Richmond)
Kindergarten Handbook for Parents, School District No. 45 (West Vancouver)
Stepping Into Kindergarten, School District No. 68 (Nanaimo)

The Committee would also like to thank David Greenberg of School District No. 57 for the photographs reproduced in this book.

Introduction

This *Kindergarten Curriculum Guide and Resource Book* presents you, the kindergarten teacher, not only with a detailed explanation of the new curriculum but also with a number of practical suggestions for translating this new curriculum into valuable classroom activities and experiences. There are two main sections to this book.

- PART I: *The Kindergarten Curriculum Guide* outlines the theoretical basis upon which this book rests, and it is most important that you familiarize yourself with its contents prior to making use of the resource book. The statement of philosophy given in this section's introduction encompasses the whole of the kindergarten experience, and the curriculum goals, which are explained at length under the heading "The Kindergarten Curriculum," define areas of growth and development that are enhanced and extended through the kindergarten experience. As much of the current research into early childhood education is reflected in the description of these goals, a number of quotations are given in the right-hand margins: These not only support the text but can also lead you to relevant sources of further information. The material presented under the heading "Children and the Curriculum" examines how children at this stage of development learn best, and it stresses the importance of creating an environment that facilitates active learning in all of the goal areas. The integration of exceptional children into the kindergarten is explored in this section as well; and finally, an examination of the purposes of evaluation, and of appropriate methods for evaluating both children and the program, is presented.

- PART II: *The Kindergarten Resource Book* contains a wide variety of recommendations, teaching suggestions, activities, and resources, all of which can help you to implement the new curriculum in ways that are suited to your individual approach and your teaching situation. Model strategies for using learning centres and content themes are presented along with sample activities based on the curriculum goals; and in addition, the resource book offers numerous suggestions for evaluating and communicating, for orienting the child to kindergarten, and for working with parents. Suggestions for equipment, materials, and supplies are included as guidelines for schools. And a bibliography of children's books, organized in two ways — around the curriculum goals and around suggested content themes — provides a starting point that should assist you in planning themes or units as well as in ordering books. Finally, a selected bibliography of professional references, ones that can further your own reading of current research into early childhood education, is provided.

The organization of both sections of the book is based on the seven curriculum goals outlined in the introduction to Part I. It is hoped that this organization will help you use this book as an "open document" that allows easy cross reference between the material in the curriculum guide and the material presented in the "Themes" and "Sample Activities" sections of the resource book. The ideas and activities presented in these parts of the book can be combined in ways that help you not only to plan your kindergarten experiences but also to employ your own ideas, activities, strategies, and resources in ways that implement the new curriculum. To this end, this book has been designed so as to provide a large amount of blank space for your own notes.

PART 1 : THE KINDERGARTEN CURRICULUM GUIDE

Introduction

Philosophy

Kindergarten contributes to the continuing growth of young children's knowledge and understanding of themselves and their world. This experience helps create awareness and appreciation of the changing world and helps foster positive personal and social attitudes in young children. In the kindergarten, opportunities for the development of aesthetic sensitivity and healthful living habits are provided. Through social interaction and participation in activities suited to their needs, children sustain and enhance their language and thought processes as learning is continually integrated and extended through play. In this stimulating, secure, and responsive environment, children experience the joy of learning as they live their childhood.

Goals

The goals of the kindergarten curriculum are
- to provide a variety of experiences that foster the child's emotional development and well-being;
- to provide a variety of experiences that foster the child's social development;
- to provide a variety of experiences that foster the development of the child's social responsibility in a changing world;
- to provide a variety of experiences that foster the child's physical development and well-being;
- to provide a variety of experiences that foster the child's aesthetic and artistic development;
- to provide a variety of experiences that foster the child's intellectual development;
- to provide a variety of experiences that foster the child's language development.

The following chapters in this section describe the kindergarten curriculum in terms of each of these seven goals.

Emotional Development and Well-Being

If facts are seeds that later produce knowledge and wisdom, then the emotions and impressions of the senses are the fertile soil in which seeds must grow.

RACHAEL CARSON, *The Sense of Wonder*

Emotional well-being and total well-being are so closely linked that efforts to help the child develop a healthy mental attitude are essential to the development of life skills and positive interpersonal relationships. The way people view themselves determines the way they feel, think, and learn. The child needs to develop positive feelings of self-worth to enhance living and learning. Experiences should be provided that help the child learn to
- develop a positive, realistic self-concept;
- accept and express emotions in socially acceptable ways;
- accept and demonstrate empathy;
- accept challenge;
- feel pride in accomplishment;
- develop independence;
- enjoy living and learning.

Developing a Positive, Realistic Self-Concept

Consideration for the emotional development of children is important not only in ensuring that their self-concept is positive and realistic but also in ensuring that they are able to develop cognitively. Children who are confident of themselves and are secure in their environment are ready for new learning. Successful learning, in turn, enhances self-esteem.

Children with self-esteem are more enthusiastic, more willing to accept challenges, and more able to concentrate and to persevere. Supportive teachers foster the natural development of self-esteem as children attempt to explore and master their own goals.

Accepting and Expressing Emotions in Socially Acceptable Ways

Children need to observe model behavior that fosters the development of interpersonal skills. Every day offers opportunities for them to deal with, and gain competence in, living with other people. Talking about problems, fears, and concerns leads children to the understanding that emotions are common to all people. The teacher's task is to help children realize that all emotions are acceptable but that some reactions to these emotions are unacceptable. Awareness of how to deal with and express emotions in a socially acceptable manner leads children to function independently and in co-operation with others. Within the safety of the kindergarten environment, children can experience the natural consequences of their actions without loss of self-worth.

Accepting and Demonstrating Empathy

Kindergarten teachers provide a model and facilitate emotional development when they use patience and perceptiveness to understand the personal point of view (egocentrism) of each child. While they can often describe their own points of view,

Characteristics of the Child
- needs to feel important
- dependent on adult
- egocentric
- sensitive
- unique

The fundamental step in helping a child feel worthwhile . . . is to believe in the intrinsic worth of all children, to believe they can grow as basic human beings. Believing in children is a powerful medicine that can work wonders.

E. L. WIDMER
The Critical Years:
Early Childhood Education at the Crossroads

Unless one loves others one cannot love self, and if one does not love self one cannot love others.

ERIC FROMME
The Art of Loving

Emotional Development and Well-Being

kindergarten children often have difficulty in understanding the points of view of their peers or teacher. When children are secure and trust the teacher, dialogue helps them accept decisions even if they cannot understand them. Egocentrism is a personal struggle towards sociocentrism.

As children receive empathy from their teacher and peers, they begin to view themselves as worthwhile members of the kindergarten society and are more likely to express empathy toward others. Children possessing a sense of self-worth, then, are capable of showing a sensitivity to others while maintaining their unique identities.

Accepting Challenge

When children are encouraged to think divergently, to express different ideas, and to experiment, they develop a belief in their own abilities. Feeling secure in the classroom serves to increase their knowledge of themselves as unique and competent people.

Personal stress that is related to insecurity may cause children to revert to easier, less challenging tasks rather than risk failure. Repetition and familiarity are comforting security aides. Some children may react by withdrawing into themselves or by resorting to physical aggression.

Emotionally secure children have the confidence to be curious and creative, to accept challenges, and to take appropriate risks.

Feeling Pride in Accomplishment

Pride in one's own accomplishments is an intrinsic feeling. Children who have learned that their attempts will be accepted and encouraged will be more likely to try. Praise may lead to tentative feelings of success but may leave children still seeking other's opinions to judge their own success. Ongoing encouragement that focuses the children's attention on the importance of valuing their own attempts helps them develop personal pride. Children who can view their work and say, "I did it, I tried my best, and I like it" do not need an adult to say, "It is good."

Developing Independence

Growth of independence can only occur when children are aware of available support and are willing to seek that support when needed. Dependence involving the healthy seeking of emotional support from others and the benefits of having trusting relationships with adults or other children is linked closely with confidence in one's self. Experience, practice, and role-playing are the basis for developing independence.

Emotional independence enables the child to internalize external expectations and to behave independently with pride of achievement.

M. A. LUCAS
"One Way of Organizing a Centre for Young Children"

Enjoying Living and Learning

By treating children with respect, warmth, good humor, and dignity, the teacher helps them to become strong emotionally. It is this emotional strength that is the key to being able to learn and find enjoyment and appreciation in the world.

If a child lives with acceptance and friendship, he or she learns to find love in the world.

DOROTHY LAW NOLTE

Emotional Development and Well-Being

Social Development

As people become more sensitive to others' feelings and more willing to co-operate for the collective good, our planet will become a much healthier and happier place to live, for all of us. Moves in this direction are absolutely essential to ensure a decent quality of life, and to ensure life itself.

TERRY ORLICK, *Winning Through Co-operation*

In order to live, work, and learn in the kindergarten and in later life, children need to develop those responses that will result in positive social interaction. Silvern (1981) refers to this process as developing "social cognition." While children will not necessarily be consistent in their behavior, they will be learning to be sociable and will be developing behavior for appropriate social interaction. Experiences should be provided that help the child to

- share;
- co-operate;
- respect and accept others;
- learn from others;
- seek and give companionship;
- anticipate consequences of actions.

Sharing

Children are always learning how to function as part of a social network. Their social behavior is restricted by their limits in vocabulary, language competence, and problem-solving strategies. Through observation and interaction with the children, the teacher models and introduces socially appropriate skills and behavior.

Co-operating

Being part of a group, planning activities, and making choices, necessitates the acquisition of the ability to co-operate. Awareness of the stages of play relevant to individual children will enable the teacher to set reasonable expectations for levels of co-operation. These expectations will be adjusted as children develop and move towards co-operation.

Respecting and Accepting Others

Just as children learn to share and co-operate with others, the respect for and acceptance of others is learned behavior. By accepting and showing respect for the children and their parents, the teacher demonstrates that all people are worthy of being treated with dignity. Such action will have a positive impact on the tone of the kindergarten. An environment where individual integrity and differing values are respected provides the setting in which children practise and develop awareness and understanding.

Learning From Others

It is recognized that social learning is important not only for intrinsic reasons but also as a critical factor in cognitive development. Acquiring appropriate social

Characteristics of the Child

- talkative
- friendly
- resolves conflict with action and words
- models behavior of others
- socially egocentric
- likes to please
- learning to co-operate with others
- beginning to play with others

Sharing is not innate; it is learned within the context of social interaction.

M. LAY and T. DOPYERA
Becoming a Teacher of Young Children

According to Piaget (1954), there are no cognitive mechanisms that are without affective elements and there is no affective state that has no cognitive element. The relationship be-

attitudes will enhance learning by increasing the possibility of interaction with and learning from others. Young children are characteristically egocentric in a social sense. They are often unaware that others also view the world from a personal perspective and that this viewpoint may differ from their own. When children are able to see that others may not share their opinions, they must then defend their ideas, justify their opinions, clarify their thoughts, and solve their own problems. Understanding and expression becomes more clear and logical.

In the social setting, much learning takes place as a result of the child's natural desire to model peers and adults. In the kindergarten classroom the child's behavior is strongly influenced by that of the teacher. The child engaged in dramatic play is not simply copying or imitating. He or she repeats an experience, utilizing specific knowledge and integrating previous observations in such a way that the task or role may be "played out" smoothly. Internal motivation and external reinforcement for interacting in socially acceptable ways results in the development of positive social skills.

Seeking and Giving Companionship

The kindergarten where children are encouraged to learn from others and to seek and give companionship offers the emotional security that makes it possible for children to interact. Learning how to make and maintain friendships is part of the social learning that should take place in the kindergarten.

Anticipating Consequences of Actions

By encouraging children to interact, use language, and solve problems, the teacher can guide children to take responsibility for their actions. Acting with forethought can be learned within the social framework of the kindergarten. Assisting children to use language to recreate and evaluate situations and to arrive at workable solutions should lead to the development of individuals who can plan and accept responsibility for their actions.

tween cognition and affectivity for him is that the latter provides the energy that makes intelligence function.

CONSTANCE KAMII
"A Sketch of the
Piaget-Derived Preschool
Curriculum Developed by
the Ypsilanti Early
Education Program"

If learning is believed to be an internally mediated process that learners can influence through their effort and hard work, the consequences for the students go beyond the mastery of subject matter to include possibly the development of a sense of self-control over one's destiny and a sense of personal responsibility for one's behavior.

M. C. WHITTROCK
"The Cognitive Movement
in Education"

Social Development

Social Responsibility

Living in harmony with other human beings may be one of the outstanding challenges for the whole human race.

VERNA HILDEBRAND, *Guiding Young Children*

The way people view the world is directly related to the early development of their attitudes and values. The child needs to develop the awareness and behavior of a socially responsible person. Experiences should be provided that help the child learn to
- develop friendships;
- participate in groups;
- become a responsible citizen;
- cope with change;
- appreciate cultural identity and heritage;
- respect cultural similarities and differences;
- respect the environment.

Social responsibility is learned through appropriate experiences beginning at a very early age. Children must be helped not only to live comfortably with themselves and others but to move beyond the personal level toward the ability to appreciate social problems and contribute co-operatively to the solutions.

Developing Friendships

The ability to form friendships is the basis of all human relationships. A friend recognizes and respects another person's point of view, values, thoughts, and feelings. The capacity to form friendships begins with one's own sense of security or well-being and allows one to move from the self toward the other person. The capacity to form friendships provides the child with the appropriate behavior patterns that apply to becoming a member of the larger kindergarten group.

Since most kindergarten children are at the egocentric stage of development, the teacher's skillful guidance will aid the young child toward awareness and acceptance of other children's points of view.

Participating in Groups

As the kindergarten child develops positive feelings of self-worth, and as participation in group activities is encouraged, an increasing sense of security as a group member will also develop. The child must become aware of appropriate group behavior such as the need to take turns, to share, to contribute meaningful thoughts or actions, to follow group direction and ideas, and to be sensitive to the needs and feelings of others. Group members must also learn when to lead or follow. Much of this behavior can be modelled by the teacher.

Becoming a Responsible Citizen

Children learn responsibility from modelling by adults and from practice in a variety of situations. Kindergarten can stimulate and reinforce behavior that creates responsible citizens by consciously drawing the child's attention to good models of behavior every day of the kindergarten year.

Characteristics of the Child

- social
- friendly
- sensitive and co-operative
- willing to help
- impressionable
- enjoys learning about the world and people
- comes from unique background and culture

Children's orientation to the social world, which begins with their earliest friendships, must be considered as part of any efforts to integrate multicultural education into the curriculum. Efforts to expand children's awareness of others, their capacity to communicate, their willingness and ability to co-operate, and their sense of social responsibility should be emphasized throughout their lives.

P. G. RAMSAY
"Multicultural Education in Early Childhood"

All good human relations are based on the inner security of the persons involved . . . We cannot value others unless we value ourselves; we cannot like others unless we like ourselves; we cannot respect others unless we respect ourselves . . . We must feel secure and adequate if we are to reach out to others.

L. S. KENWORTHY
"Accepting the Selves of Others: People Around the World"

The behavior that encourages the growth of responsibility can be learned from teacher guidance of children's involvement in daily social interaction. Natural occurrences such as conflicts between individuals can be used to teach possible ways of behaving. Instead of separating the children or settling the dispute, the teacher can guide the children to a solution of their own making. Social awareness and appropriate communication skills lead to the development of social responsibility through co-operation. The anticipation of problems that might arise during the day can also be discussed with the whole group to stimulate and create problem-solving solutions.

Coping with Change

Change occurs constantly throughout one's lifetime. Change can be gradual, sudden, pleasant, or harsh, and it may only become apparent in retrospect. Change is a healthy facet of life, and stimulates the mind and body. In kindergarten the young child can be helped to learn how to cope with change. The child is growing intellectually, socially, emotionally, and physically through personal changes.

Changes in the environment lead the child to adapt to new situations such as a change in daily routine, a substitute teacher, or a new pet. The child must understand that some events, such as the loss of teeth, occur naturally, and that some events, such as moving, are caused by people. Some of these events, such as learning to swim during swim classes, can be anticipated. It is more difficult for the child to prepare for and cope with unexpected changes. Concrete changes that directly affect a young child are the changes that can be dealt with most effectively in kindergarten because the results will be most apparent in the daily life of the child.

A child may not always have knowledge of a specific change but will respond to the emotions and stresses surrounding the change. Since the young child is egocentric, he or she views the change as a result of an action that he or she caused, or blames someone else for causing the change. The emotions of the child should never be underestimated or ignored. These strong feelings need to be recognized and accepted as prerequisites to the child's developing appropriate coping strategies.

Change evokes a variety of emotional responses. While the emotions themselves may be acceptable, the behavior that results from these feelings often needs to be dealt with. Teachers can guide children toward developing their own strategies for coping with change by discussing real-life situations with them. Children who trust their ability to cope with change have a sense of being able to control changes and are therefore more likely to react in a positive manner towards change.

Appreciating Cultural Identity and Heritage

Cultural identity is a basic human need which is developed through learning. To foster a healthy, mature attitude towards cultural identity and heritage, it is important to start in the early years. As kindergarten children learn to value themselves and form friendships, they develop the attitudes and skills that allow them to belong to and function in a group or community such as the classroom. This learning provides the basis for further knowledge, understanding, and appreciation of one's history and cultural identity.

It is necessary for the teacher to provide activities that will help children incorporate into their own framework images and experiences that foster healthy development of cultural identity. Through studying the children and their families in a group, much can be learned about family customs, physical characteristics, and history.

Children should be encouraged to develop a group consciousness and pride without feelings of superiority. Children will learn to value their roots, know their cultural history, and use the strength that comes from a shared pride and feeling of group worth to become contributing, co-operative members of our global community.

Respecting Cultural Similarities and Differences

For people throughout the world to live in dignity and at peace with one another requires an understanding of our shared interdependence. As children learn about themselves and their culture, they recognize that people share many of the same feelings and needs and yet express them in different ways.

As children learn about each other, they will note differences in appearances, customs, and habits, but more importantly (and this must be emphasized) they will learn about the similarities between people. They will note that there are many ways of handling tasks and that their own way is simply one of many and is not necessarily the best. Children need help to become aware of, and develop respect for, this diversity, which gives richness to society and reflects the creative and adaptive nature of people.

In order for children to grow up to respect other people and their cultures, we need to help them move from their egocentric view of the world towards becoming aware and tolerant of different points of view. It is this tolerance for and acceptance of differing opinions, feelings, and points of view that allows people to get along with each other and to co-operate at a local as well as a world level.

Children's concepts about other groups are based on their perceptions of their own group. If they are made to feel superior, then other groups will be viewed as inferior. Therefore, it is important that teachers help children to view their own groups realistically. Children can only assimilate new learning that can be related to their own experiences and previous knowledge.

It is important to foster an accepting, tolerant, and flexible attitude towards other individuals and groups in the classroom, in the community, and in world settings. Multicultural education can be incorporated into well-planned activities that embrace many other areas of learning. For example, at snack time foods from different ethnic groups can be used. The teacher must be aware of children's backgrounds and experiences and must use this knowledge in planning meaningful activities. We need to help children develop a global point of view as they look towards the future.

When developing a focus on a particular group of people, it is important that the people, not the stereotypes or exotic differences, are studied.

P. G. RAMSAY
"Multicultural Education in Early Childhood"

Respecting the Environment

Developing a respect for the natural and built environment requires the child to be knowledgeable about, responsible for, and understanding of human impact on the environment. By learning about the social, physical, and biological worlds, the child begins to realize the balance between man and the environment. The child's awareness level can be raised by focusing his or her attention on the reasons for respecting our environment. Utilizing everyday events as they occur will provide relevant teaching material and meaningful interactions from which the child can develop attitudes and behavior that reflect environmental respect.

Education should provide each learner with knowledge and understanding of the social, physical, and biological worlds and the balance between man and his environment and should develop attitudes and behavior leading to intelligent use of the environment.

MASSACHUSETTS BOARD
OF EDUCATION
"Coming to Our Senses"

Physical Development and Well-Being

Play and recreation activities are major contributors to the physical, social, emotional and intellectual development of children. In fact, it is seen to be as important to their growth and development as are the basic needs of nutrition, health, shelter and education.

SUZING HUM, *Play and Recreation*

Physical well-being contributes to effective living and learning. The child needs to develop healthful living habits. Experiences should be provided that help the child to
- take care of and respect his or her body;
- learn and practise safety procedures;
- be aware of and practise good nutrition habits;
- develop physical fitness and movement skills.

The kindergarten child is naturally curious, active, and interested in learning about the body and its relationship to the environment. In order to plan a balanced program, the teacher provides opportunities for a variety of experiences and a balance between the nature of those experiences. The kinds of activities, the size of groups, and location are factors that can influence the variety and scope of the program.

Taking Care of and Respecting One's Body

As well as physical activity, children need experiences that extend their knowledge of how to lead healthy lives. As opportunities arise, the teacher provides information and experiences that facilitate learning about nutrition, safety, and care of the body. By their example, teachers provide models that reinforce the importance of looking after oneself. Personal habits and attitudes established in early childhood provide a foundation for healthful living.

Learning and Practising Safety Procedures

Focusing on safety is essential in all aspects of the kindergarten program. The teacher ensures that the environment is safe and involves children in preserving that safety. The teacher provides a model of behavior and establishes conditions that should lead children to become aware of the basic necessities for safety. By giving children opportunities to be active in maintaining a safe environment for themselves and others, we help the child to become an independent, responsible person.

Being Aware of and Practising Good Nutrition Habits

Information regarding the importance of good nutrition as well as frequent experiences with a variety of foods from the four food groups will enable the child to make wise food selections. Experiences with food should help the child to understand that optimum growth and development, as well as efficient body functioning, are dependent on good nutrition habits. In addition, food is a motivating factor around which many other kinds of learning can occur.

Characteristics of the Child
- physically active
- unique
- industrious
- involves whole body in activities
- energetic but tires easily
- large muscles more co-ordinated than fine muscles
- all muscles still developing

The health and safety of children should be paramount considerations . . . We help children, learn, understand, and observe cautions as sensible behavior.

BESS HOLT and GENE HOLT
Science With Young Children

Good nutrition is a prerequisite to normal physical, mental, social and emotional growth and development of man.

E. L. WIDMER
*The Critical Years:
Early Childhood Education
at the Crossroads*

Physical Development and Well-Being

Involving children in the preparation of food on a regular basis provides opportunities for expanding cultural awareness and social, physical, and logical knowledge, and for integrating appropriate art and music activities. The discussion and subsequent recording of recipes or sequences followed when preparing food can contribute to the child's total language development.

Traditionally, a snack time has been a part of many kindergarten programs. The teacher can use this time to promote knowledge of nutrition and to further the development of concepts introduced at the food centre.

Developing Physical Fitness

Kindergarten children are physically active and energetic. The teacher capitalizes on these natural characteristics to assist the children in developing and maintaining physical fitness. By planning a variety of activities that stem from the child's need to play, move, and explore, the teacher can provide for the development of cardiovascular endurance, muscular endurance, strength, and flexibility.

Opportunities should be provided for the children to participate in activities that promote fitness and increase awareness and knowledge of the need for fitness.

Experiences that help the child to develop muscle control, co-ordination, and body-awareness should also be provided. Activities that allow children to use both functional and expressive movements should be incorporated. Such activities may include dance, drama, creative involvement, and simple gymnastics as well as simple, non-competitive games.

Knowledge of child development helps the teacher to plan suitable activities designed to encourage the child to explore and practise natural body movements. Movement experiences help the child to develop muscle control, co-ordination, body awareness, space awareness, and physical fitness. Challenges can be set to encourage the development and progression of skills. Assisting children to recognize their own potential in the security of a non-competitive environment and helping children to recognize growth and improvements should lead children to the development of a sense of personal competence.

Movement means many things to children . . . (1) life; (2) self-discovery; (3) environmental discovery, both physical and social; (4) freedom, both spatial and self-expressive; (5) safety; (6) enjoyment and sensuous pleasure; (7) acceptance.

G. ENGSTROM
The Significance of the Young Child's Motor Development

Setting attainable challenges allows children to learn to compete "with" themselves and their environment rather than "against" other people.

MOIRA LUKE

Physical Development and Well-Being

Aesthetic and Artistic Development

If I could tell you what I mean, there would be no point in dancing.

ISADORA DUNCAN, *Coming to Our Senses*

People's lives are enriched by their capacity to respond to sensory stimuli. In order for the child to develop sensitivity to these stimuli, experiences should be provided that help the child to
- develop sensory awareness;
- imagine and visualize;
- explore;
- create;
- respond;
- interpret;
- develop critical awareness;
- express and represent through a variety of forms.

Aesthetic development continues throughout the life of an individual, the degree of development varying with the child's experience with the arts. For children to become sensitive and appreciative, their involvement with art, music, drama, movement, dance, poetry, and literature must begin as early as possible and must continue throughout their education.

Reflecting on and discussing sensory experiences is important because in this way children learn to make sense of the experiences in relation to themselves, and to value the arts in meaningful ways. Hearing the views and feelings of others helps them begin to gain an understanding of and respect for attitudes and values that are different from their own, and this aids in their social and emotional development.

In addition, involvement with music, art, and drama has a positive effect on learning in other areas; in fact, cognitive learnings in kindergarten can be presented through and enhanced by experiences with a variety of art forms. Concepts can be extended and represented, and thought processes and language can be developed, through involvement with the arts.

Developing Sensory Awareness

The development of sensory awareness helps children learn about the people, objects, and events that surround them, and about themselves in relation to the environment. By listening, looking, smelling, tasting, and touching, children begin to interpret the world and to build understanding of it.

In order to develop fully, kindergarten children require a large and varied repertoire of sensory experiences.

Imagining and Visualizing

Children need to be encouraged to use and expand their natural ability to create mental images and to engage in make-believe. Picture making encourages visual representation of mental images as well as reality; dramatizing situations and experimenting with different roles is another way the child responds to and tests

---

Characteristics of the Child
- natural explorer, creator, inventor
- manipulates
- enjoys rhythm and movement
- sense of wonder
- uses all the senses
- responsive
- enthusiastic
- vivid imagination
- inquiring

Creativity cannot be imposed but must come from the child.

VICTOR LOWENFELD and
LAMBERT W. BRITTAIN
Creative and Mental Growth

Children make their greatest progress when they are curious about their environment. Questions of "why" need to be motivated so that the learner is fulfilling a personal need to find answers rather than having information that may or may not seem relevant imposed upon him.

BARBARA ANDRESS
*Music Experiences
in Early Childhood*

We learn through our senses. The ability to see, feel, hear, smell and taste provides the contact between us and the environment . . . The greater the opportunity to develop an increased sensitivity and the greater the awareness of all the senses, the greater will be the opportunity for learning.

VICTOR LOWENFELD and
LAMBERT W. BRITTAIN
Creative and Mental Growth

A person needs to think in terms of images as well as words.

L. LASKY and R. MUKERJI
Art: Basic for Young Children

---

mental images; moving in certain ways (i.e., like a cat or frog) stimulates movement in response to mental images; listening to stories causes the child to create mental images from the verbal stimuli. Recalling sensory experiences aids memory development and increases the ability to discuss mental images. In order to develop in this area, children require guidance and encouragement from the teacher.

Exploring

Children need to explore for themselves. Their inquiring minds will be stimulated and they will gain self-confidence as they make discoveries about their environment in an accepting atmosphere.

Children need time to experiment and to learn the possibilities, techniques, and skills involved in media and materials. Allowing time to explore is conducive to creating a secure environment in which children can try strategies, solve problems, and use materials in different ways.

Children must be provided with experiences that encourage them to explore with all their senses. They require a wide variety of activities that allow them opportunities to explore different art forms and thus to build up a repertoire of ways of expressing their reactions and feelings. Providing children with opportunities to be participants in and observers of dance, music, drama, and art encourages them to develop suitable modes of expression.

Creating

The degree of inate creativity varies from child to child, but in an encouraging environment this creativity can be developed to its highest potential. Children must be encouraged to use their own instincts in creating things without fear of being considered non-conformist. An atmosphere of acceptance gives them the chance to try things for themselves, to use their imagination and intuition, and to judge their own degree of success. As children represent knowledge by creating through a variety of media, the teacher gains insight into their ongoing growth and development.

Responding

Aesthetic response develops after an individual has had opportunities to be actively involved with a variety of art forms and can then react to and discuss the experiences. Only after active involvement does a child begin to understand the subject, make judgements, and form preferences. Gradually the child begins to form a concept of what is personally aesthetically pleasing.

One's response to art forms is often emotional, and children need to be helped to understand that their emotions, and those of others, can have parallels in artistic expression. Children need to be helped to understand that the art itself not only expresses feeling but also awakens feeling in the listener or observer.

Creativity is the ability to see new relationships between previously unrelated objects or ideas, to push boundaries beyond present knowledge, and to organize ideas aesthetically. Originality in action or thought is creativity . . . From a very practical point of view, it is extremely important that a person's creativity be fostered to its fullest extent.

LAMBERT W. BRITTAIN
Creativity, Art, and the Young Child

Aesthetic and Artistic Development

Interpreting

Children make sense of their environment and experiences in relation to themselves. Through their involvement in the arts, they are learning to express their feelings and are beginning to interpret the feelings expressed by others. Whether children are dancing, painting, modelling, singing, moving to music, or acting, they are communicating their interpretation of a stimulus or idea and thus are learning more about their own feelings and emotions. The interpretation children put on an experience is entirely personal and is influenced by the knowledge and background they bring to that experience. Teachers should be prepared to accept each child's response and should continue to help the child grow in this area.

Developing Critical Awareness

At this stage of a child's development, his or her judgement and preferences are very personal and definite and may change from day to day. Discussing the arts is essential in enabling children to verbalize experiences and make them meaningful. This discussion should also attempt to elicit some statements of reasoned judgement and preference.

When children have opportunities to make their own expressive statements, they learn to become critically responsive to the work of others. In seeing the world, creating images of this view, and expressing reactions through a variety of media, the child becomes atuned to his or her own art and to the art of others. In becoming aware of the natural and built environment, children can draw relationships between the arts and the rest of their world.

Expressing and Representing Through a Variety of Forms

As children sense the world around them and creatively express their reactions and responses to others, they are developing a variety of ways of representing what they know. A multitude of media, supplied with encouragement, guidance, stimulation, and freedom to explore opens up many avenues of expression and allows children to make statements that are personally relevant. Through the arts children can send important non-verbal messages from a creator or performer to a listener or observer. The arts are ideal vehicles for training the senses, enriching the emotional self, and organizing the environment. For young children, expression through the arts is especially important because they may not yet be able to verbalize their ideas fully.

To organize and substantiate thoughts and feelings is a fundamental human need. An important way of formulating and expressing ideas, feelings, and images is through the arts. By working with a variety of media, children can formulate, clarify, represent, and share their ideas.

The symbols of the arts allow us to represent our emotions, feelings, and knowledge. By creating visual, oral, and aural symbols (representation), the child organizes experience in order to clarify thinking and to communicate thoughts to others.

Dialogue enables teachers to better understand, and to make more accurate judgements about, the aesthetic development of each child.

Learning about oneself is intertwined with learning about the world of people, objects, and events. Such learning mainly takes place through the processes of sensory awareness, perceptual awareness, association, and generalization. The expressive arts help in these processes of cognitive learning about the world.

L. LASKY and R. MUKERJI
Art: Basic for Young Children

Representation—the creation of symbols—is the means by which the human being organizes his experience in order to understand or communicate it; language is one way of representing or symbolizing the world; math is another; science another—and the imagery of art is still another.

RICHARD MATHER
New England's First Fruits

Art is a personal and satisfying activity at any age, for although the arts are responsible for a greater awareness of the external world, it is also the arts that give vent to the emotions, the joys and fears of life.

VICTOR LOWENFELD and
LAMBERT W. BRITTAIN
Creative and Mental Growth

Aesthetic and Artistic Development

Intellectual Development

If intelligence develops as a whole by the child's own construction, then what makes this construction possible is the child's curiosity, interest, alertness, desire to communicate and exchange points of view, and a desire to make sense of it all.

CONSTANCE KAMII, "One Intelligence Indivisible"

It is people's ability to assimilate and use knowledge in an independent and creative manner that enables them to influence the quality of their lives and the future of their world. The child needs to develop strategies for acquiring and using knowledge. Experiences should be provided that help the child to

- sustain and extend natural curiosity;
- develop thinking processes (observing, recalling, comparing, patterning, classifying, predicting, generalizing);
- develop the ability to identify, solve, and anticipate problems;
- develop physical knowledge (physical properties of the world);
- develop social knowledge (customs, institutions);
- develop logical knowledge (classification, patterning, seriation, number, space, time);
- represent knowledge.

Intellectual development is the process of acquiring, structuring, and restructuring knowledge. The knowledge that a child brings to a situation is actively constructed from previous interactions with the environment.

The process starts with a structure or a way of thinking characteristic of one's level. Some external disturbances or intrusions (experience) on this ordinary way of thinking create a conflict and disequilibrium, and the child compensates for the disturbance and solves the conflict through intellectual activity. The final state is a new way of thinking and structuring things, a way that gives new understanding, satisfaction, and equilibrium.

The child only makes sense of the world to the extent that there is interaction and change, and this is achieved by co-ordination of both mental and physical action.

Stages of Children's Thinking

The order in which children pass through these developmental stages does not vary, but the rate at which children pass through the stages does vary from child to child. Some children reach the later stages at an earlier age than average while some linger in the early stages for a longer time.

Being in constant transition from one stage to the next, children respond in ways characteristic of more than one stage. Kindergarten children, for the most part, are in the latter period of the preoperational stage. Kindergarten experiences are designed to enhance the intelligent functioning of the preoperational mind.

These experiences enable children to function intelligently as they move through the developmental stages into adolescence. Kindergarten experiences assist the child in developing concepts and skills that are the foundation for future learning in later schooling.

Characteristics of the Child

- curious, seeking human being
- natural explorer and inventor
- mentally active and inquiring
- thinking tied to first-hand experiences with concrete material
- applies former experiences to new learning
- memory associated with experience and action
- perceives simple cause and effect relationships by association when actively involved
- becoming a conserver
- reversal of thought becoming evident
- focuses on part or whole but not both at same time
- judges on appearance rather than logic
- egocentric
- development of symbolic forms and other methods of representation are becoming evident

Piaget's Stages of Children's Thinking*

Age	Stage
0-2	Sensory-Motor
	• co-ordination of physical actions
2-7	Preoperational
	• represents thoughts through actions and language
7-11	Concrete Operational
	• logical thinking tied to real experiences
11-15	Formal Operational
	• logical, abstract thinking

** from E. LABINOWICZ
The Piaget Primer:
Thinking, Learning, Teaching*

Influences on Intellectual Development

No single factor can by itself account for intellectual development. It is a combination of the following factors and the interaction between them that influences this development. When planning experiences that will enhance intellectual development, the teacher must take all of these factors into consideration.

Factor	Characteristics
maturation	physical maturing, especially of the central nervous system
experiences	handling, moving, thinking about concrete objects and events
social interaction	playing, talking, working with other children/adults
environment	home, community, school
equilibration	the process of bringing maturation, experience, and social interaction together so as to build and rebuild mental structures

Characteristics of Preoperational Thinking

Children think differently than adults. Experiences, then, must be appropriate for their way of thinking. The child's ability to think logically is marked by inflexibility. Included in the limitations of this stage are
- the inability to reverse physical actions mentally (irreversibility);
- the inability to hold changes in two dimensions at the same time mentally (centration);
- the inability to consider another's viewpoint (egocentrism).

These limitations will begin to diminish during the latter part of this stage and as the child enters into the concrete operational stage. Since each child's pattern of development is unique, the progression is individual. During this stage
- the child is learning to conserve;
- the child's point of view is changing;
- the child perceives parts or wholes but not parts in relation to wholes;
- the child still relies on appearance rather than logic;
- the child judges quantity on the basis of space taken by objects and judges length on the basis of how far one end protrudes.

Until the child is able to organize and classify information into easily remembered categories, memory is largely associative and is linked with a particular experience or action. During this period
- the child is experiencing, distinguishing, and describing differences and similarities by color, shape, function, and number;
- the child is seeing relation between objects and is making comparisons;
- the child is beginning to show some understanding of cause and effect;
- the child is beginning to develop concepts of space and time, but has difficulty with sequence;
- the child is showing increasing awareness of symmetry and scale;
- the child is attempting to describe past events.

If children are excited, curious, resourceful, confident about their ability to figure things out and eager to exchange opinions with other children and adults, they are bound to go on learning, particularly when they are out of the classroom and throughout the rest of their lives.

CONSTANCE KAMII
"One Intelligence
Indivisible"

Providing for Intellectual Development in the Kindergarten

First-Hand Experiences

The teacher provides for first-hand experiences for the child which include both "hands on" and "minds on" activity. Children's manipulation of objects is critical to their development of logical thinking during the eleven or so years prior to entry into the formal operational stage. The more meaningful and varied the child's encounters with the real world are in his or her early years, the stronger the foundations for logical thinking and the receptivity of instruction will be.

Content must be presented in ways that children can assimilate in accordance with their stage of development. A child's lack of understanding may be due to having been presented with too much too soon. Children's inability to follow spoken or written directions is not always due to inattention or poor memory. They see and hear what they understand.

Teachers provide experiences that encourage the child to develop intellectual development, as in the following chart.

Do	Observe	Think	Interact	Communicate
experience	identify	judge	state needs	talk
touch	define	equivalence	state wants	wonder
explore	label	compare	justify	question
investigate	describe	estimate	play	inquire
experiment	count	develop	monitor	gain
test	note	concept of	direct	information
discover	similarities	space	collaborate	interpret
follow	note	develop	create	central
directions	differences	concept of	imagine	meaning
seek	remember	time	project	criticize
plan	explain	classify	model	evaluate
focus	generalize	seriate	imitate	clarify
attend	analyse	pattern	represent	anticipate
select	understand	note		predict
decide		relationships		represent
		solve		dramatize
		problems		
		infer		
		know		

Interaction Between Children and Adults

Any experience designed to foster intellectual development can be enhanced by the rich environment and quality of interaction provided by the adult. The ability to teach while talking naturally about children's activities is the teacher's challenge. A resourceful teacher can make an exciting learning experience out of the most routine event.

Almost any situation contains stimuli capable of provoking learning in children. The teacher can improve the ability to enhance children's language development by encouraging rich possibilities contained in the dialogue accompanying manipulative activities. Labelling, describing, comparing, classifying, and questioning are processes that can be used to support intellectual development.

Active manipulation of the physical world curriculum implies creating an environment favorable for the establishment of motoric representation. Young children show substantial gains in verbal fluency, language complexity, and logic when they engage in activity-based inquiry oriented programs. Such a program is especially significant because of the sensitive sensory motor and cognitive learning of the very young child.

M. LANGUIS, T. SAUNDERS
and S. TIPPS
*Brain and Learning:
Directions in Early
Childhood Education*

In dialogue with children, teachers are trying to help children to think and to communicate their thinking effectively . . . to extend the student's thinking, and to help him to find ways to expressing new ideas clearly.

JOAN TOUGH
*Talking and Learning:
A Guide to Fostering
Communications Skills
in Nursery and Infant Schools*

Because learning is accommodative, there are times when the teacher must play a direct teaching role. Teacher's questions and comments to each child play an important role in helping him or her learn.

Developing Thinking Processes

When children interact with the teacher, the environment, their peers, and other adults, they develop and refine their ability to use a variety of thought processes, as shown in the following chart.

Thought Processes	Characteristics
Observing	the perceiving of characteristics, similarities, differences, and changes through the use of all the senses
Recalling	bringing to mind previous experiences
Comparing	finding the likenesses and differences
Patterning	recognizing, duplicating, or creating regular occurence of materials, words, or events to establish predictability
Classifying	the organizing of materials, events, and phenomena into logical groupings according to common attributes or relationships
Predicting	using existing data, information, perceptible patterns, and trends to suggest non-observed or future outcomes or occurences
Generalizing	inferring a general rule from particular facts or past experiences

Growth in thinking skills is encouraged by the teacher who continually questions and suggests and who leads children to recognize problems and explore solutions.

Problem Solving

In kindergarten, children are faced with two kinds of problems — those that occur naturally and those that are presented by the teacher. Developing the ability to identify, solve, and anticipate problems of both kinds are skills critical to successful everyday living and to the solution of hypothetical challenges. Whether children are dealing with real-life problems such as social conflicts, difficulty managing materials, or working to solve a challenge set by the teacher, it is important to keep the following in mind.
- Children learn when the problem is of interest to them.
- Children learn when experiences are shared and there is the opportunity to interact with others.

We cannot expect the child to build intelligent behavior in an environment devoid of stimulating human interchange. Appropriate language-focused, adult-child interaction is required.

H. CAZDEN, MATTICK
in J. H. Stevens, Jr.,
"Everyday Experience and
Intellectual Development"

Thinking is the operating skill with which intelligence acts upon experience.

EDWARD DEBONO
"The Direct Teaching of Thinking
as a Creative Skill"

- Children learn by doing. They will incorporate and recall successful strategies for use in future problem-solving situations.

Sometimes children will use their intuition to solve problems. At other times it may be appropriate to structure the process and guide them through the steps of arriving at a conclusion. Through dialogue and by asking questions, the teacher helps the children to

- define the problem;
- reflect on past experience and gather additional information or suggest other options;
- organize and analyse the information or options;
- arrive at a solution or make a choice.

The teacher encourages the children to take the risk of facing challenges and new or difficult situations by facilitating the problem-solving process and by drawing the children's attention to the fact that there are often many ways to solve a particular problem and frequently a variety of valid solutions or answers. Once children have selected an answer or chosen an option, it is helpful to provide time for them to discuss their solutions and the process or strategies used to arrive at a conclusion. It is also important that they test and evaluate the results of their solutions in dialogue with others.

Constructing Knowledge

Knowledge is an interpretation of the real world that the child constructs through living and learning.

Although the child's cognitive processes develop as a part of the total framework, it is useful for the teacher to conceptualize the types of knowledge encompassed in this framework:

- physical knowledge;
- social knowledge;
- logical knowledge;
- representation (a knowledge within itself and of the other three).

The following example illustrates how children construct the four kinds of knowledge simultaneously through block building.

Block building allows children to develop physical knowledge about the properties of the blocks. Opportunities to classify arise spontaneously during building, and the children may discover that the large blocks don't fall down as easily when at the bottom. Subsequently, they might begin by grouping blocks by their size prior to construction.

An opportunity for serial ordering might arise when a child needs a specific block to complete the construction. The first block is too short and the second too long, so the child compares the other blocks to the first two to find a "between" length. When the child is constructing a castle or house with blocks, he or she is representing knowledge symbolically. The child who looks for a flag for every castle turret or a cup for every saucer in the doll house is experiencing one-to-one correspondence.

During block building, children use language as part of their representation, either talking to themselves or communicating to others. Here the teacher can provide the children with names of objects or events in context. Adults can even provide written labels for the construction on request. After the play, as

He is not satisfied with speaking. He must "play out" what he thinks and symbolize his ideas by means of gesture or objects, and represent things by imitation, drawing, and construction.

JEAN PIAGET
The Psychology of Intelligence

children put the blocks away, they classify them according to shape. They find the right place for each block as they match it to a two-dimensional representation or a written label.

1. *Physical Knowledge*

Physical knowledge refers to observable properties of objects and physical phenomena. The way the child finds out about these properties and physical phenomena is by
- active exploration;
- observing;
- structuring in his or her mind the characteristics of the object.

Thus, physical knowledge is structured through feedback from objects. The child will come to know the attributes of the objects in the environment and know how to go about finding out the physical nature of new, unfamiliar objects. As well, the child will be developing an attitude of curiosity and anticipation of what will happen and will form the habit of figuring out the means to achieve desired ends with objects or physical phenemona.

Physical knowledge perceived directly from objects leads to the development of concepts and generalizations such as the following.
- Objects have particular size, color, shape, and texture.
- Objects or physical phenomena float, sink, roll, grow, live, etc.
- Rain is wet.
- Snow melts.
- Birds fly.
- Ice is cold.
- Animals need food.
- Small plants grow from seeds.
- Salt dissolves in water.
- Some flowers have a scent.
- Daffodils grow from bulbs.

Activities centring on or including physical knowledge have a motivating and structuring effect on the intellectual development of young children. Essential to this development is the opportunity for children to present their views to other children as well as to adults. By exchanging opinions with others, children begin to move from an egocentric point of view and to co-ordinate their opinions with those of other children.

2. *Social Knowledge*

Social knowledge refers to social conventions that are structured through feedback from people. This knowledge includes the social rules that apply to the child's ability to behave in conformity with social expectations (i.e., knowledge that is obtained by others giving information about arbitrary conventions). It is basically knowledge that is passively received by children as they encounter various aspects of their own culture and society. It provides for transmission of culture by family, society, and school. It is external knowledge that is best imparted to children by adults and peers.

Knowledge derived from people involves knowledge about people's relationships, one's relation to individuals, one's relation to institutions, and one's

Science with young children is primarily concerned with gathering experience. Young children have a natural curiosity about their surroundings, and almost any work or play that concerns exploration of their environment results in learning with understanding.

R. RICHARDS
Early Experiences

Most teachers will agree that it is better for children to look at real things that are part of their world and to find out these things for themselves. They do so with help and guidance from the teacher by methods that are in essence scientific. Most of the knowledge a young child gains is obtained by process of trial and error. He finds when playing with water it will not run uphill; when planting seeds in the garden that those he puts too deep never appear as seedlings. He is continually comparing one thing with another and gains from his comparisons and his sorting a pattern of understanding.

R. RICHARDS
Early Experiences

Intellectual Development

relation to goods and services. Generalizations developed may include ideas such as the following.
- Firemen help to put out fires.
- Families differ in the number of members.
- Some people celebrate Christmas on December 25.
- Some people celebrate birthdays by having birthday parties.
- People live in different kinds of homes.
- People eat different kinds of food.
- Our morning meal is called breakfast.
- The flower growing from the bulb is called a daffodil.
- Nurses help people who are sick.

The more opportunities children have to interact with peers, parents, teachers, and other adults, the more viewpoints they will encounter. This experience stimulates children to clarify their viewpoint and to approach it objectively. This type of interaction is also an important source of information on customs and labels that make up social knowledge.

3. *Logical Knowledge*

In acquiring physical knowledge, the specific properties of each object are important. In acquiring logical knowledge, on the other hand, what are important are not the properties but the relationships between objects and phenomena. Children construct these relationships in their minds from their observations. These co-ordinated actions involve the reasoning processes.

Logical knowledge deals with the organization of knowledge essential to thinking:
   (i) classification;
   (ii) patterning;
   (iii) seriation;
   (iv) number;
   (v) space and time.

(i) *Classification*

The ability to classify is a thinking process that helps children to organize information gained from experiences in the world around them. Classification involves the process of noting and comparing similarities and differences in order to group things and concepts into classes according to their common attributes or relationships. Children are classifying when they put things away in their proper places, when they use behavior that is appropriate to a specific situation, when they make choices, and when they focus on a particular concept (e.g., comparing stories, finding synonyms, talking about animals in the desert, counting by two's).

When involved in classification activities, children are learning to group things into sets and are also developing their vocabularies (e.g., color words, size words, shape words, amount). Questions such as "How are they the same? We now have a set of. . . . They all . . ." help children to focus on the attribute used for sorting. It is through discussion that children clarify in their minds what has been done and learn the appropriate vocabulary for the concept being dealt with.

Logical ideas . . . cannot be transmitted by word of mouth. They must be constructed by the child through actions. Logical mathematical knowledge requires co-ordination of mental and physical action — joining, ordering, placing in correspondence.

E. LABINOWICZ
*The Piaget Primer:
Thinking, Learning, Teaching*

Intellectual Development

Children are able to classify by physical properties before they can deal with abstract ones. For example, children will be able to sort things into piles by color before they are able to do so by number. Therefore, they need diverse experiences in classifying objects by their physical properties and functions in order to understand the many different relationships among a group of objects or events.

When learning to classify, children progress through the following stages.

- *Collections:* In the very early stages children cannot sort objects into classes but will lay them out in patterns or pictures which give them a satisfying visual appearance.
- *Classifying by one attribute:* Objects are placed in piles or groups by physical attributes such as shape or color. The piles are not compared to each other to see which has more, fewer, or an equal number of members. The children are not able to shift their focus from one attribute to another. For example, when given a set of red and yellow circles and squares, they will first sort them by either color or shape. They will not be able to resort the blocks in a different way when asked to do so.
- *Classifying by one attribute and then shifting focus to another:* After sorting a group of objects in one way, the children are able to reclassify the same objects by a different attribute (e.g., texture). (NOTE: Most kindergarten children are functioning at one of the above three levels.)

- *Classifying by two attributes:* Classification at this level involves the concept of intersecting sets. Some members of one set may also belong to another at the same time (e.g., large blocks belong to one set, red blocks to another, and all large, red blocks belong to both sets). Some elements have an attribute that is common to two or more sets at the same time. Children are able to deal with intersecting sets on a concrete level before the abstract.
- *Classifying by three or more attributes:* This is a sophisticated level and is developed by older children.

The children should have many experiences in sorting and classifying physical objects by one attribute. Later, when comparing two sets, drawing conclusions, and making generalizations, it is necessary to lay the objects out in a *one-to-one correspondence* so they can be more easily compared both visually and by counting. It is the relationships between facts, rather than the facts themselves, that command attention. As these relationships are seen and discussed, concepts become clearer and some generalizations may emerge.

Another component of classification is the concept of *class inclusion.* All the members of one class may be part of a larger class at the same time (e.g., all dogs belong to the class of animals). This concept involves the ability to consider parts (some) of a class and the whole (all) at the same time. Most kindergarten children have not developed this ability. When asked whether there are more daisies or flowers while looking at a group of five daisies and three roses, most will state that there are more daisies. They are able to deal

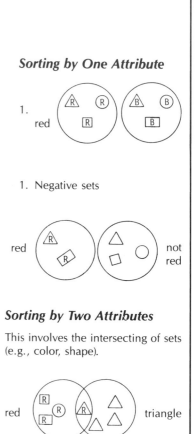

Sorting by One Attribute

1.

1. Negative sets

Sorting by Two Attributes

This involves the intersecting of sets (e.g., color, shape).

Intellectual Development

with only one aspect at a time but cannot shift from whole to part or part to whole. Responses are based on appearance of the parts, not on the relationship of some to all. When planning experiences, teachers need to be sensitive to the limits of the child's level of development.

(ii) *Patterning*

A pattern emerges when something happens regularly enough to establish a certain predictability. Being able to recognize and create patterns is related to ordering (seriation) and is a necessary development for logical thinking. Patterns may be found in materials, words, events, habits, or procedures. They are structured relationships that provide people a basis for understanding more complex processes and therefore are a valuable problem-solving tool. Helping children examine patterns is necessary because we live in patterns, are surrounded by patterns, and think, move, and speak in patterns.

Arranging and constructing patterns in a wide variety of modes contributes to an understanding of mathematics, language, and the social sciences and to a fuller understanding of the physical and social world as the search is made for order and reason. Patterning allows for the manipulation of ideas and creative thought.

Experiences that can present children with opportunities for patterning may include such activities as

- examining the sequences of the day (or even a particular activity centre), and the calendar, and the significant events in the kindergarten year;
- experiencing a variety of aesthetic, artistic, and physical experiences (e.g., dance movement, music, art);
- construction with blocks, beads, or pegs;
- examining and recognizing patterns in nature (e.g., spider webs, flowers, fruits, vegetables, leaves);
- examining their own language and the language used in stories, poems, and rhymes.

Young children require experiences that help them become aware of and able to recognize patterns and that help them explore, extend, and create new patterns. As well, they need to describe patterns in a variety of ways. We need to encourage the kindergarten child to become a seeker of patterns.

(iii) *Seriation*

The ability to seriate is a thinking process that develops in children along with the ability to classify. The child finds a common characteristic of objects and then orders the objects in the set according to the magnitude of that characteristic (e.g., by size, length, color, number). The relationship used when comparing the objects is that of relative difference. When we ask questions such as "Which group has more objects? Which stick is longer? Who is heavier?" we are dealing with seriation.

A sense of order or sequence is necessary when dealing with concepts such as first/second, before/after, heavier/lighter, softer/harder, getting up, getting dressed, and counting.

Young children are able to compare two things before they are able to do so with five or six things. They have more difficulty as the numbers of items increase. The set of counting numbers is an ordered set. Each number contains all the subsets of the smaller numbers (e.g., 5 contains the subsets 4, 3, 2, and 1).

When dealing with seriation, children are also developing their vocabulary (e.g., one, two, three; big, bigger, biggest; cool, warm, hot, boiling).

Children tend to progress in their seriation in the following sequence.

- *Pairing:* The child simply places objects together by two's.
- *Simple Ordering:* The child can order objects in a line, according to size.
- *Two-Dimensional Seriation:* The child must place an object in the appropriate spot in an ordered line. To do this the child must consider what comes before and what comes after (e.g., which is shorter and which is longer).

(iv) *Number*

Number is an abstract concept that must be constructed in the child's own mind. Number cannot be heard, felt, or seen directly with the senses as the physical properties (e.g., shape) of objects can be. By being involved in many experiences that involve comparing equal and unequal sets and identifying them with a number name, children gradually begin to grasp the meaning of the numerousness of numbers or the quantity involved for a given number. By associating the name of a number with the number of objects in a set, the child begins to relate the concrete, sensory world to the abstract one of number.

> The "threeness" does not exist physically in any one object but is abstracted from the entire set and exists in the mind of the child.
>
> E. LABINOWICZ
> *The Piaget Primer:*
> *Thinking, Learning, Teaching*

The set of counting numbers is an ordered set. Each number is one less than the number ahead and one more than the previous one.

Most young children usually learn verbal counting before coming to school. This counting is usually learned by rote and does not necessarily mean that the child has an understanding of the concept of number: he or she has simply memorized a set of words, and may not be able to associate the words with a group of objects. Later, the child may appear to count a set of objects correctly but is really only naming each individual object and not considering or including the previous ones in the set. The following is an example.

> A number is more than a name. A number expresses a relationship. Relationships do not exist in the actual objects. Relationships are abstractions, a step removed from physical reality. Relationships are constructions of the mind that are imposed on objects.
>
> E. LABINOWICZ
> *The Piaget Primer:*
> *Thinking, Learning, Teaching*

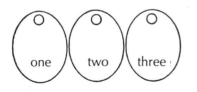

After the child has counted the three objects and has been asked to put three in a box, he or she may only put the third one in the box.

In learning to count, children pass through the following stages:

- verbal rote counting;
- counting by naming individual objects in a set without considering previous ones counted;
- counting meaningfully by considering all elements in a set.

Intellectual Development

Children who understand the concept of number are in essence classifying and must be able to determine when two numbers are the same. They must put into one class all those groups of objects with the same number and leave out all those with a different number.

To establish whether sets are equivalent or not, the child needs to match the members of each set in a one-to-one correspondence. Matching is the most direct way of comparing the equivalence of groups of objects. Children who are not ready for this may line up two rows of objects so the ends match and say that they are the same, even when one row has more objects than the other. They may even have difficulty making a correspondence between objects that show a relationship such as cups and saucers. Matching things on a physical basis can be done before a child uses numbers with understanding. For non-conservers, the ability to count objects is not a guarantee that the equivalence of two sets is a lasting one.

Children tend to progress in their one-to-one correspondence in the following sequence:

- matching identical objects and pictures;
- matching objects that show a relationship (e.g., knives and forks);
- matching members of sets with a number value to prove equivalence, more, or less (e.g., are there as many red sweaters as blue ones? After counting, prove by matching).

One-to-one correspondence is closely connected with the concept of the *invariance of number* (conservation — the concept of five never changes, regardless of the arrangement of the separate members of the set). A set of five can be compared to another set to prove whether or not they are equivalent by matching the members one-to-one. By matching the objects in two equal sets, children can prove their equivalence. When the objects are rearranged, the children who have developed conservation of number will tell you that the sets are equal because they can be matched up again. They have learned that a set of five remains a set of five, regardless of the arrangement and visual look of the members. Length of a row no longer dominates the child's perception.

Children who are not conservers are able only to focus on the end result of spreading a line out and are not able to reverse the process to where they started. Children who have not yet developed conservation of number should be involved in many activities that require matching and utilize one-to-one correspondence.

Children gradually develop the idea of conservation over a period of time. They will be able to conserve smaller numbers before larger ones.

(v) *Space*

The structuring of space is closely related to observable phenomena and is thus similar to physical knowledge. However, it is also like logical and mathematical knowledge in that concepts of space have to be constructed in the child's mind. By sorting and classifying information derived from the physical world and their movement in it, children gradually develop their perceptions and understanding of space. When children are drawing, using

. . . one-to-one correspondence doesn't depend on an understanding of number. Rather, it forms a foundation for such understanding.

E. LABINOWICZ
*The Piaget Primer:
Thinking, Learning, Teaching*

Piaget cautions that the relationships imbedded in the concept of number cannot be taught by telling. Number is not just a name for something. It is a relationship that
- indicates its place in order;
- represents how many objects are included in a set; and
- is lasting despite spatial rearrangements.

E. LABINOWICZ
*The Piaget Primer:
Thinking, Learning, Teaching*

Intellectual Development

scissors, moving about a room, using climbing equipment, or building with blocks, they are dealing with spatial concepts.

The child must learn to deal with two physical properties of space — topological and Euclidian. Topological space deals with closed or open shapes, enclosure (inclusion/exclusion), proximity (near/far), and order. Euclidian space deals with geometry — lines, angles, equalities, parallelism, and distance. Topological concepts develop in children before Euclidian concepts. For example, a child who can draw the windows correctly inside a house (topological) may at the same time draw the chimney at a right angle to the roof (Euclidian).

Young children begin to develop concepts of space in relation to their own bodies and then later in relation to other objects and people. They gradually move from themselves as the reference point to the larger world around them. Children's perceptions of distance and position are developed when they constantly handle objects (moving them together or apart) and not when they simply look at them.

To understand spatial relationships, children develop a system of reference points in the following order:

- vertical and horizontal co-ordinates;
- right and left, in front and behind co-ordinates;
- depth and distance co-ordinates.

As they grow, children need to be able to form images about space if they are to solve spatial problems. This spatial visualization involves being able to imagine how something will look if it is moved in space or how it will look from another point of view. For example, children must learn first to recognize left and right, in front of and behind, and then they must learn to transform (reverse) them. They must learn that perspective is relative to the point of view taken. To do this, they must have suitable frames of reference. For example, in drawing maps children must be able to shift their perspective to a "bird's eye" view. This shifting of point of view usually develops in the child around the ages of 7–9.

Preoperational children recognize open and closed figures before geometric shapes, can only see things from their own point of view (egocentric), and cannot realistically represent objects in a plane (e.g., putting chimneys on houses at an angle). As their ability to take another point of view develops, children become increasingly able to deal with the concepts of left/right and front/back when presented in reverse. A variety of experiences must be offered to increase each child's ability to experience and represent space in many ways.

(vi) *Time*

The concept of time as divided into intervals is a convenient classification for adults to deal with the past, present, and future. There are two aspects to the concept of time that must be co-ordinated — seriation (order of events) and duration (length of events).

Very young children are concerned with the present and have difficulty dealing with the concept of the future. The first important event related to time is bedtime. When children enter school, they learn the events of the day and week and gradually learn to name the hours and days. The most important yearly event for them is their birthday, followed by major cultural celebrations. Counting the days or weeks to an important event helps children learn concepts such as "how many days to," "before and after", and "during."

In developing an understanding of time, children first (i.e., about age three) learn concepts of "now," "going to," and "in a minute." Then they begin to use accurately past and future tenses and terms such as "for a long time" and "for a whole week" (age 4). They also begin to develop an understanding of the sequence of daily events. By age 6-7, some begin to use the clock hours to regulate or describe their activities. Experiences that enable childen to structure time into broad intervals should be offered. Smaller units come later.

4. *Representation*

Representation involves the re-creation of an experience in another form or way.

- Human beings understand their world through representations of it.
- Representational competence develops in an orderly sequence.
- Children have a desire to represent or express aspects of the world or their experiences.
- Representational competence develops fully only in response to interaction with the appropriate physical and social environment.
- The child cannot represent knowledge that has not been acquired.

In order to think about things that are absent and to exchange ideas with other people, the child needs to learn to represent all types of knowledge.

The preoperational stage is a period of major achievement where the child is increasingly able to represent objects, actions, and events, through mental images, with other objects. (Other ways include creative movement, role playing, the use of art forms, the use of symbols such as numbers, and the use of oral and written language.)

Representational thinking also frees the child from the concept of the present as a reconstruction of the past, and anticipation of the future becomes increasingly possible. Children can now represent prior experiences for themselves and can attempt to represent them to others.

Children try to symbolize the real, physical world through play and through the arts. In these outlets they repeat and relive past experiences. By doing this they relate their external world of reality to their internal world of past experiences, knowledge, mental organization, and powers of interpretation. New experiences are linked to old ones so that their minds absorb new information, and their knowledge expands.

During the kindergarten year, two major categories of representative knowledge are experienced by the child: symbolic representation and sign representation (language).

Language develops as a part of a larger system of representation. It is only one way of representing the world. The models of representation vary both in complexity and abstractness. Language is the most complex and abstract mode of representation. Whereas other forms of representation bear some resemblance to the objects or events they symbolize, language is expressed in symbols bearing no such resemblance. Unlike other forms of representation that are personal creations, language is acquired within the limits of a socially defined system. Although language often accompanies other forms of representation, and most rules of language have been constructed by age five, the child's grasp of the most complex rules and of the full meaning of words is more gradual.

JEAN PIAGET
and BARBEL INHELD
quoted in E. Labinowicz,
*The Piaget Primer:
Thinking, Learning, Teaching*

Intellectual Development

In *Symbolic Representation* the child relates the concepts, ideas, objects, events, and relationships to the kinds of knowledge being acquired (physical, social, logical). Symbolic representation refers to the following:

- creative dramatics;
- dramatic play, socio-dramatic play;
- creative rhythmic movement;
- puppetry;
- imitation;
- constructing three-dimensional models with clay, wood, paper, etc.;
- constructing two-dimensional models, drawing, painting, graphing.

In *Sign Representation (Language)* the child represents through language the knowledge that has been and is being constructed. The child develops the ability to represent things and to communicate ideas through spoken language, first

- using names for objects in the environment,
- using words to identify the properties and functions of objects,
- using words to denote location in space and location in time,
- using words that describe relationships (comparing, describing differences and similarities, enumerating, measuring, ordering),
- using words to relate physical knowledge,
- using words to relate social knowledge,
- using words to tell events and stories,
- using words to relate personal feelings and thoughts.

As the emergent writing processes develop, children will represent the above in written language and may begin to "read" the printed form. Representation through spoken language is of primary importance at this stage since it is critical for communication (and also enhances cognitive development). Through language we communicate needs and desires, gain and pass on information, and direct the actions of ourselves and others.

Language Development

Promoting the skills of using language, then, is essentially dependent on stimulating new thinking and new understanding.

JOAN TOUGH, *Listening to Children Talking: A Guide to the Appraisal of Children's Use of Language*

People clarify and extend thinking as they communicate through language. The child needs to develop and enhance his or her language. Experiences should be provided that help the child

- hear good language models;
- experiment with language;
- develop oral vocabulary and sentence structure;
- use language for a variety of purposes;
- develop the ability to listen for a variety of purposes;
- engage in dialogue with adults and peers;
- represent what is known through language;
- begin to understand the purposes of reading and writing;
- become involved in emergent reading and writing.

Language and Thinking

Language complements the thinking process. It is a complex and abstract form of representation that allows us to move away from concrete thinking towards abstract thinking. Through language we can deal with concepts of the past and future, thereby increasing the range and rapidity of thought.

Words are convenient labels representing concepts and are open to a variety of interpretations, depending upon the level of intellectual development and the personal experiences of the individual.

Thus, a child's understanding of a word may be different from an adult's. For example, a young child may use the word "brother" correctly in the sentence, "He is my brother." But in pursuing what the child's understanding of the word is, one may find that the child thinks a brother is a boy living in his house and does not understand the true relationship between them. Adults must be careful not to misinterpret the actual level of a child's understanding of words.

Children learn not only the language system of those around them but also the values and attitudes that are inherent in the way language is used. If children are never talked to except when given orders for behavior, they will learn that language is only used for control. Therefore, they will not seek out adults for conversation to learn about their world. However, if they are accustomed to talk that allows them to express what they think, to ask questions, and to form new thoughts, they will learn the value of language as a means of gaining knowledge and of understanding the world. Language thus becomes a vehicle for learning, and children will seek out conversation with others.

This has implications for schooling and further learning, as the use of language is central to our education system. The child having a rich language background, which involves the use of language for different purposes, will be able to bring a wealth of meaning to what is read. Written expression will also be more easily understood and mastered. The child who seeks knowledge and thinks about the world in further depth will be more successful in school.

Characteristics of the Child

- imitates language of others
- enjoys playing with language
- inquisitive
- experiments with language usage and structure
- listening vocabulary greater than speaking vocabulary
- asks questions

Factors Affecting the Child's Acquisition of Language

Children are born with an innate ability to learn language systems. There are several factors that affect their acquisition of language skills.

Family's Language

The language of the child's family is the greatest factor governing which language is used, how it is used, and the degree of complexity with which it is used. The sounds inherent in the social environment of the child are isolated and reinforced from the infant's early babbling as he or she first experiments with sound.

Expression of Needs and Wants

The very strong motivation in young children to express their needs and desires leads them to master the language system of their family. If children get no response to their use of language, they may not pursue it and may become delayed in their acquisition of language.

Natural Curiosity

Natural curiosity about the world requires children to use language to gain information. Attaching language to real first-hand expreiences allows children to create different ways of thinking and looking at the world and thus understanding it. This understanding leads to a greater feeling of being able to understand and influence what goes on around them.

Level of Development

The way children use language reflects their way of perceiving the world, and therefore each child has a unique way of expressing himself or herself. Young children are not using an adult system of language because their thinking processes are not fully developed. Their understanding of words as they represent concepts may be different.

Dialogue

Dialogue between people, particularly between adult and child, is essential for the continuing growth and development of language. It is the quality of verbal interaction between child and adult that governs the depth of a child's thinking and use of language. The teacher of young children must engage them in conversation dealing with their immediate physical and social environment and must help them relate (connect) this to their experiences in order for the optimum development to take place.

The Learning Stage in Language of Kindergarten Children

By the time they come to kindergarten, most children have learned the articulation of sounds and grammatical structures, a large vocabulary, and the social uses of talk. Attitudes about how and when to use language have been shaped by their environment and influenced by how the adults in their lives have used language. Children in kindergarten will exhibit many of the following characteristics in their use of language, depending upon their level of development.

As the child grows, the interest of the parents in his increasing ability in all directions, and in his capacity for responding to the world around him, is essential if he is to fulfil his potential. With this interest the parents are likely to talk with the child frequently, and it is through this interaction that the child's most important learning is accomplished. Through the use of language his curiosity about the world around him can be expressed and satisfied.

JOAN TOUGH
*Listening to Children Talking:
A Guide to the Appraisal
of Children's Use
of Language*

Thus, the current emphasis in research on child language acquisition suggests patterns . . . Such patterns emphasize
- *building opportunities for motoric development of meanings in advance of and simultaneous with verbal, semantic expectations;*
- *recognizing that what a child can say and what a child can do or can know are not equivalent;*
- *providing opportunities for young children to engage in extended monologues with adults who serve not as questioners but as involved, active listeners; and*
- *evolving educator sensitivity to children's systematic monologues and the writing process should focus on the significant role of the adult as an involved, active listener.*

M. LANGUIS, T. SAUNDERS,
and S. TIPPS
*Brain and Learning:
Directions in Early
Childhood Education*

Language Development

Listening

The kindergarten child
- understands objective language of adults better than language of peers;
- is moving from understanding simple instructions to listening to and receiving new ideas and following directions;
- is moving from listening for general rather than specific detail to listening for more detail for longer periods of time;
- may have a listening vocabulary of over 20,000 words by age seven;
- is learning to listen to ideas of others in conversations and discussions;
- may begin to pinpoint his or her own source of confusion and ask about word meanings;
- is learning to recognize purposes for listening;
- is learning to appreciate and compare prose, poetry, rhymes, music, etc.;
- is becoming more able to listen effectively to a variety of media (radio, records, films, tapes, T.V.).

Speaking

The kindergarten child
- is able to use most of the phonemes in our sound system, with the exception of some of the sounds that are closely related;
- uses language to maintain self, to direct, to report, to imagine, to reason, to predict, to project;
- shows rapid growth in language usage and structure;
- shows great range in language skill (e.g., expression, speed, volume, clarity of speech);
- uses subjective language (meaning is clear to child but not always to listener);
- needs a listener yet does not consider listener's needs (egocentric); is moving towards being aware of listener's needs;
- is acquiring his or her own grammar (uses rules to generate great variety of sentences);
- manipulates language and experiments with words;
- is moving from experimenting with word order and negative forms (e.g., "Why I can't go?") to using more conventional forms;
- ignores passive form and focuses on word order (e.g., many kindergarten children choose a picture of a cat chasing a dog to illustrate the statement "The cat is chased by the dog");
- asks many fact-finding questions leading to more how and why questions about his or her own physical world;
- seeks rules and overgeneralizes the use of rules for tenses and plurals (e.g., "I doed it", "mouses");
- uses but tends to confuse abstract terms (e.g., ask/tell, more/less, older/younger, as in "I'm going to tell my teacher if I can go");
- shows some use of compound words;
- retains some "baby talk" (e.g., "doggie");
- attempts to understand relationship (e.g., space, time);
- is moving toward narrating a story with suspense and expression and shows an increasing ability to retell stories;
- expresses ideas in loosely connected sentences and is moving towards the use of prepositions and comparative and superlative forms as understanding develops. This area continues to develop until adulthood. A child will not

usually use the more sophisticated forms of sentence structure until after the age of ten (e.g., rules for if/then, although, even though, in spite of).

Using Language for a Variety of Purposes

People speak for a purpose, and this purpose controls the type of language that is used. In order to foster language development, the teacher should be aware of the purpose for which the language is being used. This allows the teacher to recognize the level that the child is functioning at. The teacher can then guide the child to extend his or her use of language to a more complex level.

The following is a list of the ways children use language. It is one way of categorizing language usage.

Self-Maintaining Strategies

- Referring to physical and psychological needs and wants
- Protecting the self and self-interests
- Justifying behavior or claims
- Criticizing others
- Threatening others

    e.g., "I want a turn."
        "I don't like your picture."

Directing Strategies

- Monitoring own actions
- Directing the actions of the self
- Directing the actions of others
- Collaborating in action with others

    e.g., "I put this piece here and this here and . . ."
        "You throw the ball to me and I'll throw it to you."

Reporting on Present and Past Experiences Strategies

- Labelling the components of the scene
- Referring to detail (e.g., size, color, and other attributes)
- Referring to incidents
- Referring to the sequence of events
- Making comparisons
- Recognizing related aspects
- Making an analysis using several of the features above
- Extracting or recognizing the central meaning
- Reflecting on the meaning of experiences, including own feelings

    e.g., "That's the mom, there's the girl, and that's the house."
        "Your coat is just like mine 'cept it's green."

Towards Logical Reasoning Strategies*

- Explaining a process
- Recognizing casual and dependent relationships
- Recognizing problems and their solutions
- Justifying judgements and actions

Language Development

- Reflecting on events and drawing conclusions
- Recognizing principles

  e.g., "This box isn't big enough to make a house so I'm going to make it with blocks."

Predicting Strategies*

- Anticipating and forecasting events
- Anticipating the detail of events
- Anticipating problems and possible solutions
- Anticipating and recognizing alternative course of action
- Predicting the consequences of actions or events

  e.g., "The wheel will fall off if I can't stick it on."
  "I'm getting a new puppy and I'll have to get a bed and dog food and toys for it."

Projecting Strategies*

- Projecting into the experiences of others
- Projecting into the feelings of others
- Projecting into the reactions of others
- Projecting into situations never experienced

  e.g., "He's scared his mom won't come."
  "I'm going shopping with my mom and I think she'll buy me something."

Imagining Strategies*

- Developing an imaginary situation based on real life
- Developing an imaginary situation based on fantasy
- Developing an original story

  e.g., "Then the cat jumped on the broomstick and goed home."
  "We'll be the seeds in the ground. This can be the dirt covering us."

Experimenting with Language

A child's previous experiences have shaped his or her knowledge of the structure of language, grammatical forms, vocabulary, and articulation of sound as well as the value and purposes for using language. Although all children have acquired and practised language, influences such as family interactions, exposure to language models, and the child's role in family cause each child's language background to be unique.

Just as the infant experiments with sounds, the five-year old experiments with words. As he or she matures and hears language modelled, the child applies more complex language usage. The kindergarten child is hearing models and experimenting, and is discarding or internalizing language, gradually refining it to more closely match the language of the adults around him or her.

The learning environment that allows time for young children to talk and explore with other children allows each child the freedom to experiment with language.

*Strategies that serve directing, reporting, and reasoning may serve these uses also.

. . . children did not seem to acquire words simply by hearing them. Rather, they learned words related to things they could play with or manipulate. Furthermore, children who had experiences with other people or more experiences outside their homes developed vocabulary more quickly. Piaget believes that children develop concepts . . . by interacting with their environment.

R. C. SPRINTHALL and
N. A. SPRINTHALL
*Educational Psychology:
A Developmental Approach*

First, the teacher should actively involve children in experiences about which to talk and then reduce the number of questions, especially convergent ones, asked of young chil-

Children practise their language during their play. Sounds, words, and ways of speaking are explored while playing with inanimate objects such as puppets or with imaginary friends, peers, and adults. Providing a variety of settings for these experiments gives children opportunities to practise language skills that are new or are extensions of learned skills. Children need exposure to using language in dialogue between two people—adult and child, and child and child—in large and small groups. Growth in language development is most influenced by the model presented by adults around the child. Therefore the model presented by the teacher will greatly influence the child's language usage and development.

The practice derived through experimenting with correct and incorrect language usage is the child's way of sorting, organizing, and assimilating language to fit into his or her stage of development. The teacher who listens to the child's use of language will be able to judge the child's level of development.

Hearing Good Language Models

In order to understand the use of language at a sophisticated level, the child must be exposed to appropriate models in a rich language environment. The two main sources of this modelling are the use of language by other children and adults, and exposure to good literature. The former is important for the development of speech and the latter for developing the appreciation of the language of books; that is, written language. Both are important for learning and expressing ideas.

Children do not simply mimic what is heard; instead, they listen to the model, assimilating the language into their perceived system of rules. By experimenting with language features such as word order, use of tenses, and inflexions, children use the process of trial and error to refine their language.

When children haave internalized the language structure, they will apply these rules. It serves no purpose to make the young child repeat a phrase or sentence correctly. If the child says, "He goed to the store"' the best way to help the child is to accept the child's statement without comment and then model the appropriate response; (e.g., "Yes, he went to the store"). This method allows the child to feel accepted, and it also presents the child with the appropriate form of the sentence.

Hearing good language models is not enough if the extension of language skills in young children is the goal. Children must be engaged in talk. Dialogue between the teacher and the child provides the child with the practice time needed to promote language growth. The child is then exposed to a good language model and his or her skills are extended in a non-threatening manner.

Because the language used in books is different from the language of speech, children need to be exposed to many literary forms such as poetry, plays, songs, and stories. Hearing good literature introduces children to vocabulary, language forms, and ideas that may not occur in their everyday lives. Literature also offers children an opportunity to become emotionally involved in fantasy. Children who have been read to in their early years develop a familiarity with the language of books and learn that both pleasure and information can be gained through reading. Those children who have been exposed to a wealth of good literature are usually highly motivated to learn to read and write and are therefore more successful in school.

dren actively engaged in learning (Cunningham, 1977). Finally, the teacher should increase the amount of waiting time provided for answering the children's divergent questions. (Rowe, 1978.)

M. LANGUIS, T. SAUNDERS, and S. TIPPS, *Brain and Learning: Directions in Early Childhood Education*

Attitudes and values are implicit in the way in which language is used within the family and are for the most part never examined. The users are not aware that the way in which they talk to one another is reinforcing attitudes and relationships, and their use of language reflects their way of life.

JOAN TOUGH *Listening to Children Talking: A Guide to the Appraisal of Children's Use of Language*

Language provides the medium through which thinking can be expressed . . . The very use of language, and the continuous experience of being amongst users of language, influences not only the way in which the child will use language, but more important, the way in which he will think, and the kind of interpretation he will make of his experiences.

JOAN TOUGH *Listening to Children Talking: A Guide to the Appraisal of Children's Use of Language*

For a story truly to hold the child's attention, it must entertain him and arouse his curiosity. But to enrich his life, it must stimulate his imagination; help him develop his intellect and to clarify his emotions; be attuned to his anxieties and aspirations; give full recognition to his difficulties, while at the same time suggesting solutions to the problems which perturb him. In short, it must at one and the same time relate to all aspects of his personality—and this without ever belittling but, on the

Language Development

Being read to daily will help children develop a positive attitude towards books and reading. Discussion of the ideas and language used in books helps raise their awareness of the variety and uses of language. The experience of enjoying literature becomes an intrinsic pleasure for children if the interaction between them, their teacher, and their literary selection captures their imaginations and is viewed by them as a happy interlude with the spoken and written word.

Developing Oral Vocabulary and Sentence Structure

The development of oral vocabulary and sentence structure begins with the early random babblings of the infant. Through reinforcement, encouragement, and modelling by adults around him or her, the infant learns to isolate certain sounds that, when put together, form words.

At the same time that children are learning to say words, they are learning the meanings of them. Thinking and language are interdependent. Because their thinking processes are not fully developed, children's understanding of words may at first differ from that of adults. For example, in the equation "three plus two equals five," a child may use the word "equals" without really understanding that in the equation the word means "the same as." He or she has learned a rote pattern. Even though a child may use the word correctly in this situation, he or she may not be able to use the word or understand it in other contexts.

It is through concrete, first-hand experiences such as hearing words used in a variety of situations that children gradually learn the precise and varied meanings of words. For example, when first learning the word "dog," children may associate it only with the dog in their homes. Later they will associate it with dogs in general as they learn the characteristics of dogs and how they differ from other animals.

While children are learning the correct label for the concept of dog, they are also having their thinking processes extended and their vocabulary enhanced as new information is accommodated and assimilated. Thus they learn to use the word dog more precisely to label a certain class of animal.

By using correct and precise language in concrete situations, the teacher helps the child to attach language to new concepts.

It is the developmental nature of the learning process for the acquisiton of the rules of sentence structure that governs the stage the child is at and therefore the level of sophistication in the use of syntax. This is why "child grammar" is not simply verbatim repetitions of adult speech.

"As language is learned, rules are applied to general categories and then are redefined and applied to specific subgroups" (Pfaum, 1974). When children first learn the rule for adding "s" to form plurals, they will use this rule even for the exceptions (e.g., mans). They will also overgeneralize the past tense rules (e.g., "singed" for "sang"). As children develop they will "hear" the correct forms and through experimentation will be able to be more precise in the application of rules and exceptions. The structures that children learn first are the most basic elements of language. The order in which children learn the structure of language is
- subject and predicate (basic elements of meaning);
- simple sentences using auxiliary forms, negatives, and questions, structures, and inflections;
- compound and complex sentences.

Language Development

The mastering of syntax is an unconsciously acquired rule system that is usually formed by the time a child is six years of age. By this age children have also largely mastered the phonemic (sound) structure of their language, and therefore their speech is now very similar to that of adults. From this point on children refine the use of these structural rules. Vocabulary development,however, continues throughout their lives as they learn the standard, precise, and varied meanings of words and as they continually add to their vocabulary. Their cognitive development continues as new concepts are internalized.

Developing the Ability to Listen for a Variety of Purposes

Listening is directly related to language development, learning, and the total process of human interaction. Learning to listen is learning to understand and appreciate another's point of view, and this, in children as well as adults, expands perception of the world. If children can learn to be active listeners, they can internalize new ideas and thoughts and assimilate them with their own to form new thinking patterns.

Dialogue between teacher and child presents the child with a language and listening model. The child that is listened to comes to understand that what he or she says is important. Children will be more likely to listen to others when expected to, especially if they have learned that they can gain information from others.

Listening is the means used to acquire language input. Listening is an active experience serving a variety of purposes, depending on the situation. A child aware of the purpose for listening will more likely achieve a set goal than will a child who is just told to listen.

If the teacher creates an atmosphere for listening by preparing children for the listening experience and also encouraging them to feel personally involved, then they will be stimulated to listen. Children who are encouraged to talk about what has been listened to will gain some insight as to the purpose for listening. Their interpretation will reflect whether or not they have focused on the intended objectives of the listening activity.

Children need listening experiences that allow them to develop the following.

1. *Appropriate Attitudes for Listening* (e.g., marginal listening or literal comprehension)

   - develop an understanding of listening as a social behavior (i.e., part of human interactions)
   - acquire appropriate behavior for effective listening (i.e., eye contact, sitting still)
   - recognize listening as a tool for learning (i.e., learn to do an activity or learn a new song)

2. *Listening Comprehension Skills* (e.g., attentive listening or inferential comprehension)

   - gaining information (i.e., some birds fly south in winter)
   - following directions (i.e., how to fold paper to create an Easter basket)
   - understanding and interacting with the environment (i.e., in the classroom or outside of the classroom)

- criticizing (i.e., dislike or like of song or story book)
- evaluating (i.e., behavior exhibited during clean-up, and how clean the room is)
- question and problem solving (i.e., how a snack can be shared)

3. *Vocabulary and Language Competence*

- listening as it relates to speaking, reading, and writing

4. *Participation in a Variety of Listening Experiences* (e.g., appreciative listening; listening in different situations for different purposes)

- patterning, rhyming, chanting
- music, sounds of the language
- speaking with other students or with the teacher
- tapes, records, sounds

For listening experiences to be valuable to the child, the teacher must
- be a model listener;
- plan and provide the appropriate experiences;
- establish a climate that fosters appropriate listening habits.

The development of effective listening habits enhances the child's ability to learn and to communicate.

Having Opportunities for Dialogue

Children have a basic need to express themselves and learn about their world, and this leads them to communicate with others. Children need to talk with each other, but more important for the extension of vocabulary and thinking are their conversations with adults. In the context of first-hand experiences, children's ideas and views are broadened through discussions with others. Discussions guided by the teacher helps them clarify thoughts and express themselves. It must be kept in mind that a child's use of language is directly affected by the topic of discussion and by how he or she feels about being involved in that discussion.

To help sustain and enhance a child's language, the teacher must engage him or her in dialogue: that is, guided talk between teacher and child on an individual basis. The child receives the full attention of the teacher. The teacher is able to model attentive listening skills to assess the child's language level and to apply questioning techniques that will extend or foster language strategies in the child. The child's attention can be directed toward new perceptions and concepts. Having the teacher's full attention shows the child that his or her language and thought are valued, which in turn demonstrates to the child that language is important.

As a child tends to rely on learned language strategies, the dialogue technique will challenge the child to practise more complex uses of language in positive, non-threatening talk with the teacher. Dialogue that takes place when a child is busy working at a project allows the project to become the focal point around the discussion. The child feels secure in having something concrete at hand to talk about, and the teacher capitalizes on this.

Dialogue techniques that include open-ended questions stimulate a child into doing most of the talking. The teacher's role is to guide the child's utterances so the

As adults talk with him about his experiences, offer new experiences to him, and discuss them with him, so he gains new meaning for familiar experiences and is helped to build up those concepts about the world which cannot be abstracted readily from immediate concrete experience.

JOAN TOUGH
*Listening to Children Talking:
A Guide to the
Appraisal of Children's
Use of Language*

The word, handing on the experience of generations as this experience is incorporated in language, locks a complex system of connections in the child's cortex and becomes a tremendous tool, introducing forms of analysis and synthesis into the child's perception which he would be unable to develop by himself.

A. R. LURIA and F. LA YODOVICH
*Speech and Development Processes
in the Child*

To keep the uses of language in mind and become alert to the possibility each situation offers for fostering them, we will then be able to select

Language Development

exchange is useful to both the child and the teacher. The child may view the discussion as a pleasant chat, while to the teacher it represents a valuable teaching and assessing tool. Short dialogues between teacher and child, done on a systematic basis, ensure that all the children in the classroom have an opportunity to talk with the teacher. Information can be gathered about the child's language and thinking levels.

The teacher who uses dialogue in this way uses communication techniques, listening as well as questioning. Dialogue should promote thinking in the child.

The following are dialogue strategies.

Orienting Strategies

Orienting strategies are utterances, questions, and comments that set a child's thinking towards a particular topic (and use of language) and invite the child to respond. They give the child the opportunity to make an extended interpretation of the context. These orienting strategies invite the child to think in a particular way (e.g., imagining, predicting or reasoning). The child may not take up the orientation in his or her response and may choose to respond with other uses of language.

Enabling Strategies

These are utterances that are used to enable a child to move towards an extended interpretation. They help the child to reach further in the direction indicated by the orienting strategy and take three forms.

1. *Follow-through Strategies*

   These are utterances that take a child's thinking deeper or wider, following through the direction he or she has chosen. Such follow-through strategies may help the child to give further detail or to give explanations and justifications (e.g., in answer to why and how). They may help the child extend a description or invite reflection. They follow up the child's response and try to help in extending his or her interpretation.

2. *Focusing Strategies*

   Focusing strategies deliberately focus the child's attention on essential features (such as clues to a fuller interpretation of a picture) and are often in the form of closed questions or comments. They serve to focus the child's attention on a particular part of the experience, something that he or she has not taken into account.

3. *Checking Strategies*

   Checking strategies help a child to check his or her statements, to thing again, and to fill in information that is needed and has been omitted (e.g., "Is it really an elephant? Did you really mean . . .?").

Informing Strategies

These are the means by which a child is given explanations and facts as needed. Whereas orienting and enabling strategies are used to help the child express ideas, informing strategies provide information and ideas at a time when a child seems ready to receive them or when he or she needs them to complete some idea or to resolve a problem. They are the teacher's contribution to the interpretation that is

dialogue strategies deliberately and so use each situation to help the child think deeply and in the most appropriate way.

JOAN TOUGH
*Listening to Children Talking:
A Guide to the
Appraisal of Children's
Use of Language*

being built up and are intended to offer the child a new way of looking at the situation, to give an extension to the child's own interpretation, or to offer him or her some basic facts. Some teachers may be reluctant to contribute in this way, feeling that they are preventing the child from thinking independently. It is important that teachers should not do all the talking and should be prepared to listen, but a child needs both information and a model upon which he or she can base responses, and the teacher should be prepared to offer them at appropriate points.

Sustaining Strategies

These are comments that support children and assure them of the attention of their audience (e.g., "Really," "Good," "Go on," and "What else?"). Often the strategies are non-verbal, consisting of gestures and facial expressions, nod of head in agreement, the smile of encouragement, the grunt of appreciation, and the look of surprise. These strategies assure children of the teacher's interest and attention, and they prevent their contribution fading out before the interpretation is completed. Sometimes they are repetitions of what a child has just said, with an intonation indicating an expectation that he or she will continue, and providing a pause in which he or she can think further.

Concluding Strategies

These are strategies that indicate an intention to conclude the dialogue or to bring a particular topic to a close before reorienting the dialogue. It is essential to leave children with a feeling of satisfaction, either from recognition of their efforts or from knowing that their difficulties are understood as the dialogue is finally brought to a close. Examples of this strategy include statements such as "That was interesting, but I must go and see what Tommy's doing now," "Would you like to finish your picture now and I'll see it again later," and "I've enjoyed listening to your story, Tim. Will you put the blocks away now?"

Concluding strategies are not only strategies that bring the whole conversation to an end but are also strategies that deliberately conclude a particular section of dialogue when the topic seems to have been exhausted or when some more fruitful topic has been glimpsed. A concluding strategy will then serve to indicate a change of topic, and an orienting strategy will redirect the dialogue.

In this way the teacher leads from the conclusion of one topic and opens up dialogue in a new direction. The objective for dialogue is changed.

The classification given above is a simplification of the process of dialogue, but its purpose is to help teachers, and others, to distinguish different ways of using questions and comments and to study children's responses.

To gain information about a child's language development, the teacher who listens while the child talks with other children during an activity, takes note of the child's responses in teacher-directed large or small group discussions, and listens to a child's conversation with another child, will have valuable information about the child's language.

Children cannot diagnose their own problems and generally they are unaware of their difficulties.

JOAN TOUGH
Talking and Learning:
A Guide to Fostering
Communications Skills in
Nursery and Infant Schools

Language Development

Representing What is Known Through Language

During the stage of development in which we find most kindergarten children, the child's language develops as a part of a larger and more complex system of representation. Language is the most complex and abstract mode of representation. Whereas other forms of representation bear some resemblance to the objects or events they symbolize, language is expressed in symbols bearing no such resemblance. Unlike other forms of representation that are personal creations, language is acquired within the limits of a socially defined system. Language often accompanies other forms of representation and plays an important role in that representation.

Through the development of this representational system, the child is moving toward attainment of this vitally important aspect of literacy to which language is basic.

In viewing the importance of language in the kindergarten year, we are reminded that
- the teacher needs to take every opportunity to extend and enrich the child's understanding and use of language;
- children need this rich experience of spoken language as a basis for their future reading and writing activities;
- the level of language that the child has acquired in early years, and his or her understanding of the spoken language, may be the most decisive factors in his ability to learn to read and write.

The language of the child is different at the various stages of development. While the child is in the sensorimotor stage, the actions prepare a foundation for the emergence of language; the preoperational stage influences the child's construction of language. As the child enters the concrete operational stage, the child's thinking becomes truly operational or logical. This emergence of logical thought further influences the development of language and is accompanied by related changes in language usage.

Using strategies for appraising children's language will assist the teacher in recognizing the child's language, thinking, and representational abilities. The teacher needs to be alert to the language to recognize the kinds of knowledge that are being represented as the children use dialogue with adults or other children during the many kindergarten experiences. However, adults may be misled by the child's verbalism. Adults sometimes tend to credit children with a level of understanding beyond their current capacity. Since words are convenient labels for concepts, the adult is often misled to believe that the child has learned the concept as well as a label for it. On the other hand, the teacher needs to be aware that some children, though they may understand concepts and have the language, may be reluctant to talk, although they may be confident at representing their knowledge in other ways (e.g., constructing, modelling, drawing, moving, etc.).

Since we are aware that these young children develop best while involved in "hands on" and "minds on" activities, it will be crucial for the teacher to appraise and foster language representation that accompanies these experiences.

Through the use of strategies for dialogue that can be used during all activities of the kindergarten program, the teacher will have opportunities to foster the child's language and thinking. As well, the alert teacher will observe the knowledge and representational abilities of the children.

Language develops as part of a larger system of representation. It is only one way of representing the world.

E. LABINOWICZ
*The Piaget Primer:
Thinking, Learning, Teaching*

Understanding the Purposes of Reading and Writing

From the point of view of cognitive learning theory, children have a strong desire to master their environment. They select, interpret, and integrate information about their world. On the basis of this model, they make predictions about how the world works.

Piaget's theory of cognitive development allows us to understand the process of appropriating knowledge involved in learning to read and write. This position is based not only on a redefinition of reading and writing but also on a global acceptance of the learning process. Progress in literacy does not come through advances in deciphering and copying; becoming literate involves the process of appropriating knowledge of literacy. The knowledge is not truly appropriated until its means of production have been understood and until it has been internally constructed. This reflects a long developmental process from the children's initial conception of print. This process takes place in the preschool period. Some children are in the final levels of this development as they enter school. Others reach first grade at the initial levels of hypothesizing about print.

Traditional notions of reading readiness dictated the use of work/skill activities based upon inventories of isolated skills such as verbal knowledge of sound/symbol relationships and the ability to trace right-to-left progression across the page. Such skills were believed to be the prerequisites or building blocks of reading. Emphasis on the acquisition of these traditional skills reflected the demands of an instructional program rather than the nature of the reading process.

Advances in the field of psycholinguistics point toward a revised concept of reading readiness. From a psycholinguistic perspective, learning to read is viewed as a ". . . continual process of making more and more sense of written language, advancing with every reading experience and beginning with the first insight that print is meaningful" (Smith, 1980). In this sense, readiness to read implies competence in symbolic representation of meaning more than it implies facility in any given set of specific skills as seen in the program of work/skill instructions previously mentioned.

In view of recent psycholinguistic and psychogenetic research, the teacher has a vital role in developing a "set for literacy." The focus, then, needs to be on helping children acquire knowledge of literacy. To participate in the literate world the child must understand the precise connection between language, writing, and reading.

Most teachers will agree that a child's first experience with the printed word should arise naturally, bringing a sense of pleasure and achievement. Since language in its spoken, written, and printed forms is just as much a part of the child's environment as water, clay, paint, paste, and paper, we need to commend children's exploration of these aspects of their environment as well as their interest in, and exploration of, printed and written words and letters, which form an equally important and interesting aspect of their environment.

During the period of three to four years before school entry, some children have become fascinated with print and are well on their way in gaining knowledge about print as they play with reading, produce writing-like scribble, and realize that the central feature of print is that it carries a message.

There is no magical day in a child's life when it can be said that the child passes from a state of being unable to learn to read to a stage of being ready. There is no intellectual or linguistic basis for the notion of readiness. If learning to read is regarded as a continual process of making more and more sense of written language, advancing with every reading experience and beginning with the first insight that print is meaningful, then it will be seen that there can never be anything specific for a child to be ready for. Learning to read is simply a matter of reading more.

FRANK SMITH
Reading Without Nonsense

The vital learnings of this emergent stage of literacy development centre around the tasks of creating a healthy literacy set.

D. HOLDAWAY
The Foundations of Literacy

It is likely that these children have had preschool experiences with books in typical bedtime stories and that they probably come from book-oriented homes. They may have learned to write their names and to explore the creation of letters and letter-like symbols. They show intense interest in print in their environment—signs, labels, advertisements. They often imitate the forms in inventive ways. They may know the alphabet; many recognize many letters and may be able to name them.

We need to recognize that some children begin building their emergent reading and writing behavior before coming to school. Others will develop such behavior with appropriate experiences in kindergarten. Other children will still be developing knowledge of literacy in Year One. No matter; this acquisition or appropriation of knowledge of the process in the emergent reading and writing stage is vitally important for success in school. By being exposed to and immersed in written language in functional ways, children will begin to develop reading and writing behavior.

Becoming Involved in Emergent Reading and Writing Behavior

Reading needs to be a natural and delightful part of the young child's kindergarten experience. With the emphasis on enjoying stories and viewing print, it becomes woven in with all the language that the child explores in day-to-day activities. If children are exposed to and immersed in oral language, their reading behavior will begin to emerge very clearly. Many children are happy to "read" a favorite book by sitting and turning pages, commenting on pictures, and perhaps reciting a repetitive phrase from the story. This important stage can develop naturally into the reading of print. A few five-year-olds may be reading and will need a variety of books available. Other children may have had very few experiences in reading books and print.

Emergent reading and writing is based on the child making a number of discoveries about print. These discoveries come about through many opportunities to experience print in the everyday world—signs, labels, T.V., books, letters. Concepts about print are not taught directly but can be influenced by the teacher who provides many experiences for the child. The child understands that a book contains stories, that print is a way of representing spoken language.

The teacher's task is to help the child develop an ear for literary language. Predictable books appeal to young children and build concepts of language when
- there is a good match between illustrations and text;
- the child quickly predicts what the author will say and begins to chant (i.e., *Brown Bear, Brown Bear*);
- there is a cumulative pattern (i.e., *The House That Jack Built, Chicken Little*);
- there is a rhythmic pattern to the language;
- the concepts and/or the sequence is familiar (i.e., counting books);
- the story is familiar (i.e., *Three Billy Goats Gruff*).

Pattern books provide many of the aspects of prediction necessary to assist the child in gaining a set for literacy.

Orientation to book language develops in an environment of rich exposure. Repeated reading of favorite picture stories can help a child to label the pictures or to establish a story line to go with the pictures. The child develops positive associations with the flow of story language and with the physical characteristics of books.

Children begin to learn to read from the time they begin to hear language and more particularly, from the time they hear their first nursery rhymes, jingles or stories. They learn that books have a right and a wrong way up. They become fascinated with the pictures on the pages and will begin, at a very early stage, to use these pictures to help them "read" the story. They will soon learn that books mean "story time," a period of warm human sharing, enjoyed utterly by both the reader and the listener. Through this experience they will start to establish, and continue to extend, critically important positive attitudes towards books and reading that will influence their reading behaviors for the rest of their lives.

At some stage they will make an important discovery about the stories they are hearing and often repeating for themselves. They will become aware, although not necessarily with a conscious realization, that the source of the story they are hearing is not in the pictures or in the reader's head, but is actually on the pages in the black squiggles that the reader has been pointing to from time to time. They will begin to learn a whole lot of things about books, written language and reading which will set them on the road to literacy very early in their lives.

D. DOAKE
Book Experience and Emergent Reading Behavior

When learning to read, a child learns to represent one set of signs with another, the spoken with the written

Language Development

The link between reading and writing is established from the beginning, and written symbols will be introduced in the kindergarten in many different ways (such as choosing charts, poems, rhymes, songs, and recipes). This is an essential part of the learning environment.

Young children experiment with many of the functions of written language in activities such as dramatic play, making shopping lists, writing out cheques, and preparing menus. Through the use of language and "pretend" writing, children create written language.

They must discover that the writer's intentions are expressed through specifically arranged symbols, that they are related in arbitrary but precise ways to formal characteristics of speech, and that the reader can receive a message. This is a tremendous cognitive attainment for the young child.

As with reading, the foundation for writing has already been laid down for many children in their preschool experiences. From scribbling to writing recognizable stories, children display their knowledge about print.

Writing has many aspects, two of which are composing and graphic representation. It involves a psycholinguistic process of thought and language. The child recalls a personal experience or story that may be represented by composing a picture. The child talks about the picture, and the adult writes down what he says. This begins the notion of composing. As the child shows growing interest in having thoughts written down, he or she may trace, rewrite or even begin to "write" independently, using invented spellings.

Teachers may encourage children to watch them writing letters and preparing name cards, labels, recipes, and graphs. In presenting children's pictures and art creations as part of the classroom display, short captions drawn from the child can be added. These should be carefully written in clear, well-spaced letters that are large enough for children to "read" easily.

The language-experience approach to writing and reading depends upon the child's own personal experience and language. In this way, the child comes to understand the relationship of thought, spoken language, and print. This kind of activity can help the child understand that the thoughts represented through drawing, painting, or modelling can be expressed by the spoken word and written down in words.

The emergence of reading and writing behavior is critically important to the child's continuing progress toward literacy, and it develops when the child
- "re-reads" familiar books from memory;
- practises reading-like behavior;
- seeks book experiences;
- tells stories about pictures;
- shows interest in, and enjoys, books and stories;
- seeks meaning from symbols in the environment (i.e., advertisements);
- moves from pretending to read to attempting to match the flow of language to print;
- begins to develop interest in dictating stories and is able to recall the general meaning of stories;
- is aware that meaning can be sought through picture and print;
- is able to listen to continuous language of story length being read or told;

ply this in relation to reading he will need to have had much experience of using symbols to represent one thing by another.

JOAN TOUGH
Talking and Learning:
A Guide to Fostering
Communications Skills in Nursery
and Infant Schools

Therefore if we wish to meet the needs of children to acquire literacy in its fullest sense we can view it (literacy) as the top rung of the ladder of representational growth. Early developmental stages of symbolic play may then be seen as the means of moving up the rungs of the ladder.

C. H. WOLFGANG
and T. S. SAUNDERS
"Defending Young Children's Play
as the Ladder to Literacy"

Knowledge is not truly appropriated until its means of production has been understood; until it has been internally reconstructed.

E. FERRIERO and A. TEBEROSKY
Literacy Before Schooling

Language Development

- is able to attend to the language of books;
- practises writing-like behavior;
- experiments with producing written language;
- gradually shows interest in learning to print;
- attempts to trace over or print under dictated stories;
- is aware that meaning can be conveyed through print;
- watches adults read, pretends to read, and is beginning to learn book skills;
- attempts to match own flow of language to print;
- can trace over, and/or copy under, names, words, and short stories (with assistance);
- may learn to print name(s), words, and short stories;
- may watch as words are written;
- tells stories about a picture and may show interest in having the story printed;
- may "read" dictated stories;
- may show an interest in letters or words.

In the psycholinguistic view, these concepts develop as a result of many experiences with books and reading through a growing awareness of print as a whole. This process includes writing and early composing.

To foster emergent reading and writing behavior, the kindergarten experience must include the following.
- The teacher needs to read to children; the stories should have a predictable structure and use highly patterned language.
- The children need to be exposed to song, chants, poems, and rhymes for choral reading.
- Print should be clearly visible to children (intensive use of enlarged versions). Children should be encouraged to join in and chant the predictable parts.
- Story books should be available to children (taped stories, records, volunteer adults, and older children need to be available).
- There must be a time and place for reading, a book centre, visits to the library, and daily story time.
- Writing must be given importance. It should be read to the children and displayed for others to read.
- There must be a print-saturated environment with a wide range of materials available (labels, directions, recipes, menus).
- Children need to be encouraged to use patterns of language and story structures in sociodramatic activities.

For those few children who already read when they come to school, the teacher must keep in mind the complexity of the development of emerging reading and writing behavior in order to enhance the program and develop a literacy set for each child.

Language Development

The Learning Environment

The learning environment consists in part of the settings, the people, the program and the resources that influence the kindergarten child's learning during this year. The child's background and early experiences, and the child's interests inside and outside the classroom, also influence learning. Previous experiences and interactions with people will affect the learning and have a bearing on the knowledge, needs, and interests of the child. All these factors are considered when the teacher plans, provides, or facilitates the experiences that comprise the kindergarten program.

Through orientation sessions, home visits, parent interviews, the phasing-in program, dialogue with children, and observations, the teacher learns a great deal about the previous experiences of the children. The teacher's knowledge of the characteristics and needs of the children, and of the goals of the program, is crucial to the preparation of the kindergarten environment. In the kindergarten setting, the teacher builds on the child's previous knowledge and experience and incorporates children's needs and interests to provide new learnings. The environment is adjusted to meet needs of individuals or groups of children and is shaped to reflect the nature of the community.

The environment of the kindergarten is strongly influenced by the attitudes, knowledge, and beliefs of the people who are responsible for the program. Children and their parents feel welcome in an environment where they are accepted and respected. The teacher is the key factor in the creation of a positive classroom climate. The way in which the teacher interacts with the children, the parents, and others involved in the kindergarten program provides a model for the children.

The life of the classroom is reflected by the positive (reflective) manner in which the teacher facilitates, guides, directs, assists, interacts, suggests, and extends the learning. The teacher respects the child's development and always keeps in mind the characteristics of five-year-olds, their stage of development, and the manner in which they learn best.

The kindergarten year provides a continuation of group experiences. Many children have attended preschool (some for two years)—a fact that must be recognized and accepted. Continuous learning and stimulation programs must be provided to facilitate the transition from preschool to kindergarten.

Learning centres allow the children to pursue the learning of a variety of concepts and skills at their own rate. The environment is adapted to their stage of development and is success oriented. Each task can be pursued according to the individual child's ability.

Because the kindergarten curriculum reflects the child's integrated way of learning, the physical space, equipment, and materials are organized so that children can learn while pursuing activities of interest to them. The differing needs of all children can be met when a variety of experiences and activities is provided. One child may be acquiring knowledge about the physical properties of sand, water, clay, and wood, while another may be ready to undertake measurement tasks using the same materials at the same learning centre. Similarly, some children may be at the stage of exploration with books and other print materials while others are ready to read books and write about their experiences. Many children can use the same materials or be involved in the same activity, but each child will personalize the experience. Through first-hand experiences, children accommodate new information and assimilate it to their present way of thinking about themselves and the world, thereby forming a new way of perceiving reality. They extract from the experience what they are ready to internalize. The activity and resources are common denominators, but the learning is individual in rate and depth for each child.

Some centres (such as sand, water, woodworking, modelling, food, music, art, construction, manipulation, and dramatic play centre) remain in use throughout the year, but the materials available at these centres are changed to provide for a variety of learning experiences. Other interest centres are developed as needs arise from a theme, a visitor, or a field trip or through items children bring to school. Careful consideration must be given to the individual child's interest and to providing follow-up activities that arise from this interest.

Bringing in interesting objects and artifacts, and having resource people come to share experiences, can expand and enrich the environment. Experiences arise from various sources. Most are planned in advance and are provided by the teacher on the basis of the needs and interests of the children in the group. Some are initiated by children (and are facilitated by the teacher) as they explore areas of special interest. Some arise spontaneously as the teacher focuses on events at hand to further the goals of the program.

Most learning-centre activities involve individual and small groups, but the whole group can gather at a learning centre for opening time, story time, or snack time, or for a variety of activities directed by the teacher. Activities such as movement, drama, and music may take place in small groups or large groups and may be set in another environment (i.e., outdoors, gym, activity rooms). Such factors as themes, visits, and resource people also influence the grouping and the environment. The teacher plans sessions carefully so that children are exposed to a balance of quiet and active experiences.

Although the teacher may not be able to alter the provided facility, kindergarten supplies and equipment are arranged to provide for individual, small-group, and large-group activities. Furniture and equipment are placed to provide a safe and attractive atmosphere. Children can move around the space without disturbing others. A variety of equipment is readily accessible. Tools, equipment, and resources are suitable for this age group and are of the best possible quality. Things that stimulate discussion and exploration are included in the environment. By creating an environment that is rich in sensory input, the possibilities for high-quality learning are increased.

When children help to create and maintain their environment, they learn to plan, develop responsibility, and feel that their opinions are valuable. The learning environment reflects an organization and order that is helpful to the learner. The teacher provides a framework in which children can learn to become socially responsible and independent. By involving and observing the children, the teacher evaluates the effectiveness and appropriateness of the classroom environment and then rearranges, adds, or removes things as necessary. Challenging new materials and centres are added regularly.

The learning environment does not stop at the classroom doors. Its horizons are those of the children, and these can be extended as the teacher plans new experiences for the children both inside and outside the classroom and the school. Children gain a feeling of security about being at school as they become familiar with the facility. As they become confident in their ability to find their way around the school, they are better able to make use of the resources available. Field trips

The Learning Environment

are a natural extension of the classroom. Through such experiences, children are given the opportunity to explore and hence to understand more fully the world around them.

The teacher provides a supportive, non-threatening environment with a variety of materials and experiences that will challenge the children yet allow them to learn at their own rate. Time is an important factor as all children need time to be involved, to reflect, and to learn at their own pace.

The best possible use is made of the available space, time, people, and materials in the kindergarten environment to ensure that the learning opportunities for each child are of high quality. The teacher evaluates the learning environment continuously in order to provide a strong program and to assess the progress the children make in that environment.

THE INTEGRATED CURRICULUM

To the young child the experiences of living and learning are inseparable. Learning that takes place in kindergarten is part of the total experience of living. Separating learning experiences into blocks of time or into subjects taught in isolation is contrary to what is known about how young children learn.

The most effective learning takes place as a result of combining new learning with that which is already known. When teachers provide experiences that help children make connections between new learning and what they know already, children's knowledge skills and concepts are developed and extended in all aspects of the curriculum. The teacher provides experiences that allow the children to learn in a naturally integrated way. This approach to learning is the basis for an effective program.

The kindergarten program reflects the characteristics, needs, and interests of five-year-old children. Kindergarten children come from a variety of backgrounds and cultures and are at different stages of development. Yet they all need to learn through first-hand experiences. An integrated curriculum is flexible, open-ended, and planned. When preparing activities and organizing materials and equipment, the teacher plans first-hand experiences that are the vehicles for the children's learning. Each activity or experience in kindergarten encompasses possibilities for developing and expanding learning in several of the kindergarten goal areas. Similarly, through a single theme, each child is exposed to a wide range of possible learning.

The teacher provides those facilities and activities that will encourage children to explore their world in a relaxed yet guided way. An integrated curriculum provides kindergarten children with the freedom to explore, probe, think, and use their senses. The teacher is aware of the (traditional) subject areas but presents activities and experiences embracing many content areas.

For example, if the teacher plans experiences developed around the theme "Rain," the boundaries of several disciplines will be crossed. Rain can be experienced by each of the five senses. Vocabulary will be introduced; language will be developed and expanded; pictures, books, and films can be shared and discussed. The children have the opportunity to gain social knowledge by learning about weather forecasters or about customs that have evolved as a result of human experiences with rain. Information about the physical world can be gained as children participate in activities that help them form concepts about measurement, temperature, wetness and dryness, and the varying physical states of water (e.g., vapour, rain, sleet, hail, snow). As the teacher investigates possibilities, provision can be made for the children to anticipate, identify, and solve problems using rain as the vehicle for study (e.g., "What are ways to keep dry in the rain?"). The teacher also plans activities that foster talking, drawing, painting, dramatizing, constructing, and labelling and writing captions for their representations. Each teacher develops experiences around a theme in a way that meets the needs of each group of children. Depending on the teacher and the children, the number and nature of the activities vary, but each activity allows for a variety in learning.

As children come into contact with people and materials, teachers should continually ask, "What is being learned?" Observation will reveal that the children are learning and developing physically, emotionally, socially, and intellectually. A single activity presented to a group of children will result in experiences that are different for each child. In addition, while the teacher plans learning activities aimed at specific learning outcomes, some incidental learning may also take place.

To continue with the previous example (planning experiences around the theme "Rain"), the teacher may decide to have the children experiment with the effects of water on sand, dirt, and rocks. By mixing water with these materials, the children can be encouraged to observe changes, classify results, and perhaps arrive at conclusions and make generalizations. One child may simply recount the experiment. Another may incorporate previous knowledge and newly introduced vocabulary to explain the results of the experiment. One child may experience only the sensory aspects — the grainy, wet sand, the cool, sticky mud, and the solid, damp rocks. Another child may want to draw pictures of the experiment and write captions to describe the process. The teacher may act as the recorder, printing on a chart the various ideas and observations made by the children. The activity presented is constant, but what each child learns and understands will differ, depending upon his or her experience and level of development. The teacher provides the setting and opportunity to capitalize on the interest and capabilities of individual children.

Kindergarten children have a desire to exchange points of view. They are alert and curious in their attempts to effect and control their environment. When talking to children, teachers draw out and build upon their natural motivation to investigate their environment. Children can be encouraged to develop and extend their thought process by observing, comparing, classifying, generalizing, and solving problems. The kindergarten environment that provides for integrated learning contributes to the child's present development and strengthens and extends the base for future learning as well.

Learning through Play

Play is the fundamental, natural, universal activity of children. Play is what children do, what they have always done, and what they must continue to do. Play is intrinsically motivated for personal satisfaction and a way of learning. It is the expressive activity resulting from the child's desire to make sense of the world.

The child learns through the process of play because of his or her inner drive to explore, experiment, and discover. The integration of the child's intellect, emotions, and inner drive promotes the development of the whole child. This integration may be accomplished through the provision for high-quality play experiences in the kindergarten. As children play, information gained through experience is explored, tested, and represented in a variety of ways.

Types of Play

Understanding the types of play, as classified by Parten and Newell (1974), guides teachers in their program planning.

- *Unoccupied Behavior:* To an observer, the child appears not to be playing at all but is occupied with watching anything that happens to be of momentary interest.
- *Solitary Play:* The child plays alone and independently. Interest is centered on his or her own activity without any reference to what others are doing.
- *Onlooker Behavior:* The child watches others play, talks to them, asks questions, or makes suggestions, but does not enter into the play.
- *Parallel Play:* The child plays with other children and uses similar materials to them, but not necessarily in the same way.
- *Associative Play:* The child plays with other children and shares materials in similar activities. The activity is not organized. Each child acts as he or she wishes.
- *Co-operative or Organized Supplementary Play:* The child plays in a group that is organized for the purpose of making something, attaining a goal, dramatizing a situation, or playing a formal game. There is a marked sense of either belonging, or not belonging, to the group. Each child plays a role in relationship to other members of the group.

Although associative and co-operative play are the types encouraged most often in the kindergarten, all six types of play may occur simultaneously. It is important that the teacher recognize that the types of play listed are not stages and that children will select the type of play that meets their needs. For example, one child may need to be the observer until he or she feels confident enough to participate. Another child who usually takes an active part in group activities may become fascinated by a particular experience and feel the need to explore it independently. Just as adults vary their behavior according to needs and circumstances, children also participate in different kinds of play.

Stages of Play Related to Cognitive Developmental Stages

As children develop intellectually, the types of play in which they engage reflect this development. Play may be categorized in three stages: practice or functional play, symbolic play, and games with rules.

- *Practice or Functional Play:* Play at this stage involves the sensorimotor explorations of the very young child (birth to two years). The games played are very functional as the child manipulates toys and play objects, explores his or her physical capabilities, and experiences the environment.

Play is by no means a simple thing; it is, in fact, a very complex thing. It is the only activity in which the whole educational process is fully consummated: when experience induces learning and learning produces wisdom and character.

N. V. SCARFE
Play Is Education

Recent expansion of research in the area of play and its effects on learning firmly supports the notion that concrete objects and experiences manipulated by children at play are the prerequisites to successful acquisition of more skills.

LANCE M. GENTILE
Kindergarten Play:
The Foundation of Reading

Learning through Play

- *Symbolic Play:* In the early stages (preoperational stage — two to seven years), the child substitutes a symbolic object for a real object (i.e., a block becomes a telephone). Symbolic play becomes more sophisticated as the child dramatizes the actions surrounding that object (i.e., the child imitates dialing the telephone). Later, symbolic play incorporates true imitative behavior and reaches the most sophisticated levels of symbolic play: sociodramatic play (two children have a conversation over the "telephone").
- *Games with Rules:* At this stage (concrete operational stage — seven to eleven years approximately), the child learns to accept prearranged rules and to adjust play accordingly. The child learns to control his or her behavior, actions, and reactions within established limits. This form of play accompanies us into adulthood. Because kindergarten children are only beginning to develop the ability to consider things from a point of view other than their own, involving them in games with rules is often inappropriate and may cause undue stress.

The Role of Play

Play is a facilitator of cognitive development. When children are involved in symbolic play, they combine and practise concepts that they have already assimilated. They also learn to put together thinking skills in new ways to fit the play situation where they lack full knowledge of the real situation (e.g., 12:30 on a digital clock. A child "playing" at telling the time may say "Oh, it's 1, 2, 3 o'clock").

Symbolic play is essential if the child is to develop the understanding that one thing can represent another. This knowledge is prerequisite to understanding the symbol systems used in mathematics and language.

Sociodramatic play, the most sophisticated form of symbolic play, requires an ability, developed through previous play experiences, to share that imagination with another. Language develops as children explore, test, and construct new ideas and vocabulary to accompany their sociodramatic play. Children represent what they know about their world as they imitate, role play, pretend, fantasize, dramatize, and create.

Opportunities that allow children to assume "as if" roles are essential for the development of abstract logical thought as well as for promoting social and emotional development.

The basic material in a kindergarten activity centre may remain constant throughout the year. By the addition of simple props and the provision of stimulating preparatory experiences, for example, a small table may be represented as a shop counter, the bridge in *Three Billy Goats Gruff,* a fire engine, a hospital operating table, a Japanese tea house, or whatever representation is necessary for children to become absorbed as they learn through symbolic and sociodramatic play.

Symbolic play can foster literacy development in two ways. First it provides an opportunity for children to use representational skills that serve as the basis for representation in literacy. This focuses on the relationship between the process of symbolic play and literacy development. Second, symbolic play provides a safe environment in which children can practise the skills and social behaviors associated with literacy activities. This focuses on the relationship between the literacy content of symbolic play and literacy development.

J. ISENBERG and E. JACOB
"Literacy and Symbolic Play:
A Review of the Literature"

Learning through Play

Providing for High-Quality Play Experiences

An activity such as playing with sand results in different learning for each child. When children choose to play the sand table, they may explore, observe and investigate, experiment, create, interact, discuss, compare, classify, record experience, and learn.

Spontaneous play is an integral part of the kindergarten environment. Because the outcome of spontaneous play is not always predictable, the teacher observes and interacts in order to plan with the child for extension of the child's learning. This develops the child's ability to sustain, enrich, and thereby improve the quality of his or her play.

Planning, Observing, and Extending Play

Effectiveness in providing for high-quality play experiences is enhanced as teachers provide experiences that allow kindergarten children to be engaged in exploring, testing, imitating, constructing, discussing, planning, problem solving, resolving disputes, dramatizing, creating, generating ideas, and experimenting.

The teacher learns about each child by observing and reflecting and can plan a variety of experiences that will encourage the child to participate in play at the appropriate level of development. When confronted with unfamiliar situations or phenomena, children will often need to explore and test their perceptions before moving to the more symbolic stage of imitation and to sociodramatic play (where they are involved creatively in using the new information they have assimilated). Through play, children reflect what they know and use elements of their knowledge to create, to express themselves, and to further explore their environment. The teacher supports, sustains, facilitates, extends, enhances, and enriches the child's ideas and endeavors expressed through play, and children come to understand their world by organizing and processing information and by altering their perceptions accordingly. Play can be a deeply satisfying, creative endeavor as well as an adventure in self-expression and exploration.

. . . the teacher plays a vital role by providing a rich physical and social environment that is essential to support children's play.

JUDITH SCHICKENDANS
" 'You'll Be the Doctor and I'll Be Sick:' Preschoolers Learn the Language Arts Through Play"

Play creates many practical situations in which the child discovers and observes, and reasons and solves, problems.

WILLARD C. OLSON
Child Development

When children play they are taking an active part in their growth and development.

D. JEFFRIES
"Focus on Childhood"

CHILDREN WITH SPECIAL NEEDS

Children with special needs are typically more like than unlike other children. Unfortunately, it is often the areas of weakness that become the focal point of our efforts. These children exhibit the same needs and requirements as other children. With the exception of special recommendations, they should be treated as are all other children in our care. The goals for kindergarten are congruent with the needs of exceptional children.

Integration of exceptional children is most common and natural at the kindergarten level. The curriculum is child-centred and thus offers a high possibility for success. Each child is considered in light of individual strengths and weaknesses, and it is accepted that all children will be at varying stages of their development. The exceptional child is given the opportunity to model the behavior of peers, and other children are encouraged to accept and respect the differences between individuals.

One of the responsibilities of educators is to enable children to function appropriately in the school setting and to prepare them for life in the "real world." That world will be the same for all children. We are charged with the task of encouraging children to make the greatest possible use of the capabilities they have and of establishing a balance for reasonable expectations. To expect too much is to risk frustration and failure; to expect too little can result in failure to attain full potential.

Given these considerations and the specific kinds of special needs, it becomes apparent that more is being asked of today's teacher. It may be necessary to change our attitudes, adapt our behavior, and adjust our teaching styles and strategies. Fear of the "unknown" is one of the biggest factors in teachers who are not used to working with exceptional children. Teachers are therefore encouraged to seek information and support from a variety of sources. The child's family is often well informed as to the nature and degree of their child's special needs. They can provide background information and suggestions for useful strategies, and they are often able to give assistance in the classroom. Teachers can make use of the human resources in the class by establishing a "buddy system," by utilizing aides, and by encouraging parent participation in the program. At the school level, the learning assistance teacher, the special class teacher, and/or the resource room teacher may be able to provide valuable suggestions. District Special Education Consultants, the Ministry's Special Education Division, and independent societies and agencies can provide information, materials, contact with others, or consultative services.

Approaches

Whether your district has established policy for planning programs for children with special needs or not, procedures commonly include the following steps.

1. *Diagnose the specific learning difficulty.* Because a label for a child is less important than a descriptive statement of educational strengths and weaknesses, teachers are encouraged to familiarize themselves with the characteristics and nature of their students' special needs. Emphasizing this positive approach eliminates the debilitating effect that can occur when children are merely labelled.

2. *Establish long-term educational and social goals as well as short-term instructional objectives.* This process should be conducted as a team effort. All those who will be working with the child (parents, teachers, counsellor, principal, agency professionals, and consultants) should be included in this phase.

Somehow the requirements for teaching these children are the same as those for teaching other children . . . only more.

BERNARD SPODEK
Teaching in the Early Years

Resource Agencies

- Special Education Division
  Ministry of Education
  Parliament Buildings
  Victoria, B.C.
  V8V 2M4 (387-4611)

- Education Clinic
  Faculty of Education
  University of British Columbia
  Vancouver, B.C.
  V6T 1W5 (228-5384)

3. *Plan a program specifically aimed at developing skills.* Once the goals and objectives of the individual program have been established, the teacher or team must identify the kinds of materials to be used, the special services that are needed, the steps to be taken in order to attain the objectives, and the responsibility of each team member. Each has a role in this process, and all must work together. Providing for the needs of the child is a shared responsibility. It is important to accept the child at his or her present stage of development and, if necessary, plan the program in small segments to ensure success for the child.

4. *Assess progress in skill areas.* The parents, teacher, and professionals will have established a date for review of the program. The roles and responsibilities of all will have been clearly set. At the time of program assessment, all information available will be compiled and related to the original goals and objectives.

5. *Consider future placement of the child.* Long-term planning for the child's future placement in a school setting must be considered throughout the team meetings. The questions that should be considered include, "What is available in the district?"; "What can the parents cope with?"; and "Where would the best, *least restrictive* environment be?"

The Role of the Teacher

Teachers who are sensitive to the needs of exceptional children are
- knowledgeable about normal growth and development patterns as well as the exceptional nature of abilities or disabilities;
- familiar with the particular learning characteristics of each child;
- aware of basic techniques of education for exceptional children;
- able to gain access to information and service delivery, to work as an effective group member with outside agencies, consultants, and experts, and to keep individuals informed;
- capable of encouraging student independence.

The Nature of Special Needs

The following subsections are intended to assist the teacher with the first steps in providing for the needs of the exceptional child in the kindergarten classroom. The statements and definitions provided have been extracted in full or in part from the *Special Programs Manual of Policies, Procedures, and Guidelines,* section 11; "Program Guidelines and Information." The following labels can assist the teacher seeking information and support services, but teachers are cautioned to keep in mind that the label is the *least* important piece of information, that it serves only to establish a beginning point from which a statement of educational strengths and weaknesses can be developed.

Special Needs Resources

- *Special Programs: A Manual of Policies, Procedures and Guidelines.* (Ministry of Education: Division of Special Education, Special Programs Branch)

Severe Learning Disabilities

The Ministry of Education recognizes the *severely* learning disabled as pertaining to that one–two per cent of children in the schools whose hindrances to learning are so severe as to almost totally impede educational instruction by conventional methods.

Learning disabled children have one universal characteristic: in one or more learning areas, performance consistently falls short of estimated potential. Given

Resources Concerning Severe Learning Disabilities

- Co-ordinator
  Learning Assistance and Learning Disabilities
  Ministry of Education
  Parliament Buildings
  Victoria, B.C.
  V8V 2M4

the complex task of defining the learning disabled population and the deficiencies of each of the many definitions currently proposed in the literature, the following definition is advanced by the Ministry of Education:

> Children with learning disabilities are those who show a significant discrepancy between their estimated learning potential and actual performance. This discrepancy is related to basic problems in attention, perception, symbolization, and the understanding or use of spoken or written language. These may be manifested in difficulties in thinking, listening, talking, reading, writing, spelling, or computing. These problems may or may not be accompanied by demonstrable central nervous system dysfunctions.

Mentally Handicapped Students

The Special Programs Branch recognizes that there are some children whose sub-average cognitive, motor, social, communication abilities, developmental skills, and adaptive behavior are such that they require special education services to assist them in attaining age-appropriate coping skills and in reaching their potential.

Depending on their present level of functioning, these children are referred to by classical disability categories based historically on the results of I.Q. tests which are used to classify them as mildly, moderately, severely, or profoundly mentally handicapped.

- *Mildly Mentally Handicapped Children* (E.M.H.; E.M.R.) are those who may not be able to progress satisfactorily in standard programs in regular classroom without the provision of support services of an instructional and/or curricular nature.
- *Moderately Mentally Handicapped Students* (T.M.R.; T.M.H.) are those students who demonstrate sub-average intellectual and social functioning to such an extent that they are unable to experience success with programs for the mildly mentally handicapped.
- *Severely and Profoundly Mentally Handicapped Students* are those who because of severe/profound below-average intellectual and social development have extraordinary needs that necessitate specialized supportive services. Increasingly, school districts are offering educational programs for severely and profoundly mentally handicapped children. These programs are expensive and require specialized staff and support services.

Physically Handicapped Students

Physical handicaps are as varied as the students who have them. Included in this category would be disorders of the nervous system, musculoskeletal conditions, congenital malformations, and other crippling and health impaired conditions.

Physically handicapping conditions are usually identified on the basis of medical classifications:

- disorders of the nervous system (e.g., cerebral palsy, convulsive disorders—epilepsy—multiple sclerosis);
- musculoskeletal conditions (e.g., scoliosis, Legg-Perthe's, rheumatoid arthritis, muscular dystrophy);
- congenital malformations (e.g., malformations of the heart, limb deficiencies, spina bifida, hydrocephalus);
- other crippling conditions (e.g., conditions due to accidents, infectious diseases, birth injuries);
- impaired health conditions (e.g., cystic fibrosis, leukemia).

- Vancouver Neurological Centre
1195 West Eighth Avenue
Vancouver, B.C.
V6H 1C5 (734-2221)

Resources Concerning Mental Handicaps

- *Special Education Core Curriculum Supplement: A Resource Guide for Teachers of the Mentally Handicapped,* (Ministry of Education; Curriculum Development Branch, 1983)
- *The Physically/Mentally Handicapped Student in the Regular Classroom,* (Alberta Education, 1982)
- B.C. Association for the Mentally Retarded
155, 1200 West 73rd Avenue
Vancouver, B.C.
V6P 6G5 (266-1146)
- Woodlands
Ministry of Human Resources
9 East Columbia Street
New Westminster, B.C.
V3L 3V5 (521-2611)

Resources Concerning Physical Handicaps

- Cerebral Palsy Association of B.C.
204, 579 Granville Street
Vancouver, B.C.
V6C 1Y7 (660-0756)
- B.C. Epilepsy Society
1721 Richmond Road
Victoria, B.C.
V8R 4P9 (595-1433)
- Canadian Paraplegic Association (B.C.)
780B S.W. Marine Drive
Vancouver, B.C.
V6P 5Y7 (324-3611)
- Kinsmen Rehabilitation Foundation of B.C.
2256 West 12th Avenue
Vancouver, BC.
V6K 2N5 (736-8841)

Children with Special Needs

Hearing Impaired Students

Hearing impaired students include those students whose hearing impairment results in such a substantial educational handicap that they require special education and/or related services from trained and qualified teachers of the hearing impaired. These students may be described as deaf or hard of hearing.

Visually Impaired Students

Visually impaired students include those students whose visual impairment results in such a substantial educational handicap that they require special education and/or related services from trained and experienced teachers of the visually impaired. These students are commonly referred to as blind or partially sighted students.

Students with Speech Disorders

Through school district consultative services or the Public Health Unit, information, services, and support are available for those children with speech disorders or communication difficulties. Teachers are cautioned to keep in mind, however, that many children of kindergarten age will exhibit speech peculiarities that will disappear with maturity.

Autistic Students

The definition of autistic students used by the Ministry of Education is derived from the short definition endorsed by the Canadian Society for Autistic Children (October 1977).

> Autism is a severely incapacitating life-long developmental disability which typically appears during the first three years of life. It occurs in approximately five out of every 10,000 births and is four times more common in boys than girls. It has been found throughout the world in families of all racial, ethnic, and social backgrounds. No known factors in the psychological environment of a child have been shown to cause autism.

Resources Concerning Hearing Impairment

The following materials are available from Publication Services Branch
- *Math Resource Book for the Hearing Impaired*, 1982
- *Speech Resource Guide for the Hearing Impaired*, 1982
- *Life Skills Resource Book for the Hearing Impaired*, 1983
- *The Hearing Impaired Student in the Regular Classroom: A Guide for Teachers*
- *Selected Characteristics of the Hearing Impaired, School Age.*

The following resources are available from the addresses indicated.
- Western Institute for the Deaf
  2125 West Seventh Avenue
  Vancouver, B.C.
  V6K 1X9 (736-7391)
- *The Signed English Dictionary*
  Gallandet College Press
  Gallandet College Bookstore
  Gallandet College
  Washington, D.C. 20002

Resources Concerning Visual Impairment

- Canadian National Institute for the Blind
  350 East 36th Avenue
  Vancouver, B.C.
  V5W 1C6 (321-2311)

The following materials are available from the Publication Services Branch.
- *The Visually Impaired Student in the Regular Classroom.*
- *Orientation and Mobility for the Visually Impaired.*

The symptoms are caused by physical disorders of the brain. They must be documented by history or present on examination. They include the following.

- disturbances in the rate of appearance of physical, social, and language skills;
- abnormal responses to sensations (Any one or a combination of sight, hearing, touch, pain, balance, smell, taste, and the way a child holds his body are affected.);
- the absence or delay of speech and language (Specific thinking capabilities may be present. Immature rhythms of speech, limited understanding of ideas, and the use of words without attaching the usual meaning to them are common.);
- abnormal ways of relating to people, objects, and events (Typically, autistic children do not respond appropriately to adults and other children. Objects and toys are not used as normally intended.).

Autism occurs by itself or in association with other disorders that affect the function of the brain (such as viral infections, metabolic disturbances, and epilepsy).

Students with Severe Behavior Problems

Children with severe behavior problems are those who exhibit excessive deviant behavior that seriously interferes with the learning process for him/herself as well as for other students. Some examples would be physical and/or verbal aggression, attention seeking, unusual or excessive fears, lack of interaction with peers and/or adults, etc. These children almost always exhibit a significant discrepancy between academic performance and potential.

Gifted and Talented Students

The most popular definition of the gifted is that of the U.S. Office of Education, endorsed by the Council for Exceptional Children in Canada and the U.S., which states

> Gifted and talented children are those . . . who by virtue of outstanding abilities are capable of high performance. These . . . children require differentiated educational programs and/or services beyond those normally provided by the regular school program in order to realize their (potential) contribution to self and society. Children capable of high performance include those who have demonstrated any of the following abilities or aptitudes, singly or in combination:
> 1. general intellectual ability;
> 2. specific academic aptitude;
> 3. creative or productive thinking;
> 4. leadership ability;
> 5. visual and performing arts aptitude;
> 6. psychomotor ability.

E.S.L. and E.S.D. Students

English as a Second Language/Dialect programs are designed to provide services to students who do not speak standard Canadian English as a "home" language. The regular curricula will need to be adapted and/or modified to meet the needs of the English as a Second Language/Dialect students until they can attain the ultimate goal of working in the regular curricula.

In many instances, we find multiple handicaps . . . or other combinations of divergencies from the normal. A crippled child may be gifted. A deaf child may be blind. A cerebral-palsied child may be visually impaired, hard of hearing, mentally retarded (or gifted), and defective in speech.

SAMUEL A. KIRK
Educating Exceptional Children

Resources Concerning Gifted and Talented Students

- *Enrichment and Gifted Education Resource Book* (Ministry of Education: Curriculum Development Branch, 1981)
- Co-ordinator of Gifted Programs Division of Special Education Ministry of Education Parliament Buildings Victoria, B.C. V8V 2M4

Resources for E.S.L. and E.S.D. Students

The following materials are available from the Publications Services Branch.
- *English as a Second Language/Dialect Resource Book for K-12* (Ministry of Education, 1981)

Children with Special Needs

E.S.L./D. students bring to school a wealth of ideas and experiences which are encoded in the language of the home. They are cognitively as well developed as their standard-English-speaking peers; they simply express themselves in a different linguistic form.

The Special Programs Branch of the Ministry of Education assists school districts, in consultation with the native community, to meet the special learning needs of Indian children in the public schools. To achieve this objective, special approvals may be generated by school districts which are aimed at academic skill building, and, in the process, should reflect the cultural, linguistic, and social background of Indian children as integral to that success.

Conclusion

The goals for kindergarten, the integrated nature of the curriculum, and the emphasis on theme development are congruent with the needs of some children for broader or deeper educational experiences. By supplementing the curriculum, extending activities, and increasing or decreasing the levels of inquiry, the teacher can adapt, enrich, or expand experiences in order to meet the needs of all children.

- *Language Arts for Native Indian Students* (Ministry of Education, 1982)

The following materials are available free of charge from the Division of Special Education, Ministry of Education, Parliament Buildings, Victoria, B.C.

- *New Strategies in Indian Education Utilizing the Indian Child's Advantages in the Elementary Classroom* (by Saul Arbess, Maureen Murdock, and Penelope Joy)
- Videotapes (¾" or ½" UHS) "Telling Our Stories" "Curriculum Content" "Interaction in the Classroom" "Instructional Strategies"

EVALUATION

Purposes of Evaluation

In order to evaluate effectively, the teacher considers the purposes of evaluation as well as the child as an individual in relation to goals of the curriculum. Evaluation has several purposes.
- It provides a developmental profile.
- It provides a basis for diagnosing individual needs.
- It provides a basis for program evaluation.
- It provides relevant information to include in reports to parents.

Developmental Profile

Teachers develop and utilize evaluation procedures in order to gain a clear developmental profile of each child. The data collected reveal individual student's strengths and help to identify those areas needing further attention.

Diagnosis

Information gained from evaluation not only provides a profile of development but is also used for diagnostic purposes. From this information the teacher plans experiences to reinforce or expand the child's understanding, growth, and development or prepares activities suitable to the needs of groups of children.

Program Evaluation

The teacher can use information collected to help determine the effectiveness of the total program. The suitability of experiences, the balance of activities, and the implementation of the curriculum must be considered. This process provides the information necessary for critical evaluation and further program planning and modification.

Reporting to Parents

Ongoing assessments are also made to provide meaningful information to parents about their child. Parents require information about the child's adjustment, participation, and progress in the kindergarten program. Appropriate evaluation procedures should provide realistic and meaningful information.

The Evaluation Cycle

Ongoing evaluation in the kindergarten involves a systematic, cyclical process. Because children are growing and developing daily, evaluation is a multi-faceted and ongoing part of the program. The evaluation cycle consists of four stages:
- Collecting and Recording Data;
- Organizing, Analysing, and Interpreting Data;
- Ongoing Program Planning;
- Re-evaluation (i.e., continuing the cycle).

Ongoing assessment then becomes a natural part of the daily activities of the kindergarten.

Collecting and Recording Data

Through systematic observation and recording, the teacher gathers a large amount of information about each child. This provides either *background information* or *ongoing information*.

- *Background Information:* Background information can be gained through a variety of sources. When the child is enrolled, information is supplied through forms and often through an interview. School questionnaires and public health forms can provide the teacher with a considerable amount of valuable information. Home visits can provide background information as the teacher gains a better understanding of the child in the home and family environment.
- *Ongoing Information:* Observation is one of the most useful modes for collecting data because this method provides information that is specific and relevant. Observations must be ongoing and purposeful. The information gained can be recorded in a variety of ways.
- *Dialogue with Children:* When teachers engage children in dialogue that elicits and extends their observations and ideas, the ways in which children are able to use language become evident. This information can be recorded and used as a basis for planning future dialogue and activities. Experiences that stimulate new kinds of thinking and expression can be provided.
- *Collecting Materials:* Keeping samples of work produced by the child is an effective means of accumulating information about how children represent their knowledge as they continue to mature. Over time, the teacher can see (and can demonstrate to parents) both the rate and quality of development. Photographs, tape recordings, and videotapes can be used to save that which cannot be recorded in more convenient form. For example, a block construction, a child's accomplishment with a particular set of concrete materials or piece of apparatus, or speech development can be documented as a reminder of abilities, can serve as proof of the event, or can be preserved for later analysis.

Organizing, Analysing, and Interpreting Data

Once observations have been made and rough data compiled, the teacher must decide how to organize the information and must then analyse the results. This important and necessary step in the evaluation cycle enables the teacher to plan experiences and provide the best possible learning situation for each child, to report information to parents in a meaningful way, to diagnose individual difficulties, and to evaluate aspects of the program.

- *Sequential Organization:* Recorded information serves to form a profile of individual growth and development as well as to indicate patterns of development within a class. Dating materials and examining information in sequence provides a profile of the child's development from the entry point to the present. The examination and interpretation of data is a time-consuming yet critical process.
- *Seeking Patterns and Analysing Content:* Knowledge of child development serves as a framework for evaluation. The teacher has a view of the stages that allow for the development of expectations and reference for comparison. By evaluating children's responses, the level of complexity of the use of concrete materials, or the content of representational information, the teacher gains information regarding the child's development to this time. Patterns begin to emerge in both the work of individuals and the class as a

whole. From such analysis, the teacher then decides what intervention may be necessary and what experiences would be appropriate to provide for continued growth and development.

Ongoing Program Planning

Evaluation is an integral part of the planning for the kindergarten program. Effective planning is dependent upon accurate observation, systematic recording, and thoughtful interpretation. Systematic evaluation provides the teacher with continual feedback with regard to the effectiveness of instruction and suitability of the program. It forms the basis for program decisions. Systematic evaluation helps the teacher decide what objectives to prepare for each child, or what experiences are appropriate for groups of children.

Re-evaluation

The teacher continually reassesses individual student progress to provide meaningful information to parents, to determine the effectiveness of the program, and to plan according to the ever-changing needs of the children. The evaluation component is a natural and relevant part of the everyday activities of the kindergarten. The teacher systematically observes, records, analyses, and interprets information. On the strength of the evidence collected, improvements and modifications can be made as needed.

Communication with Parents

One of the fundamental purposes for ongoing and systematic evaluation is to provide parents with meaningful information about their child. Parent-teacher communication enables the home and school to provide complementary and supplementary experiences for the child. Some ways to facilitate this process are as follows.

Home Visits

Visiting with children and parents in their own home has many potential benefits. The teacher can observe the interaction of the child with the family members in his or her home environment. Being away from the school and in an informal atmosphere increases the possibility of gaining a better understanding of the child.

Observations Made by Parents

Teachers may wish to include parents in the activities of the classroom. Providing parents with some specific behavior or activities to observe will often help focus their observations on their own child and make the experience more meaningful. Setting aside a short time at the end of the visit allows the parent and teacher to compare and discuss their observations.

Written Reports

Stated observations describe growth and development over a period of time. Observations also provide insight into the needs of a child at a particular point in time. Interpretations can be thought of as the teacher's description of the child's growth and development. Since development is a transitional process, comparing children with others, or defining behavior with respect to success or failure, is irrelevant. The teacher describes the child in terms of his or her growth and development in relation to the goals of the program. The child is viewed as a unique individual who is learning many new things.

Interviews

Conferences provide parents and teachers with the opportunity to share information about the child. The teacher can provide information gained from observing the child in the classroom setting. The parent may be able to relate information pertinent to the teacher's observations and may be able to add additional insights. Mutual concern and the two-way exchange of information enable parents and teachers to begin to co-operate in planning experiences that will benefit the child.

Expanded Evaluation

If the teacher has used the evaluation techniques described and yet finds that the child is not progressing as expected, it may be necessary to request assistance from supportive professionals. A child who exhibits developmental "lag," whose behavior interferes with learning or who appears to be in need of special programming (handicapped or gifted), may require a more comprehensive evaluation.

Using the teacher's evaluation as a base, supportive professionals may add new information and expand the individual student's profile. Outside personnel can offer additional information through observations, test results, and insights that result from their expertise and experience.

PART 2: THE KINDERGARTEN RESOURCE BOOK

THE INTEGRATED CURRICULUM

The Kindergarten Day

A Sample Plan

In keeping with the philosophy of an integrated curriculum, the kindergarten day is divided into large blocks of time. The outline below illustrates a sample order for the experiences provided for the children. While the order in which these experiences occur may vary, it is suggested that these blocks of time and experiences are provided each day.

- Opening
- Activities and Learning Centres
- Book Time
- Snack Time
- Movement Education
- Group Time
  —Story Time
  —Music
  —Drama
  —Activities
- Closing

The ways in which the goals for kindergarten are related to the activities and experiences of the children within these blocks of time are indicated on the large, fold-out chart entitled "The Kindergarten Day — An Integrated Curriculum" that is inserted at the back of this book.

The sequence used to organize the kindergarten day will be unique for each classroom. Factors such as available resources, space within the school, and the activities of other children will determine the order of these sessions (e.g., gym, library, activity room, music, kitchen, playground). It is important to consider the children's needs for a balance between:

- active and less active sessions;
- large group, small group, and individual actitivity;
- child-directed and teacher-directed experiences.

The teacher may also see the need to adjust the sequence and length of activity in order to reflect the tone, interests, and needs of the particular group as well as to incorporate spontaneous events (which can be accommodated by maintaining a focus on the goals). This flexibility serves to personalize aspects of the curriculum and allows children to share ownership of the program. Such experiences have benefits beyond the educational value of the event itself because they allow the child to exercise some control and to be involved in the process of decision making.

The criterion for selecting a system of indicating and recording choices must be fair, enjoyable, time-saving, and informative. It should facilitate movement from centre to centre and maintain a record of the children's activities. The teacher may wish to use a pocket chart or some variation to facilitate the selection of activities.

Opening

A whole group meeting at the beginning of the kindergarten session provides opportunity for the children to focus on issues of importance to them and to discuss and establish plans for the day. This is a time for greeting, talking, and sharing news or information. Routines such as the calendar, attendance, birthday celebrations, helpers, and class graphs are attended to. The teacher may wish to introduce a new theme, discuss activities, and make plans with the children concerning coming events.

Activities and Learning Centres

The activity time is an essential part of the day. As children make choices and interact with their environment, they learn. Whether working alone, in small groups, or with adults, much incidental as well as planned learning takes place. This *child-directed but adult-supported* period allows the child the necessary time to complete tasks and projects and to become actively involved in experiences that further concept development, utilize thought processes, and develop language.

As the children use the learning centres, the teacher interacts, assists, and observes. The information gained is used to evaluate and adapt the program and the environment in order to meet individual and group needs. New centres may be added; centres may be removed or changed; and materials from one centre may be combined with another to maintain a high level of interest. The arrangement and physical structure of these centres may vary from classroom to classroom, but the important consideration is that the materials provided are attractive, accessible, challenging, and inviting.

Constraints imposed by room size and location as well as the purpose, function, and content of specific learning centres may determine that there be an overlap and blending of physical spaces within the kindergarten. For example, a quiet area, a listening centre, a library centre, and an aesthetic centre may all function in the same area or vicinity. Materials from one centre may overlap and support another. For example, art, collage, construction, painting, modelling, woodworking, drawing, and writing can all be used to complement each other.

Although children are encouraged to clean up as they leave centres, using a portion of the activity time for general clean-up helps to develop independence and shared responsibility for the classroom.

Transitional Activities

Since the children will not finish cleaning up at the same time, a productive and enjoyable way to provide a transition between activities and the next part of the program should be planned. Some teachers find this to be an appropriate time for involving children in discussion leading to personal evaluation of the activities they participated in.

Book Time

The value of including a book time in the kindergarten day is that it encourages children to spend time with books and to practise emergent reading behavior. Providing time for children to experience and enjoy books lays the foundation for developing reading habits and attitudes that can lead to a life-long love of books.

A time and place for practising reading behavior should be provided each day so that children can explore favorite and new stories. This gives each child the opportunity to represent what he or she knows about reading and to extend that knowledge naturally. The teacher plays a critical role as model by reading books so children can observe appropriate reading behavior and come to appreciate the pleasure and purpose found in print. As a facilitating resource, the teacher asks and answers questions and comments on, encourages, and promotes discussion with children about their books and the process of reading.

Snack Time

The snack activities in kindergarten can be a valuable teaching and learning experience. Manners, safety, cleanliness, and acceptable ways of handling food can be encouraged. By participating actively in the preparation, distribution, and eating of food, the child has many opportunities to learn. Snack experiences provide opportunities for learning concepts when no other kind of activity will suffice. For example, when teaching children about bread making, the most appropriate activity would be to make bread with the children. Recording and planning the process of cooking foods gives the children practical experience in observation and representation. Knowledge and awareness of a variety of types of foods from differing cultures and sources can influence and change nutritional habits. Relating snack activities to field trips, themes, and special interests, and to the cultural backgrounds of the children, integrates food into the total program. By combining snacks and snack preparation with the other experiences in kindergarten, the children are provided with food energy throughout the day and gain an understanding of how food affects their lives.

Encouraging parent participation in snack activities reinforces and expands the scope of the experience. As part of ongoing communication with parents, the teacher can share recipes and snack plans in newsletters, cookbooks, or calendars. Parents can become involved in cultural and nutritional programs through staging events such as a "Nutrition Afternoon," a "Cultural Food Fair," or a "Family Breakfast."

Sample Snack Calendar

A calendar such as the following might be prepared and sent to parents to illustrate how their snack fees were used in a given month.

Week	Monday	Tuesday	Wednesday	Thursday	Friday
1	—apple slices —milk	Cooking Day —nuts and bolts —orange juice	—nuts and bolts —milk	Cooking Day —french toast —apple juice	—½ orange
2	—½ banana —milk	—peanut butter and crackers	Cooking Day —turkey and vegetable soup —crackers —milk	—nuts and raisins	Cooking Day —home-made butter served on baking powder biscuits —apple juice
3	—½ orange —milk	Cooking Day —cranberry muffins —cream cheese	—dried fruit —milk	Cooking Day —chicken soup with rice	—½ apple filled with peanut butter and raisins
4	Cooking Day —pizza	—nuts and raisins —milk	Cooking Day —pancakes with maple syrup —orange juice	—½ banana —milk	—apple slices with cheese and crackers

Whether the daily snack originates in the home or at the school, it is critical that children be allowed planned and varied experiences in the preparation, handling, and cooking of food.

Movement Education

During the portion of the day devoted to movement education, the teacher plans experiences that challenge children to develop their ability to move both their bodies and objects in a variety of ways. As children play, they explore the patterns and learn the language of movement. Whether in the classroom, in the gymnasium, or outdoors, children are introduced to activities designed to promote development of large and small muscles, co-ordination, body awareness, and familiarity with equipment. The daily physical activity necessary for total growth and development of the young child is basic to providing a balanced kindergarten program. Music, dance, and drama can be an integral part of movement education. Routines and activities learned are useful transitions or focus points that provide a change of pace throughout the day. For example, children may walk like space creatures with accompanying music during clean up, play "Simon Says" before a group meeting, or participate in singing movement games such as "Punchinella" as a way of bringing the group together.

Group Time

This is a time for teacher-initiated activities and for both teacher and child input. As individual group members talk and listen, they gain information and learn to respect the ideas of others. This time provides an opportunity for children to gain recognition as the teacher and other children let them know that their contributions are valuable and essential. The interest of children is stimulated by discussion, drama, puppetry, mime, films, film strips and videotapes, demonstrations, graphing, recording, games, chants, poems, songs, and stories related to current themes or arising spontaneously.

At group time, the teacher and the class gather to share ideas, information, and literature. They participate in reading and listening to books (big and small, child-made, and commercial). Making and reading language experience charts and stories helps children develop literacy, and daily story time provides special shared reading experiences for all children.

Sensitivity to the children's enjoyment, responses, and eagerness to pursue a topic of activity, and the flexibility to respond and incorporate the children's interests, result in a program designed to meet the needs of the group of children.

This is the time of the day that reflects the tone or mood of the relationship between the teacher and the children. Cohesion of the total program is accomplished as the children share experiences.

Closing

Whether it is incorporated into the group time or a separate experience, some form of closure to their kindergarten day is required by children. A song, a chance for children to comment on the activities of the day, or a chance talk about plans for the next day bring a sense of group unity. A short review of the day helps children prepare for discussing the events with their families. Providing time to finish the day helps personalize the kindergarten experience.

Organizing and planning a time for children to collect their belongings and projects at the end of the session provides opportunity for conversation and for dealing with the concerns of individuals.

Communication with parents is strengthened when children are involved in reading and discussing the messages or letters they deliver home. Children are encouraged to be responsible for telling their parents about activities at school and sharing news about their day. Establishing a routine of being available in the classroom or taking children to meet waiting adults in an ideal way to develop pleasant and informal contact with parents. It also demonstrates to children the partnership between their home and school.

Learning Centres

Learning centres in the kindergarten classroom provide one way of arranging, storing, and presenting materials to facilitate implementation of the curriculum. This organization reflects attempts to foster all aspects of the child's development. Children can choose activities that vary in complexity and difficulty. Centres may appeal to the different senses and acknowledge a variety of learning styles. Working independently or in groups encourages children to direct their own learning for some time during the kindergarten day.

Centres should be flexible and adaptable rather than rigid and static. The number, kind, and contents of the centres will vary and change during the year. The choice of which centres to include in the learning environment is influenced by a number of factors, such as current themes, physical space, interest level, and capabilities. However, there are some learning centres that should be a constant and integral part of the daily life of the kindergarten. The suggested learning centres are presented in the following section with a description of purposes, function, suggested materials, and activities.

Consideration must be given to where a centre is located as well as to what materials it contains. Placement of centres is governed by awareness of safety, possible interference caused by noise, space available, and movement patterns. Locating centres so that materials and activities of one centre facilitate, supplement, and complement those of another supports integration and allows the child to select from and adapt the environment to suit his or her needs. The list of centres given in the margin is organized to show centres that could be enhanced by being located in proximity.

- Group Meeting Area
  Library Centre
  Listening Centre
  Quiet Area
  Aesthetic Centre
  Drawing and Writing Centre
  Art Centre
- Construction Centre
  Modelling Centre
  Woodworking Centre
  Painting Centre
- Water Centre
  Sand Centre
  Interest Centre
  Exploration Centre
  Table Toys and Games Centre
  Block Centre
- Dramatic Play Centre
  Puppet Centre
  Cooking Area
  Music Centre

Group Meeting Area

This is the place where new ideas and activities are introduced, where familiar activities are reviewed, and where field trips and other experiences are remembered and reflected upon. Parts of the program carried out at this learning centre provide children with fresh input and ideas and with the opportunity to learn or try new things, to review and enjoy the familiar, and to reflect, talk, and reason about their experience.

Suggested Activities for the Group Meeting Area

This is a place for large group, teacher-directed activities such as
- opening and closing activities;
- looking at books and enjoying stories;
- learning about food and nutrition;
- planning, discussing, developing language and thinking;
- music, movement, singing, dancing, drama, and appreciation of "the arts";
- counting, graphing, grouping, comparing, and other mathematical activities;
- writing letters, reading recipes, charts, songs, and poems, recording experiences, and other literacy-related activities.

Suggested Materials

- carpeted space and/or small carpet pieces (one for each child)
- chart stand and paper
- flannel board
- chalkboard
- magnetic board
- big book easel
- teacher chair or stool
- record player
- rhythm instruments
- bookcase

Library Centre

The library centre provides opportunities for children to have daily access to familiar and favorite books, new stories, and research and resource books. A special feature of the class library are the child-authored and scribe-written books.

Suggested Materials

- big books with accompanying small books and tapes
- selected variety of good children's literature

Concept books, pattern books, big books, and a variety of children's literature from the book centre are read to children during storytime and are available for rereading and for close and repeated inspection on a regular basis. Children are encouraged and given time to "play at" reading. In this manner, emergent reading patterns can develop. Language experience materials are stored here and maintained on an ongoing basis so that children can use them as references.

Suggested Activities for the Library Centre

- Read and reread favorite stories.
- Share observations; discuss and answer questions about books, stories, and other print materials.
- Re-tell favorite stories or encourage children to "read" into a tape recorder.
- Role-play characters or situations from stories. Consider using puppets or flannel board and cutouts to facilitate dramatization. (These can also be used for ordering and matching.)

Listening Centre

This learning centre provides the opportunity to read and reread favorite stories, to listen to music or stories on the earphones, or to enjoy these with a group and respond with movement, rhythmic speech, dramatics, or song. Small versions of big books can be made available at this centre. Some teachers have found it beneficial to develop the library and listening centres in close proximity.

Suggested Activities for the Listening Centre

- Listen to stories accompanied with read-along books, records, or tapes.
- Tape the children's language, stories, or songs and listen to them at the listening post.
- Listen to poems, chants, choral-speaking activities. For example, the children can actively participate in the repetitions found in the poems "Chicken Soup with Rice" or "Alligator Pie."
- Develop oral language by providing a model and having children approximate the words and patterns used by the teacher.

Quiet Area

Like adults, children have a need for being alone at times. Provide one or two spaces in the classroom where a person who wants to be alone may seek shelter. A place for quiet reflection, resting, or observation can be established close to the library centre or group meeting area.

Suggested Activities for the Quiet Area

- Look at or read a book.
- Rest.
- Play individual games.
- Cuddle a stuffed toy.
- Talk to a friend.

- pattern books
- class-made and child-authored books
- research and resource books for a variety of topics related to themes, interest centre, seasons, field trips
- class news board
- poems
- song charts
- language experience charts
- pictures with captions
- calendar, graphs, helper charts
- name tags
- tape recorder

Suggested Materials

- tape recorder
- record player and records
- adaptor
- earphones (6 or 8)
- listening post
- taped stories and book sets, big book sets
- taped music/songs (these can be teacher-made, child-made, or commercially prepared)
- soundscapes or sound effects tapes that provide sounds such as walking, house noises, country/ city situations

Suggested Materials

- large refrigerator carton or packing barrel converted to resting spot
- pillows or mats
- carpet pieces
- stuffed toys
- snake coil pillow
- rocking chair

Aesthetic Centre

Children develop their sensitivity to beauty in the man-made and natural environment when beautiful things are cherished and lovingly displayed. The child's fistful of dandelions has a place in this centre alongside a famous artist's painting or a photograph of springtime. Children should be given the opportunity to touch and wonder about objects and to discuss, enjoy, and share feelings evoked by the environment.

Suggested Activities for the Aesthetic Centre

- Provide a variety of experiences with textures, patterns, and shapes. Through their senses and dialogue, children can begin to develop an appreciation for the integrity of individual items.
- Encourage children to share items they have found on the way to school or brought from home. Ask the child who is sharing the item to describe it and to identify some aspect that evoked interest.
- Provide materials for creating displays. Children can be invited to arrange and rearrange items until they are displayed in a form they find pleasing.

Drawing and Writing Centre

Drawing provides the child a way of saying things that cannot easily be said in words. This non-verbal representation of thought is closely linked to oral discussion, which can be extended to the written expression of those thoughts. This centre provides a place where children can play with literacy materials. This is not a place of instruction but rather a place where children explore the nature, purpose, and function of written language, each operating at his or her own level. The teacher responds to the children's requests for information or help with the conventions of print.

Concrete experience provides the foundation for all forms of representation for young children. Recording children's language and thoughts with written words and developing activities and projects that incorporate this kind of writing will provide a source of meaningful reading material for children. Motivation and interest in writing and reading occur as children see a purpose for it and for their involvement in these processes. Beginning slowly and developing complexity and depth, language experiences occur as children's interests and attention spans develop.

Providing opportunities for children to collect and learn phrases or words builds up the child's knowledge of the features and characteristics of printed language. Chosen meaningful words (key words) may be printed on large cards. Children can say the word out loud, trace over the letters with their finger, and "feel" the print. Words are stored and always accessible. As the word collection grows, and activities and opportunities to use the words take place, the children will remember and eventually read the words on the cards.

The successful use of key words in the kindergarten is dependent upon levels of motivation and interest on the part of the child. Key words can be introduced in response to the needs of individual children and may not be appropriate for all children.

Suggested Activities for the Drawing and Writing Centre

- Explore and experiment with a variety of materials.
- Describe drawings and paintings. Trace or copy a sentence recorded by the teacher.
- Write notes or cards to friends and family.
- Prepare labels for artifacts or objects in various centres. If the Dramatic Play Centre is set up as a restaurant, children could make signs, write menus and prepare "orders" for "customers."
- Write instructions for others to follow.
- Record recipes or copy teacher-made charts.
- Make books based on themes, interests, and personal experiences.
- Record sequences of pictures and phrases to accompany familiar songs, stories, and poems by using known words and symbols.
- Evolve personal symbols for common yet meaningful objects.
- Write a script for a puppet play.
- Work with an older student partner (scribe) to produce child-authored books.
- Explore and experiment with the printed word and various media available. For example, children could make words or numerals by drawing on chalkboards, rolling out dough, and painting or cutting words, letters, or numerals from magazines.

Art Centre

The art centre houses and features the art materials in the classroom. Materials are provided and skills, techniques and processes are explained and demonstrated so that children will have the opportunity to explore, experiment, and represent their feelings and ideas. Depending on the theme, interest, or topic of the moment, the teacher chooses and introduces appropriate activities and materials and demonstrates various media and techniques, thus encouraging the children's initiative.

Suggested Activities for the Art Centre

- Draw with oil pastels.
- Paint using a variety of painting techniques such as finger painting, table painting, spatter painting, sponge painting, roll-on painting, and blow/straw painting.
- Use a variety of techniques such as mural making, chalk picture making, cutting and tearing paper collages, off-loom weaving, tie dyeing, batik making, stitchery and quilting, mobile making, kite making, and string art.
- Crayon resists with paint and crayon.
- Use a variety of print-making techniques using materials such as rollers, sponges, Styrofoam, cardboard, vegetables, "junk," leaves, feathers, hands, feet, thumbs, etc.
- Make sculptures from boxes, wood, and "junk."

Suggested Materials

- crayons
- oil pastels
- chalk
- finger paint
- liquid paint
- cake paint
- screens
- empty deodorant bottles for roll-on painting
- sponges
- Q-tips
- cotton balls
- brushes
- straws
- toothbrushes
- fabric
- wool
- string
- "junk"
- tissue paper
- crêpe paper
- raffia
- various objects for printing
- leaves
- foods
- feathers
- Styrofoam sheets (tops of egg cartons)
- wax
- staplers
- scissors
- glue
- paste
- felt pens
- hole punches
- variety of papers

Construction Centre

The construction centre houses and features a wide variety of materials. By supplying a few simple materials in September and adding to them throughout the year, teachers provide children with the opportunity to handle the materials and learn techniques and skills at gradually increasing levels of complexity. Depending on the theme, interest, or topic of the moment, the teacher chooses and introduces appropriate activities that may be integrated with the drawing and writing centre and the modelling centre. The teacher models the combining of various media and techniques, thus encouraging the children's initiative.

Suggested Activities for the Construction Centre

- Explore and create using a variety of materials and techniques.
- Create collages or "junk" pictures by tearing, cutting, and gluing pictures, fabric, or objects to cardboard scraps.
- Weave paper strips, yarn, or wool through prepared cardboard frames.
- Construct box sculptures, models, or mobiles using scraps available at the centre. Encourage children to design, plan, and construct their projects through to the stage where they are completed.
- Make puppets using a variety of materials. As the children work on their creations, encourage them to experiment and to select materials independently.

Suggested Materials

- wallpaper
- poster paper
- gummed shapes
- gummed starts
- paper scraps
- cardboard scraps
- carbon paper
- tracing paper
- paper plates
- cellophane
- tissue paper
- waxed paper
- aluminum foil
- Styrofoam
- Kleenex
- crêpe paper
- yarn or wool
- string
- thread
- straws
- net
- lace
- cloth
- ribbon
- rickrack
- felt scraps
- glue or paste
- tape
- paper fasteners
- staples
- paper clips
- glitter
- safety pins
- straight pins
- Pollyfilla
- small boxes and containers
- Styrofoam chips
- egg cartons
- paper rolls
- buttons
- screws
- nails
- washers
- toy parts
- wire screen
- wood scraps
- jewellery
- hole punch
- chalk
- "tracers"
- pencils
- felt pens
- crayons
- scissors
- pinking shear
- rulers
- shells
- leaves
- cones
- twigs
- rocks
- sand
- rock salt

Learning Centres

Modelling Centre

Creative play with modelling materials allows children to delight in the joy of handling materials. Concepts of texture, pattern, size, and shape develop as the children mould the materials into different forms and discuss what they are doing.

Time is needed to manipulate and mould with the hands before tools are introduced. The modelling centre provides an area of interest and avenue of representation for children who need to express their ideas in a concrete tactile form.

Suggested Activities for the Modelling Centre

- Encourage free exploration and experimentation with the medium. Children will discover the properties of modelling materials as they roll, press, squeeze, pull, stretch, and try to make things.
- Invite children to participate in the mixing of clay and water or preparation of playdough. Once children have had the experience under supervised conditions, many will be able to prepare recipes for modelling materials independently.
- Plan and construct a large table model as a group project. Individuals or groups of children can be responsible for carrying out part of this co-operative effort.
- Create sculptures to represent people, animals, or other objects that are part of the child's experiences.
- Use hands or utensils to create impressions, patterns, or decorative texture effects on slabs of modelling material.

Recipes for Modelling Materials

- *Cornstarch Clay*
  1 part cornstarch
  4 parts salt
  4 parts boiling water

  Boil to soft-ball stage and knead until malleable. Keep in plastic bag.

- *Sawdust Modelling Mixture*
  2 parts sawdust
  1 part wallpaper paste

  Add enough cold water to paste to make creamy mixture. Add sawdust.

- *Reusable Clay*
  250 mL water
   30 mL salad oil
    1 L flour
  350 mL salt
  food coloring

  Combine oil, water, and food coloring in a covered jar and shake. Mix flour and salt together. Add the water mixture to the dry ingredients a little at a time, working with the hands to mix thoroughly until consistency of firm bread dough.

- *Breadcrumb Dough*
  250 mL soft breadcrumbs
  250 mL salt
    5 mL powdered alum
  Beaten egg white

  Mix and color if desired.

- *Salt Beads*
  2 parts table salt
  1 part flour

  Mix salt, flour and water to create dough consistency. Break off small pieces and form into beads. Pierce with toothpick and allow to dry. String.

- *Play Dough*
  500 mL flour
  250 mL salt
   30 mL cream of tartar
   75 mL salad oil
  500 mL water with food coloring or powdered tempera mixed in

  Mix in a cooking pot and put on stove to boil. Stir and boil until the dough no longer sticks to the bottom. Knead. This dough is far spongier and nicer feeling than plain uncooked dough.

Suggested Materials

- plasticine
- playdough
- ingredients for making playdough
- clay
- rolling pin
- arborite sheets to work on
- bread dough
- sand
- papier-mâché
- mud
- garlic press
- spoons
- forks
- potato masher
- meat hammers
- pie plates
- cake tins
- child-safe knives
- plastic containers for storage
- cookie cutters
- popsicle sticks
- found objects that make impressions

Woodworking Centre

Woodworking provides a simple and satisfying activity for children. Hammering, sawing, gluing, and clamping can help children increase their visual-motor abilities, their overall co-ordination, and their sense of accomplishment. Woodworking requires careful preparation and selection of materials and conscientious teaching of basic techniques so that children can have successful, safe experiences. If noise is a factor, use glue on a regular basis and save the hammer and nails for special times or outside use.

Suggested Activities for the Woodworking Centre

- Explore freely, using a variety of materials and basic techniques.
- Create patterns by hammering nails, tacks, or bottlecaps into pieces of wood.
- Create simple representations such as boats, planes, houses, etc.
- Store tools on a pegboard. Outlining each tool on the pegboard provides a good matching activity at clean-up time.

Safety Notes

- Limit the number of children at one time in the woodworking centre and ensure that activities are carried out under the supervision of an adult.
- Provide safe storage for tools.
- Do not allow the use of woodworking tools in other learning centres.
- Label containers for nails.
- Insist that tools be put away as they are used, not just at the end of the session.
- Teach children how to hammer and saw: place wood in a vice.
- Avoid cedar, since some children are allergic to cedar splinters.

Painting Centre

Paints and paper are materials children need to use freely and creatively. They enjoy painting for its own sake; and although adult interest provides encouragement, painting is essentially a private activity. The opportunity to paint should be available every day for every child. Easel painting enables the child to experiment with color and technique, to explore the properties of various media, to evolve and elaborate upon personal symbols, to create and respond to pictures, and to represent what is known from experience. The opportunity to try a variety of papers, paints, colors, and techniques for applying media is offered at the painting centre and is incorporated at the easel for subsequent use.

Children are encouraged to talk about their pictures and seek assistance with recording captions or sentences. As the year progresses, children can do more of the writing themselves.

NOTE: Paints should be mixed thickly so that they don't run. This gives children a sense of control over the paint.

Suggested Activities for the Painting Centre

- Explore freely, using a variety of materials and techniques.
- Create illustrations for songs, poems, experience charts, stories, and big books.

Suggested Materials

- workbench with vice/clamps
- construction hats
- painters caps
- tools (e.g., hammers of appropriate weight and size, work aprons, coveralls, large-headed nails, saws, pliers, square rule, level, vise, coarse sandpaper, clamps, ruler)
- wood glue
- wooden wheels
- dowling
- broom handles
- spools
- string
- Styrofoam
- toothpicks
- bottle caps
- driftwood
- small wood scraps (hard wood for gluing, pine and spruce for sawing and hammering)
- "found objects"
- cardboard
- paint
- balsa wood
- containers

Suggested Materials

Surfaces
- easels
- tabletops
- floor

Paper
- white rolls
- butcher, banner, Kraft, or wrapping papers
- white drawing paper
- construction paper of assorted colors
- mill screening paper
- fingerpaint paper, coated
- tagboard, assorted sizes
- watercolor paper
- wallpaper sample books and end rolls
- wrapping paper, brown
- old newspapers
- newsprint
- computer papers
- Japanese rice papers

- Create paintings that represent some aspect of a theme currently studied.
- Create patterns such as those found on wallpaper and wrapping paper to use in association with other projects. For example, children could make and use their wrapping paper.
- Paint for the joy of painting!

Recipes for Powder Painting

- *Powder Paint*
  75 mL powder paint
  75 mL water

Add liquid starch or liquid detergent (detergent aids in removing paint stains from synthetic fabrics). Add wintergreen or peppermint to prevent sour smell.

  If having difficulty mixing red, violet, or orange, add a few drops of alcohol.

  For pastels, start with white and add color.

  For glossy paint add glycerine, liquid starch, or evaporated milk.

  For painting on glass or metal, add soap flakes.

  For chalk-like effect, use buttermilk instead of water.

Recipes for Fingerpainting

To keep all recipes from drying, add 30 mL of glycerine. Add wintergreen to keep from souring.

- *Starch and Soap Finger Painting*
  125 mL instant cold water starch
  300 mL soap flakes
  150 mL water

  Beat together until consistency of whipped potatoes. Add food coloring.

- *Talcum Powder Finger Paint*
  3 parts laundry starch
  1 part talcum powder
  13 parts boiling water
  3 parts soap flakes
  dry paint or food coloring

  Mix starch with a little cold water until creamy. Add the boiling water and cook until the mixture becomes clear. Stir constantly. Add talcum powder. Allow mixture to cool a bit, then add the soap flakes and stir. Keep covered.

- *Cornstarch Finger Paint*
  1 part cornstarch
  2 parts boiling water

  Dissolve the starch in a small amount of cold water and gradually add hot water. Cook until clear.

- *Liquid Starch Finger Paint*
  liquid starch (or thin white paste)
  powder paint

  Pour 15 mL of liquid starch in the centre of a sheet of dampened paper. Add a small amount of powder paint. Mix.

- *Sugar Finger Paint*
  1 part sugar
  2 parts flour
  2 parts water

  Combine. Add slowly to 5 parts boiling water, stirring until thick.

Paints, Colors, and Other Ingredients
- powdered tempera
- liquid tempera (mix to thick consistency)
- finger paint, commercial
- liquid starch (to extend paints, to make fingerpaint, to use with chalk)
- liquid soap (to extend fingerpaint)
- shaving cream (to fingerpaint with)
- oil pastels, assorted colors
- pastel chalk
- kindergarten-size crayons
- tempera blocks, assorted
- transparent watercolor paints
- marking pens, watercolor

Brushes and Other Tools
- easel brushes
- large painter's brush
- feather dusters
- tongue depressors or chopsticks for mixing paint
- ice-cream sticks for mixing paint
- small juice or fruit cans for holding paint
- plastic containers or milk cartons for holding paints
- aluminum foil (for covering paint cans)
- Q-tips
- sponges
- straws
- rollers
- toothbrushes

- *Flour Finger Paint*
  2 parts flour
  1 part sugar
  1 part cornstarch

  Mix ingredients to a thick heavy paste in cold water. Pour on enough boiling water to make a thick, heavy starch, stirring constantly until clear.

- *Wallpaper Paste Finger Paint*
  2 parts wallpaper paste
  3 parts cold water

  Dissolve, beat with egg beater. Store in refrigerator.

Recipes for Silk-Screen Painting

- *Liquid Starch Silk Screen Paint*
  liquid starch
  powder paint

  Add starch to paint until consistency of light paste.

- *Tempera Silk Screen Paint*
  tempera paint
  soap flakes
  water

  Add a small quantity of soap flakes to the tempera. Add water as necessary to create the consistency of cream.

Recipes for Printing Ink

- *Varnish Base Printing Ink*
  3 parts powder paint
  1 part varnish

  Will dry quickly. Use on non-absorbent, smooth finish paper.

- *Oil Base Printing Ink*
  2 parts powder paint
  1 part linseed oil
  1 part varnish

  Mix to consistency of smooth paste. This ink will spread evenly but will not dry quickly.

Water Centre

A water centre provides opportunity for manipulation and exploration using water in a variety of ways. Children gain new insights through water play by interacting with each other and with the teacher, who provides suggestions or questions that enhance and extend the experiences. Children extend their physical and logical knowledge as they engage in activities that utilize water and additional materials.

Suggested Activities for the Water Centre

- Explore the properties of water and the pleasure of playing with it.
- Measure, weigh, and record the amounts of water held by different containers.
- Add color to water and study its diffusion.
- Melt snow and ice. Boil water or let it evaporate from dishes. Encourage children to discuss the physical properties and states of water.
- Mix bubble solution and make blowers for creating bubbles.
- Challenge the children to discover or make things that will float and things that will sink. Record observations, using drawings to illustrate materials that have been classified through experimentation.
- Displace water with large, smooth stones in buckets.

Suggested Materials
- water table
- water
- sponges
- towels
- containers that vary according to size, shape, and function
- sponges
- cardboard
- cartons
- cork
- cups
- watering can
- eye dropper
- measuring cups
- bowls
- baster
- straws
- siphon
- pouring spouts
- egg beater
- sieve
- strainers
- plastic fish

- Explore, experiment, observe, and classify contrasting kinds of objects (porous and non-porous; metal and wood).

Note: Precaution must be taken when adding food color to water to ensure that it does not cause allergic reactions in students.

Using Water as a Theme

Any of the following topics could be integrated into experiences for the children.
- evaporation and drying (wet objects become dry)
- absorbancy (some materials soak up water)
- dissolving (some substances disappear in water)
- water has weight
- water can move objects
- water for washing and cooking
- rainy days and puddles
- rivers, streams, ponds, and seashore
- water animals

Recipes for Water Materials

- *Bubble Solution*
  200 mL liquid soap
  70 mL glycerine or sugar
  1 L water

  Make own bubble pipes. One pipe is a Styrofoam cup with a plastic straw poked near end of one side or bottom.

Sand Centre

A sand centre provides opportunity for manipulation and exploration using sand in a variety of ways.

The activities at the sand centre are child-initiated. However, the teacher facilitates learning and development of concepts with challenges and open-ended questions as well as the provision of special materials.

Suggested Activities for the Sand Centre

- Explore both wet and dry sand. It can be shovelled, packed, poured, measured, and weighed. Through dialogue and experiences, the children's play promotes both language development and understanding of physical properties.
- Construct theme-related maps or models such as buildings, pools, rivers, roads, castles, or the surface of the moon.
- Make sand clocks to measure time.
- Make tracks, patterns, and impressions in wet and dry sand.

NOTE: If the sand found in your area is dusty and fine, or of a poor quality, buy clean sand at a supply store (i.e., a retail outlet for concrete). Sand is not all that expensive when you consider how important it can be in a learning centre.

Suggested Materials

- squeeze bottles
- clear plastic tubing or hose
- objects that sink or float

Suggested Materials

- two sand containers (dry sand table, wet sand table)
- dust pan or broom
- a variety of containers and objects for pouring, measuring, and making things (e.g., cans, jello moulds, cookie cutters, funnels, graduated measuring objects, watering can, bucket and shovel, spoons and scoops, sieves and strainers, salt and pepper shaker, strainers, collander, cars and trucks, animals, balance scales, egg timer).

Interest Centre

Collections are created in conjunction with various themes. Children like to contribute to these and may bring collections of their own from time to time to share with the group.

As children explore at this centre, they sort, match, measure, estimate, group, classify, describe, discuss, label, graph, and/or record their observations.

Collections provide rich opportunities for extending social, physical, and logical knowledge for stimulating language and thinking skills.

Suggested Activities for the Interest Centre

- Examine, handle, and manipulate the objects. Discuss observations.
- Make comparisons by examining different attributes such as size, shape, color, texture, where things are found, their use, etc. Encourage children to explore individual objects and groups of objects thoroughly.
- Sometimes collections are made by the teacher to introduce new or unfamiliar things to explore such as cogs, clocks, a plug, a kaleidoscope, spoons, magnets, a glass stopper, an old radio, or weights.
- Invite a person who has a special collection to visit the kindergarten.
- Label the items in the collection.
- Group the items into categories according to function or use.

Exploration Centre

Providing the opportunity to explore and experience a variety of materials in a systematic way is done by offering carefully prepared activities to children. Materials should be selected on the basis of their ability to reveal natural phenomena, their ability to be used in different ways to encourage experimentation, and their capacity to motivate.

While the children are playing in this centre, the activities engage them in many processes. They observe, using their senses to perceive similarities, differences, and changes. They classify, organize, and sort materials, events, and occurrences into groupings. They quantify, comparing objects or events by length, area, volume, mass, temperature, force, and time. They communicate their understanding to others through oral language, charts, graphs, and language experience. Finally, they infer (based on past observations) and predict future occurrences.

Suggested Activities for the Exploration Centre

- Mix colors (food coloring and water) or paints and examine the colors of light as seen in a prism or rainbow.
- Plant a garden. Encourage children to care for the plants, observe changes, and keep a record of growth.
- Care for and observe small animals. Compare habitants, foods, and special care necessary for different animals.
- Bring a number of simple machines to class. Encourage the children to take the machines apart and to reassemble them. Children can trace and label parts, draw diagrams to illustrate the machine, or "invent" machines of their own.

Suggested Materials

- table or space for display
- labels
- magnifying glasses
- scales
- ruler
- magnet
- paper and pencil

Suggested Materials

- water
- magnets
- magnifying glass
- weighing tools (balances, scales)
- plants
- small animals (hamster, lizard, chameleon, gerbil, newt, crayfish, turtle, hermit crab, garter snake, land snails, a bird)
- terraria for different animals (desert for lizard; forest or jungle for newt, garter snake, snails; pools for crayfish; pond life for turtles and frogs)
- batteries and bulbs
- thermometers
- magnetic board
- classroom garden materials (old wading pool, seeds, pots)
- simple machines and gadgets (telephone, old radio, control boxes, circuit boxes, clocks)
- tools (screwdrivers, pliers)
- collections
- touch and feel box
- texture hunt materials (leaves, netting, lace, fabric, wood grain, brick, cement)
- sheet or clothes pins
- lamp

- Play with shadows. Dramatize stories using shadow puppets or compare the size and shape of different kinds of shadows. Trace silhouettes or experiment with hands to create shadow "monsters" and shapes.

Recipes for the Exploration Centre

- *Crystal Garden*
  Place broken pieces of brick or terracotta clay in glass bowl or jar. Pour following solution over pieces.

  4 parts water
  1 part ammonia
  4 parts bluing
  1 part Mercurochrome
  4 parts salt

  Add more solution each day until garden has grown to desired size.

Table Toys and Game Centre

Opportunities to manipulate toys and puzzles and to engage in games and activities with others stimulate both intellectual and social activity. Further, children are given the chance to refine their fine muscle co-ordination. They can build constructions and incorporate their creations into dramatic play. They are encouraged to draw or map their creations, to talk about them and write labels, and to make signs or captions where appropriate. The teacher provides verbal challenges and activities for extending the experiences.

The equipment can be used by individuals or in small groups. Planning, discussion and co-operation become necessary to facilitate the use of space, time, and materials.

Suggested Activities for the Table Toys and Games Centre

- Explore and create, using a variety of toys and games accompanied by dialogue with the teacher as appropriate.
- Use small toys and building and constructing equipment for dramatic play activities.
- Use small toys such as plastic animals and vehicles for ordering and classifying activities.
- Provide children with many opportunities to work in small groups and to take turns playing games. It is often helpful to have an adult or older child participate as a player with the kindergarten children.
- Encourage children to share and communicate with each other while they play.

Suggested Materials

- puzzles (animals, occupations, objects, literature, nursery rhymes, concepts, dinosaurs, sequences, numerals)
- snakes and ladders
- lotto games
- card games and playing cards
- dominoes (geometric, wooden, picture, plastic)
- construction toys (Lego, Beaufix, Play Plax, connector sets, Tinker Toys, interlocking blocks)
- puzzles (animal, nursery rhymes, cars, trucks, dinosaurs)
- advanced puzzles (inlay, boxed, color pattern, foam)
- stacking toys (rings, beakers, nested boxes)
- puzzle storage case
- fastening materials (buttoning games, zippers, lacing boards, nuts and bolts, locks with keys, beads and laces, threading blocks)
- peg boards with pegs
- magnetic shapes

Block Centre

As children play in the block centre, they represent their thinking and imagining in three-dimensional form. Intellectual development occurs as children sort, classify, measure, evaluate, and solve problems. Concepts such as size, space, and time develop. Children represent what they know from experience by constructing, planning, talking, and engaging in dramatic play. The conversation and co-operation necessary to plan work with others on construction projects and the satisfaction gained promotes social and emotional development.

Children are encouraged to draw, paint, map, label, talk, or write about what they are doing as a further extension of their activities.

Suggested Activities for the Block Centre

- Explore and create, using a variety of materials. Dramatic play usually accompanies this activity.
- Construct buildings, roads, an airport, docks, cities, train stations, farms, parks, construction sites, a playground, and anything else children can think of. They should be encouraged to label buildings, create roads, and add paper creations and to engage in dramatic play.
- Challenge the children to extend theme- or interest-related knowledge by suggesting block representations of such things as a castle, a circus, a firehall, or a post office.
- Make patterns using the blocks. Encourage the children to try both linear and circular patterns.
- Match or sort blocks by attributes such as color, shape, size, or thickness.
- Seriate a set of blocks.

Dramatic Play Centre

A dramatic play centre allows the children to interact, experience, and recreate real or imaginative situations, places, or role-dramas. Either as individuals or in groups, children can plan, rearrange, and execute changes to the centre, which reproduce real-life experiences. Participation stimulates intellectual, social, and liguistic development as children become involved in detailed planning, sharing, and co-operation. Emergent reading and writing (writing plans, making signs and labels, etc.) are encouraged wherever appropriate. Encouraging children to bring items from home to facilitate a dramatic play motivates involvement.

It may be useful to store some items in separate "prop boxes" or small suitcases. An overabundance of materials can make clean-up difficult for the children. Once you have determined the kinds of prop boxes you wish to have and how you will store and label items, you can begin to sort and add to collections of materials you already have available. Children and parents will contribute items if you provide a stimulating list to get the process started. Other items can be "scrounged" from stores, repair shops, lumber companies, garages, newspapers, printers, and so on.

Suggested Materials

- block and toy shelves to house wooden blocks (unit), cardboard bricks, table blocks (Froebel), hollow centred wooden blocks, pattern blocks, Beaufix, multilink, cuisinaire, geometric shapes, attribute blocks, and pattern blocks
- toys and props to enrich block play (trucks and vans, airplanes, cars, boats, trees, trains, buildings, wooden people, animals, hats, set of traffic signs, masking tape for roads, paper roads, water, runways, tracks, plastic caps, lids for "turrets" or towers, toilet paper rolls, fabric scraps for curtains, pens or paper for signs or labels, directions, paper cores and cylinders for wheels, books)

Suggested Materials

- furniture (child-size furniture and equipment — stove, refrigerator, sink, tables, chairs, cupboards, dresser, clothes basket, ironing board, iron, cradle, broom, dustpan)
- table setting (tablecloth, dishes, cutlery, cooking and serving utensils, placemats, napkins, dishpan, dishcloth, soap, drying rack, containers)
- dolls (doll clothes, carriage, bed, bedding, high chair, dishes, cutlery, cooking utensils)
- dress-up clothes and props (hats and caps, boots and shoes, purses and bags, wigs, glasses, brushes, barrettes, first-aid kit, aprons, fabric, "wings," gloves, jewellery, full-length mirror)

Suggested Activities for the Dramatic Play Centre

By planning and providing appropriate props,

- Create role-drama situations such as home, hairdresser's, bus ride, train ride, airplane ride, post office, fire hall, bakery, moving house, occupations, tea parties, birthday parties, dinner time, supermarket, shoe store, cafe/restaurant, shopping centre, bank, pet shop, spring cleaning, washday, picnic, packing for holidays, zoo, space ship, and space station.
- Create role-dramas involving getting ready for Christmas, New Years, etc.
- Encourage spontaneous dramatic play accompanied by dialogue with the teacher (when appropriate) as an aid to solving problems, extending knowledge, or clarifying thought.

- food (food models made with flour and salt dough, hardened, baked and painted; food pictures — mounted and laminated; cans, food packages, bags, shelves for storage.
- stores (play money, cash register, bags, counter, signs, items for sale)
- hairdressing (mirror, hairpins, hairnets, curlers, dryer, towels, combs, magazines, empty bottles, plastic basin, money, emery boards)
- car repairs (clean, used motor parts; hammers, pliers, screw driver; funnels, empty boxes and cans, flashlight, wire, pump, keys, gloves, auto supply catalogues, rags, old shirts)
- camping (canvas for tent, knapsack, rope, grill, small logs, flashlight, blankets, books on nature, binoculars, food models, etc.)
- doctors/nurses (first-aid kit, scissors, tape, hats, white clothing, dolls, bandages, cotton, stethoscope, gloves, bag)

Puppet Centre

Children take great pleasure and need time for free exploration using puppets to dramatize real or imaginary situations as well as to develop characterizations based on favorite stories. Opportunity to plan, practise, produce, perform, and present plays or "shows", as well as to make a variety of styles of puppets, involves an elaborate network of concepts and skills.

Children should be encouraged to create their own scripts, to tape record their stories, and to use a variety of voice tones and inflections that enhance their ability to reproduce a vision of themselves as a character over and over again.

Suggested Activities for the Puppet Centre

- Explore and manipulate puppets. Use them for singing songs and for other simple activities.
- Introduce the children to a wide variety of handmade and commercial puppets. Encourage them to create their own simple puppets such as stick puppets, finger puppets, sock puppets, bag puppets, and so on.
- Adapt a story or create an original store to be produced as a puppet play. If appropriate, write a script to be followed.
- Make a puppet theatre or prepare backdrop scenery for the production of a puppet play. If several scene changes are necessary, groups of children can be responsible for individual sets.
- Make tickets and invitations to attend the puppet play. Invite another class to come and view the show.

Suggested Materials

- commercial puppet theatre
- refrigerator box
- empty TV cabinet
- curtains
- commercial puppets
- material for handmade puppets (socks, bags, sticks, paper, yarn, buttons)

Cooking Centre

Reserving work space for a cooking centre and locating necessary materials for food preparation in one central area facilitates cooking in the kindergarten. Cooking with small groups of children and utilizing the assistance of parents can enable food preparation to be a regular part of the kindergarten program.

Suggested Activities for the Cooking Centre

- During group planning and discussion, children will be involved in the reading of rebus-style recipes and in accepting jobs as helpers. Throughout this kind of activity children participate in problem solving and decision making in an experiential sense.
- Children can participate in much of the food preparation. They can wash and cut food, mix ingredients, and so on. Following preparation of a recipe, children should also be involved in the clean-up of utensils and workspace. Others can set tables and serve the food.
- Make a class cookbook. Recipes can be printed or typed, and children can draw the illustrations. Duplicate a copy for each child.

NOTE: Safety precautions concerning equipment and food allergies should be taken.

Sample Holiday Snacks

- *Thanksgiving*
  turkey soup
  corn on the cob
  pumpkin pie
  fresh fruit
  fresh vegetables
  cranberry sauce
  popcorn

- *Halloween*
  pumpkin seeds
  pumpkin muffins

- *Hanukkah*
  potato latkes
  bagels/cream cheese
  kugel

- *Christmas*
  mini Christmas cakes
  tarts

- *Valentines*
  red foods
  heart-shaped foods

- *Pancake Day (Shrove Tuesday)*
  pancakes

- *St. Patrick's Day*
  baked potatoes
  soda bread
  stew

- *Easter*
  omelets
  scrambled eggs

- *Victoria Day*
  picnic foods

Suggested Materials

Child-Safe Utensils
- knives
- bowls
- measuring spoons
- egg beater
- flipper
- serving trays
- small bowls
- muffin tins
- small plates
- loaf pans
- placemats
- apple slicer
- serviettes
- potato peeler

Equipment
- stove
- fridge
- water
- popcorn popper
- electric frying pan
- food dehydrator
- mix master
- blender

Additional Resources

- KINDERCOOKS
  School District No. 38
  (Richmond)

- Milk Foundation of B.C.
  2940 Main Street
  Vancouver, B.C.

- Information booklets published by Health and Welfare Canada, Public Health Units

Learning Centres

Music Centre

Experience with musical sounds helps to increase auditory acuity. Perception can become more acute when children are given opportunities to enjoy, create, and respond to music. Children are encouraged to improvise individual responses through dance, drama, and movement.

Activities introduced during group sessions are often practised spontaneously during the activity/centre times.

Suggested Activities for the Music Centre

- Explore informally both homemade and commercially produced instruments.
- Make instruments and experiment with the sounds they produce.
- Use instruments from the music centre to enhance dramatic play. Children can create a "band," assemble a parade, or incorporate instruments with known singing and movement games.
- Make big books of songs by recording the lyrics and having the children illustrate the verse or separate segments.

Suggested Materials

- collections of song and rhythm books
- rhythm instruments (drums, triangles, bells, tone bells, cymbals, sticks, maracas, castanets, tone blocks, tambourine, xylophone, sand blocks)
- piano
- records and record player
- tape recordings and tape player
- rice in a box
- beans or dimes in a jar
- spoons, rattles
- comb and waxed paper kazoos
- foil and cellophane
- bottles with water in them
- papier-mâché maracas
- gourd shakers
- streamers on sticks
- pom-poms
- fans, hats, scarves
- songs recorded on charts
- big book songbooks
- Orff instruments, activities, and songs
- materials for "writing" scores and lyrics

Field Trips and Visitors

Learning is relevant to young children when it is based on first-hand experiences and appeals to their natural curiosity. Classroom visitors or field trips into the community can make learning much more meaningful to young children. For example, kindergarten children better understand the function of a post office if they have the *shared experience* of visiting the office or having a postal worker come and speak to them. Simulated situations are not as effective.

Field Trips

Field experiences can be used to introduce new skills or concepts through guided study or to provide the opportunity to apply skills and concepts introduced in the classroom to practical situations. Through field studies, children have the opportunity to pose questions and examine alternatives. They can gather data at the source and organize and analyze it once they return to the classroom.

Field trips are most appropriate when they are incorporated into the overall program and not experienced in isolation. For this reason, thorough planning and careful preparation of pre-trip, on-site, and follow-up activities are key components to their success.

Examine potential sites carefully and select those that offer a maximum number of learning opportunities. If interaction with people at the site has been planned, it is helpful if you can give your hosts information beforehand regarding the children's interests, concentration span, and vocabulary levels. Also, it is especially important to let your hosts know how you view the visit in relation to what the class is studying in school.

When children are encouraged to take an active role in preparations, they have an opportunity to develop or refine a variety of skills and to make a cognitive connection between in-class learning and field-based learning. They may predict what they think they might see on an outing. They may think about the kinds of questions they could ask. They can be encouraged to remember things about the trip that would help them carry out a follow-up project such as converting the dramatic play centre, building a model, writing a group story, or making a book.

Planning and preparation are important to the success of the experience, but once on the site it is not unusual for the child's interest to be captured by the unexpected. These special moments can become valuable learning experiences.

While procedures for planning field trips will vary from district to district, the following checklist of suggested considerations is included to assist you with preparations.

Suggested Field Trip Checklist

Teacher Planning

1. Specific or general objectives decided. .... ☐

2. Destination and route to be followed, pre-visited, and decided. .... ☐

3. Permission obtained from principal and contact person at destination. .... ☐

4. Transportation and volunteer help arranged. .... ☐

5. Letter to explain objectives, to provide information regarding time, place, and clothing needs, and to obtain parent permission. .... ☐

6. Behavior expectations and trip objectives explained to children and volunteers. .... ☐

7. Equipment assembled. .... ☐

8. Groups assigned and named. .... ☐

Preparation for Children

Discuss with children:

1. Reason for field trip. .... ☐

2. Safety (travelling and on site). .... ☐

3. Behavior expectations. .... ☐

4. Activities children will be involved in, both group and individual. .... ☐

5. Responsibilities of groups and group leaders. .... ☐

Activity Planning

1. Pre-trip activities planned. .... ☐

2. Field trip activities planned. .... ☐

3. Post-trip activities planned. .... ☐

4. Thank-you notes written. .... ☐

5. Evaluation. .... ☐

Field Trips and Visitors

Sample Planning Guide

1. Field trip # _____, Proposed date _____

2. Purpose _____

   _____

3. Mode of transportation _____

4. Departure _____ Return _____

5. Permission from principal _____

   Permission from contact person at site _____

   (details) _____

   _____

   _____

   Permission slips to parents _____

   to be returned by _____

6. Contact transportation services _____

7. Resources: Parents _____ _____

   _____ _____

   Materials for the trip _____ _____

   _____ _____ _____

8. Meeting with parents _____

9. Follow-up:

   * Note to principal _____

   * Thank-you letter to people
     facilitating visit _____

   * Thank-you letters to parents _____

10. Comments _____

Sample Letter to Parents/Guardians

_____ school,

_____ street,

_____, B.C.

Dear Parents/Guardians,

As part of the program in kindergarten, we are learning about the post office and what happens to a letter after it has been written. Each of the children has prepared a "letter" (a picture painted and labelled at school). I will address the envelopes, and we will take the letters to the post office for mailing.

Our field trip to the post office will be on March 3rd. We will be travelling to the post office by bus. The bus will pick us up at the school at 9:20 and return us by 11:00. Please meet your child at the regular dismissal time of 11:30.

We will need five volunteers to supervise groups of children. In order to discuss plans and organize the activities, volunteers are asked to meet with me on February 24th at 11:30 in the classroom.

The children are excited about the trip and I am pleased we are able to provide this kind of experience for them. Please call me at _____ if you have any further questions.

Thank you.

_____

Sample Permission/Information Sheet

I give permission for _____ _____ to go on the

field trip to the _____post office on

March 3, 1984. I understand the children will be transported to and from the
centre by school bus and that regular kindergarten hours will be observed.

_____
(Parent/Guardian)

PLEASE RETURN THIS FORM BY February 17, 1984.

. . . .

I am able to attend the meeting on February 24, 1984 at 11:30 and will be
willing to assist with the field trip.

Name _____ Phone Number _____

PLEASE RETURN THIS FORM BY FEBRUARY 17, 1984

* to be attached to the letter to parents/guardians

```
┌────────────────────────────────────────────────────────┐
│       Sample Outline for Parent's/Guardian's Meeting (Feb. 24th)       │
│                                                          │
│  Purpose of this trip _____  │
│  _____  │
│  _____  │
│  _____  │
│                                                          │
│  My responsibilities _____  │
│  _____  │
│  _____  │
│  _____  │
│  _____  │
│                                                          │
│  Group # _____ Children _____  │
│                      _____  │
│                      _____  │
│                      _____  │
│                      _____  │
│                                                          │
│  Notes _____  │
│  _____  │
│  _____  │
│  _____  │
└────────────────────────────────────────────────────────┘
```

At the meeting with the parents, the teacher will want to discuss the purpose for the trip — the activities the children will be involved in and how they are to be carried out. In addition, it is wise to make clear the respective responsibilities of the group leaders and the teacher. If a leader experiences difficulty with a child or if there is an emergency, it's a good idea to have done some pre-planning in this regard. Organizing the groups prior to the day of the trip can eliminate potential problems. It is suggested that this (or similar procedure) be followed for each trip.

If you are relying on parents to transport students, some schools require that teachers leave this information at the office prior to departure. (See sample).

Field Trips and Visitors

```
┌─────────────────────────────────────────────────────┐
│           Sample Form — Volunteer Drivers            │
│                                                       │
│  Name of Driver _____ │
│                                                       │
│  Licence number _____  Insurance _____ _____ │
│                                                       │
│  Occupants of car _____ │
│                                                       │
│                   _____ │
│                                                       │
│                   _____ │
│                                                       │
│                   _____ │
│                                                       │
│                   _____ │
│                                                       │
└─────────────────────────────────────────────────────┘
```

Visitors

The field-based experience is one way to provide children with a shared experience. An alternative is to bring people from the community into the classroom to share their expertise with the children. In this way the community becomes an integral component of the children's in-class experiences. And children have an opportunity to interact on a personal level with people who represent, or have an impact on, the world they are exploring.

Classroom visitors may include a child's grandmother telling folk talks to the class, a parent cooking with a small group of children, a local firefighter showing slides of the equipment used in fire fighting, or a drama group presenting a puppet play. To aid a visitor's planning for the presentation, the teacher should explain specific objectives, share insights into the children's interests and attention spans, and indicate teaching aids that the speaker might have access to that would appeal to the children. Visitors should be advised to bring items that the children can touch and handle. It is helpful for the visitor to have the date, time, and place specified in writing. A phone call to confirm the visit will help ensure that children aren't disappointed. Children benefit from having an opportunity to actively participate in as much of the preparation as their maturity will alllow and should have the opportunity to practise asking questions prior to the visitor's arrival. Deciding on a speaker and the timeline for the visit, designing the questions to be asked, acting as guides to the classroom for the guest, and planning further activities are examples of how children can become involved. Some form of follow-up activity will encourage them to recall the experience and reflect upon it.

Note: Sample "Parent Interest Forms" appear in the "Orientation" section of this book.

Follow-up Activities

Follow-up activities are important whether the children have been involved in discussions with classroom visitors or on field trips. Examples of activities that could be used to extend the children' experiences have been included throughout the "Themes" section of this resource book. Such activities will allow students to integrate their new skills and concepts into the total scope of the program.

THEMES

Overview

Themes provide *one* approach to planning and organizing a kindergarten program. By relating a number of activities and experiences to a central theme, a teacher presents opportunities for development in an organized and integrated manner. Keeping in mind the various centres in the kindergarten, the teacher relates the goals of the program to a theme or themes. The result is a variety of activities related to a single topic. This way of presenting experiences is intended to take into account the interrelatedness of the child's perception of the world. Using this framework can help to clarify the nature of the children's experiences. Thus *the themes presented in this section of the Resource Book can be related to goals, content areas, or learning centres.*

Themes are vehicles for delivering the curriculum. They provide the flexibility needed to develop an interesting and challenging learning environment for children. At the same time, theme development provides the teacher with a structure for planning, teaching, and evaluating.

The length of time devoted to, and the scope of activities involved in, a single theme will vary according to the children, their needs, their interests, and the classroom environment. Some themes will lend themselves to longer periods of activity (a month or more), while others may last for only a few weeks or days.

Some themes can be considered "classics," and you may want to repeat them each year. Others may be appropriate only for a particular group one year. Some themes are broad enough to be applicable to all aspects of the program, while others are more limited. When a theme is related more easily to some goals than to others, it may be helpful to plan parallel themes to complement each other. While "major" themes are developed, "minor" themes or experiences can be provided simultaneously.

Theme planning can be facilitated through graphic layouts relating the theme to the goals, to content areas, or centres. Individual teachers will evolve methods for planning that best suit their own ways of thinking and working with children.

Theme planning can be an exciting and creative venture. At times the teacher may have planned a theme only to discover that the children have different interests or experiences that could be developed. The ability to support, integrate, and facilitate the development of themes based on the children's ideas and interests is an important facet of planning for kindergarten. So, too, is the ability to take advantage of unexpected occurrences. The goals of the program can be related to child-initiated interests, spontaneously arising events, teacher-initiated experiences, and theme-related activities. Balance among these elements can be achieved over the year.

A great deal of information and resource material can be gathered in relation to a chosen theme, and literally hundreds of activities are possible. While examining and considering the myriads of possibilities and alternative experiences available for planning, it is important to remember that themes should last only as long as the children's and teacher's interests and abilities can maintain.

We don't have to search long or far for topics. They can be found almost everywhere and can be drawn from any curriculum area. However, the most successful are likely to be those that develop from the experiences, environment, and interests of the children. Children are interested in so many things in their everyday world that if we are sensitive to their concerns, questions, and delights, there should be no difficulty in finding topics for study.

Although every goal cannot be addressed in relation to every theme, care should be taken to ensure that all the goals of the kindergarten are implemented in a balanced way.

It cannot be overemphasized that the experiences described are suggestions, offered as *samples* from which the individual teacher can plan and develop a variety of other experiences. *Teachers are encouraged to select* those activities that are most appropriate for their group or that hold special interest for the teacher. People and places selected should be of immediate interest and concern to the children.

A list of books chosen to complement each of the themes included in the "Children's Book" section of this resource book. Teachers are encouraged to note their favorites in the space provided at the conclusion of each theme.

Teachers will want to select and adapt the ideas that appeal to them on the basis of the needs, interests, and abilities of the children in the group. In addition, themes may be chosen to reflect regional significance, cultural relevance, local resources, or materials available. The goals of the program can be implemented in relation to virtually *any* subject matter. The latitude to select, adapt, plan, implement, and evaluate theme-related activities is subject to the professional judgment of the teacher.

Regardless of the reason for choosing a particular theme, it will be more meaningful and exciting to the children if it has emotional relevance and impact for the group or the teacher. Even if the children are interested in a topic, it will not be successful without the enthusiasm and skill of the teacher as he or she questions, guides, organizes, and models behavior throughout the learning experience. The willingness to be open and flexible in planning and scheduling, accompanied by a commitment to acknowledge and incorporate input from the children in developing the designs for their own learning, are necessary components to the success of the theme approach. The combined energy and thoughts of the teacher and children can produce high-quality, theme-related experiences and can convey the message that what the children contribute is considered valuable. It is these contagious "sparks of excitment" that will motivate, stimulate, enhance, and extend learning in all dimensions of the kindergarten program.

Themes can be designed to extend and enrich field experiences within the community.

- Bakery
  Fast Food Outlet
  Grocery Store
  Cannery
  Vegetable Market
  Pizza Place
  Home Economics Class
  Restaurant
  Smokehouse

- Animal Hospital
  Kennels
  Bird Sanctuary
  Duck Pond
  Veterinarian
  Zoo/Aquarium
  Pet Shop
  Undersea Gardens

- Homes
  Schools
  Neighborhood
  Apartment Block

- Bowling Alley
  Ice Rinks
  Yacht Basin

- Post Office
  Television Studio
  Radio Station
  News Stand
  Printing Shop
  Telephone Booth

- Lumber Yard
  Pulp Mill
  Newspaper Plant
  Woods
  Log Construction

- Orchard
  Farm
  Berry Picking
  Pumpkin Patch
  Ranch
  Vineyard
  Rodeo
  Greenhouse
  Fair Grounds
  Flower Gardens
  Dairy
  Sheep Shearing
  Elevator
  Irrigation System

- Airport
  Train
  Sea Bus
  Boat
  Bus
  Wharf
  Car Wash
  Gas Station
  Road Construction
  Gravel Pit
  Roundhouse
  Bridges

- X-ray Clinic
  Ambulance
  Hospital
  Doctor's Office
  Drugstore

- Glass Blower
  Factory
  Watchmaker
  Hairdresser
  Hardware Store
  Jewellers

- Clock Shop
  Upholsterer
  Tailor
  Shopping Centre

- Power Station
  Weather Station
  Quarry
  Oil Well

- Hills
  City Dump
  Kelp Beds
  Waterfall
  Nature Park
  Beach
  Fish hatchery
  Fields
  Tree Farm
  Lake/River
  Botanical Garden
  Island
  Reservoir
  Dam

- Totem Poles
  Artist's Studio
  Hobby Show
  Orchestra
  Library
  Theatre
  Museum
  Magic Show

- Planetarium
  Observatory
  Science Lab

- Police Station
  Polling Booth
  Fire Station
  Fire Alarm Boxes

Themes can be designed to accompany special times for celebration as a response to ethnic and multicultural backgrounds of the children.

- Yom Kippur
  Remembrance Day
  New Year
  St. Patrick's Day
  Father's Day

- Thanksgiving
  Hanukkah
  Chinese New Year
  Easter
  Groundhog Day

- Halloween
  Christmas
  Valentine's Day
  Mother's Day
  Festival of Lights

Themes can be developed to reflect the nature of the school community.

- The School
  Playground
  School Neighborhood
  Secretary
- Patrol Guard
  Principal
  Aide
  Nurse
- Custodian
  V.P./Administrative
    Assistant
  Librarian
  Learning Assistant

Themes can be developed around people who would be willing to share information about their occupations, hobbies, culture, traditions, and travel.

- Fire Fighters
  Police
  Doctors
  Nurses
  Dentists
  Bakers
  Grocers
  Merchants
  Drivers
  Delivery People
  Zoo Keepers
  Orchardists
  Carpenters
  Farmers and Ranchers
- Weavers
  Authors
  Artists
  Potters
  Musicians
  Actors
  Sports People
- Dancers
  Translators
  Storytellers
  Crafts People

Themes can be developed as a response to changes or special features of the environment.

- Weather: rain, wind, snow, fog, sun, storm
- Seasons: fall, winter, spring, summer
- Ecology: plants, animals, earth, garbage
- Plants: flowers, trees, houseplants, growing seeds, gardens
- Water: rain, clouds, rivers, lakes, streams, ocean
- Tracks: animals, mud, imprints, rubbings, fossils
- Shadows: light, dark, puppets
- Backyards: plants, animals, spaces
- Playgrounds: equipment, play, toys, games

Themes can be designed to develop a particular concept.

- Observation
  Time
  Number
  Identification
- Change
  Classification
  Patterns
  Exploration
- Collections
  Colors
  Shapes
  Size/Weight

Themes can be developed to expand the child's knowledge or awareness.

- Safety
  Me
  Animals
  Seasons
  Life Cycles
  Cities
- Nutrition
  Senses
  Plants
  Machines
  Transportation
- Health/Cleanliness
  Families
  Physical Properties
  Days/Weeks/Months
  Buildings

Themes can be developed to build appreciation and positive attitudes.

- Environmental issues
  Friendship
  Feelings
- Nutrition
  Citizenship
- Physical Fitness
  Cultural Understanding

Themes can be developed in response to "issues of the moment" or because the children have indicated a special interest or a strong emotional response to certain topics.

- Space
  Teddy Bears
  Nursery Rhymes
  Circus
  Toys
- Monsters
  Fairy/Folktales
  Music/Records
  Sports
  Whales
- Dinosaurs
  Fantasy
  Babies
  Kites

The Process of Planning Themes

The items that follow are suggestions to assist you with planning. You are encouraged to use or adapt the activities in such a way that they will be suitable for the children in your class. Each of the themes presented here has been developed as a single format. A sample outline is provided for your use. Each of the themes is expressed to reflect this model for planning experiences and activities related to a single topic. This model is not intended as a "blueprint" but rather as a starting point for planning. Teachers are encouraged to develop a planning format most suitable to their needs or teaching style.

Topics

Begin by selecting a theme or topic.

Goals

Identify the goals of central relevance to the chosen theme. It is useful to list the specific theme-related concepts for each goal area. The list will vary from classroom to classroom and from theme to theme in accordance with the teacher's knowledge about the needs and abilities of the children.

Experiences, Activities, and Organization

Develop a list of diverse experiences and activities designed to further the goals central to the theme. One technique for planning a theme in the beginning stages is to draw a web chart. This kind of diagrammatic representation shows the possible directions in which a theme could lead the teacher and the children.

Develop a list of all the different ideas that occur to you about a theme. One idea will lead to another, and soon the paper will be filled with ideas and activities. Relationships between these ideas will emerge and can be grouped or classified under the goal headings. The next step in planning and organizing is to determine which ideas should occur first, the flow of one activity to another, and the development of a naturally blended sequence of activities.

Following this stage of planning, it is necessary to consider the length of time needed for the children to participate in the experiences.

Although the "classic" web chart often resembles a wheel with spokes or a "flow chart," it is important that each individual adapt and alter the working model to meet his or her needs and personal style. The important criteria (the goals for kindergarten) should remain constant.

Involving the children in a "brainstorming" or planning session would help to identify those aspects of the theme that are of greatest interest to them. One of the advantages of a web chart is that it is open-ended and can be changed; new thoughts and ideas can be inserted, and it can be adapted at various points during development.

Materials and Resources

Identify those materials and resources that will be necessary and basic to the success of the chosen theme. Books, songs, games, pictures, filmstrips, charts, or films can all be listed, located, and gathered together. Having identified themes in the planning for the year allows for development of a system for collecting materials and resources. Labelling containers with theme titles is a convenient way of building and maintaining an ongoing collection.

Teacher knowledge, background, and interest are factors that can provide greater depth and scope in planning specific themes. Research, reading, exploration, and preparation by the teacher will be necessary. Informing parents of plans for themes can lead to contributions of resources and materials as well as increased participation and interest on their part.

Implementation

Having organized the ideas into experiences, the concepts by goals, and the activities in logical sequence, the teacher then considers how each of these co-ordinates and dovetails with the dayplan.

THEME _____

EMOTIONAL DEVELOPMENT AND WELL-BEING	SOCIAL DEVELOPMENT	SOCIAL RESPONSIBILITY IN A CHANGING WORLD

Note: The goals of providing experiences to foster growth in emotional and social development are inherent in and intrinsic to all other goals. Therefore, it is understood that much related activity and concept development occurs at all times.

PHYSICAL DEVELOPMENT AND WELL-BEING	AESTHETIC AND ARTISTIC DEVELOPMENT
Health and Safety	Art
Nutrition/Snack	Music
Movement Education	Drama

INTELLECTUAL DEVELOPMENT

Social Knowledge

Physical Knowledge

Logical Knowledge

Representation

LANGUAGE DEVELOPMENT

Listening

Language

Emergent Reading and Writing

Resources

<u>Books for Children</u> (See the "Children's Books" section of this resource book.)

<u>References for Teachers</u> (including Field Trips/Visitors)

<u>Media</u> Because access and availability of media resources varies greatly from district to district, the "Media" section for each theme explained in this resource book has been left open to allow teachers to make note of available materials.

"Me"

Due to the egocentric nature of kindergarten children, the most important person in their lives is themselves. The world of the child, the people, and the things in his or her everyday life, provide the foundation for a place to begin the year in kindergarten. As a theme, "Me" can be of short duration and/or ongoing throughout the year. Each child brings to the program his or her own special background and experiences, thus forming the basis for a growing understanding that each person is unique but shares common needs and feelings. The theme "Me" naturally extends into discussion of the family and community. The following activities are intended to foster development in the seven goals of the kindergarten curriculum.

Emotional Development and Well-Being

- Discuss individuality. Children can begin to recognize that each person is special and unique by focusing on specific topics such as
    "My favorite T.V. shows";
    "My interests/hobbies";
    "My favorite books";
    "My pets";
    "My favorite places."
- Make banners of "Things I Like/Things I Don't Like."
- Discuss why each is so unique or special. Encourage children to ask themselves "What are the things that make me happy, or sad, or embarrassed?" Ask "How do you feel when your Mom hugs you?" "How do you feel when your friend shares something with you?" "How do you feel when someone you love goes away?"
- Use a sharing circle to discuss things about each other. The thing I like best about _____ is _____. Each child is given the opportunity to make one contribution. The other children listen. Using a sentence frame, recall in turn what each child has said. For example, "I remember Sam because he said _____." Then Sam has a turn to recall what another child said.
- Create "Me Exhibits."
- Discuss the idea of self-worth. Topics might include
    "I am a likeable person . . ."
    "I can learn to like/love others . . ."
    "I belong to different groups of people . . ."
- Recall first memories. Draw pictures of self as a baby. Record earliest memories and important "firsts" in each child's life. You may have to enlist the help of parents with this activity.

Social Development

- Choose the "Special Person for the Day" to be the teacher's "helper". Keep a chart so that everyone gets a turn.
- Bring baby pictures to school. Organize them in sequence and have the children guess "who is who?".
- Discuss "What is a friend?" "What does it mean to be a friend?" "What does it mean to have a friend?"
- Bring objects for "Show and Tell" from home. Each object should clearly illustrate a focal interest of the individual child.
- Participate in a "hand squeeze." Stand in a circle; hold hands; send a squeeze around the circle.

- Represent the relationships in which the child participates. For example, I am part of a family/group/class/neighborhood/etc.
- Discuss the meaning of birthdays. Celebrate birthdays at school. For those children who have summer birthdays, let the child select a day on which to celebrate his or her "un-birthday."

Social Responsibility

- Discuss the similarities and differences among people, kinds of homes, and the size and composition of families. Encourage children to describe these.
- Discuss family origins. Children can bring information and photos from home. Countries of origin, race, traditions, and customs can all be discussed within this context.
- Examine the rights of individual children and the needs of the group. Each child has a right to his or her feelings, a share of the time, and use of the materials.
- Encourage children to understand that each has ideas he or she wants to express. Others have ideas too.

Physical Development and Well-Being

Health and Safety

- Discuss recreational activities the children like to participate in. For each activity listed, discuss suggestions for carrying out these activities within a safe environment. Ask children with special skills to demonstrate or bring equipment to show to and discuss with the others.
- Discuss the parts of the body and the characteristics and functions of each.
- Discuss the five senses and the role each plays in how one learns about the environment. Are the children aware of the need to care for their eyes, ears, etc.?
- Display a growth chart on the wall. Measure the heights of the children at varying times throughout the year. Are the children aware of the changes in their own growth?

Nutrition and Snack

- Discuss the value of caring for the body through proper nutrition. Discuss and prepare healthy snacks and plan menus for nutritional meals.
- Make initial-shaped cookie cutters. Bake cookies with nutritional ingredients.
- Have an assortment of toppings available for baking pizzas. Encourage the children to make their own choices. The same idea could be utilized when children are involved in other food activities such as choosing the flavors for yogurt toppings or fruit milkshakes or choosing the fillings for sandwiches or tacos. Emphasis is on the differences of choices from within a variety of nutritious options.

Movement Education

- Discuss and demonstrate knowledge of parts of the body, the ability to move in space, and simulation exercises (e.g., "Move like a . . ."; "Pretend you are a . . .").

- Any of the following songs would be suitable movement activities:
  "Looby-Loo"
  "Hokey-Pokey" (*Sound Beginnings*, p. 71)
  "Punchinella" (Mary Helen Richards)
  "This is What I Can Do" (*Sound Beginnings*, p. 76)

Aesthetic and Artistic Development

Art

- Make silhouettes.
- Make "Me" collages from drawings, photos, magazines, or pieces of scrap paper and fabric.
- Make replica doll or puppet of self. By tracing the body, decorating it with features, and then stapling or stuffing the doll with newsprint, large dolls can be dressed and displayed in the classroom or in hallways.
- Bake, paint, and glaze dough people to reflect the image of individual children.
- Draw self-portraits. Use a mirror or sets of individual mirrors to assist with the noting of details.
- Use fabric crayons, felt pens, or dye to paint a self-portrait on cloth or to create a personalized T-shirt.
- Paint pictures of self involved in a variety of activities. Show family outings, get-togethers, and activities as they happen during the year.
- Create a class mural to depict all of the children in the class. Make a "Friend Ship." Each child draws his or her face on the porthole space of a large ship mural.

Music

- The children might enjoy learning and singing the following songs.

Raffi	"The More We Get Together"
	"All I Really Need"
	"I Wonder If I'm Growing"
	"I'm in the Mood"
Mary Helen Richards	"Here We Are Together"
	"Mary Wore a Red Dress"
Sound Beginnings	"Your Shadow" (page 180)
	"Me, Myself and I" (page 108)
This is Music for Today	"When I Grow Up"
	"My Family and Pets"
This is Music	"If You're Happy and You Know It"
Marlo Thomas, et al	"Free to Be You and Me"
Hap Palmer	"Growing Song"

Drama

- Use a hat or other articles from a prop box. Ask the children, "Who do you become?" Pantomime a new role and have the other children guess who you are.
- Mime common activities. After the role play is completed, have the actor ask the children, "What was I doing?" and "Can you guess who I was pretending to be?"

Intellectual Development

Social Knowledge

- Discuss friendship. Ask "What is a friend?" and "What does it mean to be a friend to someone else?"
- Discuss the similarities and differences between people. Encourage the children to talk about their homes, their families, and the community.
- Make a large model map of the neighborhood around the school. Use small boxes, blocks, and "found" objects in the kindergarten to represent the features of the neighborhood.
- Discuss the individuality and uniqueness of the children. Make and compare fingerprints, footprints, and handprints.
- Discuss "What is a family?" Encourage the children to consider what families do together as a group and how activities, roles, and responsibilities differ between family members and from one family to another.

Physical Knowledge

- Make a "Growth Chart" with the children. Use pieces of string or Multilink or Unifix cubes to measure body length.
- Compare a child's present height with a measure of his or her height at the time of birth.
- Make fold-out booklets about "My Five Senses."
- Provide life-sized floor puzzles of children (available commercially). It may also be useful to trace the outline of children on hard paper and then cut it into puzzle segments.

Logical Knowledge

- Graph information such as
    - —My shoes (by size or by method of closing)
    - —heights and/or weights
    - —eye color or hair color
    - —birthdays
    - —"Things I Like/Dislike"
    - —"My Favorite _____"
    - —"Our Pets"
    - —"Lost Teeth"
- Discuss the relationships of family members. For example, "How can someone be a father, brother, uncle, and husband all at the same time?"
- Illustrate personal lifelines. A parent helper can assist the children to record captions at various points along the line.

Representation

- Act out the roles and activities of various family members at the dramatic play centre.
- Use the blocks to create representations of people or of the children's own homes or yards.
- Provide many opportunities for the children to talk about themselves, their interests, their families, and their feelings. Help them to reflect, compare, and draw conclusions about their own experiences and those of others.

Language Development

Language

- Encourage the children to recognize their own names and the names of other students in the classroom by making use of cards with individual names printed on them.
- Learn "Hickety, Tickety Bumble Bee" (Mary Helen Richards) to facilitate the learning and use of children's names.
- Use the poem, "Color Me" to facilitate oral language development. Each child chooses a color and develops a statement about the choice made. For example:

> Color me yellow
> Bright and happy like the sun
> The color of butter, daisies, and bees.
>
> Color me blue,
> Like a bright, cloudless sky,
> Like a bluejay, like midnight, like my new bike.

Listening

- Tape record the children talking in turn. When each child has had a turn, play the tape back and encourage the children to guess the name of the speaker.
- Listen to "soundscape" recordings. Can the children guess what the individual sounds are? What kind of impressions are gained from the combined sounds? How are people's impressions similar? How do they differ?

Emergent Reading and Writing

- Make booklets on the topics "My Best Friend," or "My Family," or "About Me."
- Create language experience charts using any of the following titles.
  "What is a Friend?"
  "All About Families"
  "My Wishes"
  "My Toys"
  "My Favorite . . ."
- Use sentence patterns for completion. Write the sentence stem on the chalkboard or chart paper. Have the children complete the sentence in their own words. For example,
  I can _____.
  I have _____.
  I like _____.
  My legs can _____.
  My arms can _____.
- Make a class book using older children or buddies as scribes; assemble the single pages. Children could illustrate and describe their own page, using any of the following.
  "Myself"
  "I feel happy when . . ."
  "Things I like are . . ."
  "Who am I?"

Vocabulary

- I
- me
- you
- mine
- myself
- we
- they
- us
- family
- feeling
- home
- house
- neighborhood
- names of body parts
- names of actions
- colors for skin, hair, eyes
- his
- hers
- ourselves
- you
- yours
- theirs
- them
- help
- share
- like
- love
- friendship
- friend

Resources

Books for Children (See the "Children's Books" section of this resource book.)

Useful Toys and Equipment

- dolls
- tape recorder
- people puppets
- mirror
- magnifying glass
- home centre
- dress-up clothes
- wooden people for block centre

References for Teachers (including Field Trips/Visitors)

- "Additional Facts the Teacher Should Know," in B. M. Flemming, D. S. Hamilton, and J. D. Hicks, *Resources for Creative Teaching in Early Childhood Education* (New York: Harcourt Brace Jovanovich, 1977), 90–96.

- children's homes
- the teacher's home
- shopping centre
- hospital
- parents
- police officer
- ambulance attendant

- grandparents
- relatives
- pets
- friends
- doctor
- nurse
- dentist

Media

"Me"

"Apples"

The choice of the topic "Apples" for theme development allows the teacher to incorporate a number of interesting experiences for the children. This theme could be adapted to include foods from a particular food group. The following activities are intended to foster development in the seven goals of the kindergarten curriculum.

Emotional Development and Well-Being

- Ask each child to bring an apple to school. Sit in circles (groups of five or six children). Tell the children to look at their own apple very carefully and, after noting distinguishing features, to take a turn describing the apple to the other children in the group. Have the children put the apples in the centre of the circle, walk around once, and try to find their own apple. Talk about how apples are different and how they are similar. Expand the discussion to focus on the similarities and differences between people.

Social Development

- Focus on taking turns in activities and discussions. Encourage the children to work co-operatively and demonstrate appropriate behavior in school and while on field trips.
- Make applesauce or a fruit salad by combining apples or other fruit the children have brought from home. Talk about the co-operation necessary for completion of this activity.

Social Responsibility

- Focus on caring for, sharing, and tidying up the equipment and materials used in the classroom.
- Encourage the children to bring from home stories, pictures, or items that are related to the theme. In this way children can participate actively and assume some responsibility for their own learning and that of others.

Physical Development and Well-Being

Health and Safety

- Wash hands and apples in preparation for eating. Discuss the necessity for having cleaned the food and your hands.
- Discuss the use of sharp knives in the preparation of food.

Nutrition and Snack

- Use apples to introduce the fruits and vegetables food group.
- Discuss types of apples. Vary the kinds to be sampled raw and demonstrate a number of different ways to cut and serve raw apples.
- Discuss the benefits of eating foods such as apples.
- Make applesauce, apple juice, apple muffins, apple pie, or dried apples. Recall the steps taken in preparation. Record and read recipes.
- Make a collage of other fruits and vegetables, using pictures from magazines. Label the food items.

- Plan with children for future snacks that may include apples as part of the snack or an accompaniment to it.
- Classify and make lists of snacks (e.g., "Snacks that are red" and "Snacks that are fruit").

Movement Education

- Introduce movements associated with apples or trees. Have children suggest ways to display falling, bending, shaking, rolling, swaying, spinning, and so on.

Aesthetic and Artistic Development

Art

- Make prints and rubbings of sections of apple trees or leaves or of the parts of the apple that can be used to make prints.
- Paintings can be done on apple-shaped paper. Draw or paint pictures to illustrate activities connected with apples. For example, one child may decide to make a picture of the trip to the grocery store while another may make a picture about making applesauce.
- Using play dough, the children can create models of apples, tarts, pies, trees, and so on. Provide rolling pins, muffin pans, and pie plates to facilitate play.
- Children can construct pictures about apples using scraps from the construction centre — bits of red paper, fabric, or colored tiles for mosaics could all be used.
- Create a large mural to depict seasonal changes and the apple tree — the development of an apple from blossom to fruit and what happens to apples after they are harvested.
- Look at a print of Cezanne's *The Big Apples*. Set up a still life near the paint easel and encourage children to paint pictures.
- Encourage children to paint a picture of an apple and tell the class about it.

Music

- Discuss the Raffi record *Corner Grocery Store* and invite children to bring other Raffi records to share with the class. Songs such as "Shake Your Sillies Out," "Sembalina," or "Knees Up Mother Brown" would be suitable choices.
- Listen to the song "Apple Pickers' Reel" or the record *1, 2, 3, 4* by Sharon, Lois, and Bram.

Drama

- Dramatize songs, stories, and poems where appropriate.
- Mimic the sequence of events associated with shopping for or cooking with apples.

Intellectual Development

Social Knowledge

- Take a trip to an orchard or yard to see apple trees and pick fruit; to a juice plant, cannery, or packing house; or to a grocery store to see other kinds of apples and fruits. Find examples of apple products and labels throughout the store.
- Recall the places where apples can be found.

Physical Knowledge

- Bring apples from home and discuss the resulting collection in terms of color, size, shape, kind, stem, bruises, or other distinguishing features.
- Observe and discuss "What's inside an apple." Learn the names for the parts of the apple and describe each.
- Dry apples. Observe and record the changes in appearance, texture, and taste. Think of other ways apples could be changed, and experiment.

Logical Knowledge

- Group apples in the collection on the basis of various characteristics. Count the apples, record findings, and make picture graphs.
- Some apples are red. What other things are red? Make lists. Start a "red table" and encourage children to bring items from home to be displayed on the table.
- Estimate how many apples will fit into various containers. Try the experiment, count the apples, and record the results.

Representation

- Convert the dramatic play centre into a store or roadside fruit and vegetable stand. Record plans for the conversion, make signs and labels, and collect the items necessary.
- Build a model, in the block centre, of an orchard, a shopping centre, a packing plant, etc.
- Recall and record sequences as they relate to the activities carried out relevant to the study of apples.

"Apples"

Language Development

Listening

- Can the children recognize the sound of someone crunching into a fresh, crisp apple?
- Listen to the story or record of *Johnny Appleseed* (Walt Disney).

Language

- Discuss the parts of the apple and the apple tree. Predict what will be observed when an apple is cut open.
- Discuss the characteristics of different apples (colors, shapes, sizes, weight, texture, or flavor).
- Discuss how apples get from the orchard to the grocery store.
- Taste different kinds of apples. Discuss preferences and graph them. Record and analyse the results.
- Think of all the places apples are found.
- Hide an apple in the classroom. Ask questions and give directions so that the children can discover its location.

Emergent Reading and Writing

- Write sentence strips for centres where a challenge has been posed. For example, "Can you paint a picture about apples?" or "Can you count the apples on these apple trees?"
- Use apple-shaped paper and booklets at the drawing and writing centre. Encourage children to draw and write their names on their work.
- Discuss the trip to the grocery store to buy apples. Write an experience story to reflect the children's recollections. Paint pictures to illustrate the story.

Resources

Books for Children (See the "Children's Books" section of this resource book.)

Vocabulary
- apple
- red
- green
- yellow
- fruit
- skin
- core
- seeds
- stem
- flesh
- juice
- applesauce
- pie
- muffins
- tree
- leaves
- orchard
- boxes
- canning

Useful Toys and Equipment
- juicer
- apple corer or slicer
- apple peeler
- apple sectioner
- blender

References for Teachers (including Field Trips/Visitors)

- Visit an apple orchard.
- Visit a nursery to see fruit trees.
- Invite a person to bring apple dolls or to demonstrate how to make them.

Media

"Hoedown"

Children have long enjoyed mimicking the behavior of cowboys and cowgirls and will engage in sociodramatic play based on their experiences from television and movies. The theme "Hoedown" permits the teacher to expand on a topic that is highly motivating to the children. The following activities are intended to foster development in the seven goals of the kindergarten curriculum.

Emotional Development and Well-Being

- Encourage children to participate in discussions about the relationship between cowboys and their horses (i.e., relying on something or someone else — "A good cowboy always takes care of his horse").
- Encourage children to participate in discussions about working together on a ranch.
- Encourage children to participate in discussions about the satisfaction of being able to ride a horse, care for animals, be independent (self-sufficient), care for the land, or do a good day's work.

Social Development

- Participate in and plan for the rodeo and hoedown as a group member.
- Discuss sharing of the harvest.
- Talk about working together in co-operation on a ranch or farm.
- Participate in a "Jeans Day."

Social Responsibility

- Discuss any of the following with the children:
  responsibility for the care of animals;
  using guns;
  hunting versus survival;
  land use (farming versus ranching or hunting).

Physical Development and Well-Being

Health and Safety

- Make a list of safety rules that farm workers should observe when working around animals and farm machinery.
- Discuss safety with ropes, lassos, and nooses.

Nutrition and Snack

- Prepare any of the following with the children:

Butter	Hash
Hamburger	Chili
Stew	Scrambled eggs
Beans	Egg nog
Corn on the Cob	Milkshakes

Movement Education

- Sing and play the traditional "Farmer in the Dell" game or adapt the game with the children.
- Introduce folk dancing, square dancing, or circle dancing activities.
- Imitate the actions and movements of farm animals (horses run, gallop, trot, walk).

Aesthetic and Artistic Development

Art

- Design a brand. Mount or frame the brand and take turns elaborating on choice of symbols.
- Design a bandana. Decorate plain red cotton fabric with white and black patterns.
- Design a belt buckle out of cardboard covered in tinfoil.
- Make a belt out of brown paper. Design as if tooling leather.
- Make a brown paper bag vest. Complete with fringe of paper, string, or wool.
- Make a hobbyhorse with papier-mâché over a balloon that has been tied to a stick.
- Paint pictures at the easel. Depict own or imagined experiences of life on a ranch or farm.
- Create a mural of a range, farm, or ranch. Discuss and plan carefully before beginning. Draw, cut out, and paint life-sized farm animals for wall mounting on butcher paper. Include buildings, machinery, and people.
- Make a patchwork quilt from paper or fabric. Have each child design a square and then (perhaps with the assistance of a parent) join the pieces together.
- Make a farm scarecrow as a class project. Old clothing can be stuffed with newspaper or straw and then stapled or sewn together.
- Make a table model of a ranch or farm.

Music

- The children might enjoy learning and singing any of the following songs.

Sound Beginnings	"All the Pretty Little Horses" (page 69)
	"Old MacDonald" (page 184)
	"Quilting" (page 104)
	"Yankee Doodle" (page 137)
Sharon, Lois, and Bram	"Apple Pickers Reel," *1, 2, 3, 4*
	"Old Texas", *1, 2, 3, 4*
	"Riding Along," *Smorgasbord*
Fred Penner	"Cat Came Back"
	"Ghost Riders in the Sky"
	"I Had a Rooster"
John Denver	"Grandmother's Feather Bed"
	"Thank God I'm a Country Boy"
	"Take Me Home, Country Roads"
Mary Helen Richards	"Oats Peas Beans and Barley Grow"
	"Old Brass Wagon"
This is Music For Today	"Goodbye Old Paint"
	"I am a Cowboy"

"Hoedown"

Roy Rogers and Dale Evans   "Happy Trails to You"
Raffi   "Biscuits in the Oven"
       "Listen to the Horses"
       "She'll Be Coming Round the Mountain"

Drama

- Act out any of the following roles or situations:

cowboys/cowgirls	planting
farmer	rodeo
harvest	branding
chores	

- Perform a hoedown for parents and school audience. The children would be involved in the following kinds of activities:

  learning square dancing;
  designing and making costumes;
  practising songs;
  getting bales of hay;
  decorating gymnasium or schoolyard with animals, corral, barn, hats, boots, lassos, and guitars.

- Make puppets of farm or ranch animals and people. Create and enact situations. Stage a puppet play.

Intellectual Development

Social Knowledge

- Take the children on trips; show films and filmstrips; look at pictures and invite visitors to provide shared experiences and to facilitate the development of concepts such as the following.

  Food is grown on a farm.
  Animals need care.
  Animals can work for us.
  Animals have families too.
  A celebration in "the west" is called a hoedown.
  Establishing the "Old West."
  Discuss urban life compared to rural life.

Physical Knowledge

- Demonstrate how water moves from a container through a plant by using coloured water and a celery stalk. Discuss the conditions necessary for growing plants.
- Grow plants in the classroom from seed or use carrot tops, potatoes, or avocado seeds to motivate observation and discussion about growing things.
- Identify and recognize types of animals by using pictures and models.
- Collect pictures or samples of the kinds of food eaten by a variety of animals. Encourage the children to identify the foods and name the animals that eat that particular food.
- Discuss original sources of food (beef and milk from cows, pork from pigs, eggs and meat from chickens). Discuss products and by-products in more specific terms.

Logical Knowledge

- Classify pictures or model of animals according to where they live (farm, ranch, wild, city) or by what they do (work, provide food, pets).
- Classify pictures and models of animals by size and color.
- Seriate farm animals by size or predict weight (heaviest to lightest).
- Graph preferences for colors of hats or horses, food likes or dislikes, number of legs on animals.
- Use a seed catalogue for classification and sorting.

Representation

- Ask children to tell others about their experiences on ranches and farms. Help them to compare similarities and differences as they talk about their experiences.
- Transform the dramatic play centre to depict the rodeo grounds, the farmhouse or kitchen, or the barn. Enlist the help of the children in the planning and collecting of materials.
- Encourage the children to create corrals, fences, fields, and buildings and to incorporate the use of farm animals and people models in their play with the blocks. Encourage dialogue as children plan and carry out these activities.
- Model animals or people using clay or play dough. Encourage the children to think and talk about the details they incorporate in their models.
- Make a table model of a ranch or farm. Complete the model using the animals or people the children made themselves.

Language Development

Language

- Label theme-related items.
- Discuss stories, events, activities, and films experienced in the course of studying this theme. Help children project into the experiences and feelings of others in different situations.
- Make group plans for a hoedown. Help children recall and carry out their plans. Assist them in solving problems that may occur.
- Take photos on field trips; label and discuss.
- Learn the names for the male, female, and offspring of farm animals.

Listening

- Provide time for the children to listen to any of the following:
  Fiddle or guitar music;
  "Wagon Train" theme;
  William Tell Overture (Lone Ranger Theme);
  Western music and cowboy songs;
  Selections from Rogers and Hammerstein's "Oklahoma";
  Soundscape of "Life on a Ranch" (animal and machinery sounds).

Vocabulary

- brand
- rodeo
- cattle drive
- herd
- corral
- range
- saddle
- train
- break
- round up
- hogtie
- bridle
- hay bale
- thresher
- lasso
- cowboy
- scarecrow
- hayloft
- barn
- pasture
- cow
- dogie
- bandana
- chaps
- holster

Emergent Reading and Writing

- Develop brands with individual children. These can be used as signatures for their art work.
- Make an "If I Were a Cowboy I Would _____" book.
- Make shape booklets about farm animals, horses, ranches, or barns.
- Make an "Old MacDonald Had a Farm" big book. Write out the words to the song and encourage the children to make the illustrations. Read the book together as a group.
- Have seed catalogues and farm implement catalogues available for reference. Produce class catalogues using the same format.
- Keep a daily "farm journal."
- Make experience charts to accompany "events."
- Record votes taken to determine likes and dislikes about various aspects of the theme. For example, "Who liked beans for snack?" or "What color is your horse?"
- Have each child make a picture. The teacher can then develop a pattern to accompany it and encourage the children to express their descriptions of the pictures using the pattern. For example, "I went to the farm and I saw a _____." "The _____ went _____ _____ _____." (sound)
- Send thank you notes to visitors and field trip hosts.

Resources

Books for Children (See the "Children's Books" section of this resource book.)

- spurs
- cowgirl
- cowboy
- chuckwagon
- wagon train
- guitar
- mane
- mare
- tail
- stallion
- colt
- foal
- stable
- hay
- paddock

Useful Toys and Equipment

- bridle
- boots
- hat
- holster
- tin badge
- western saddle
- bed roll
- canteen
- model of chuckwagon
- plastic farm animals and horses
- barn (Fisher Price farm)
- tin dishes
- hay bale

<u>References for Teachers</u> (including Field Trips/Visitors)

- Arrange a square-dance demonstration by older students, parents, or a local dance club.
- Invite a veterinarian to discuss the animals he or she would treat as well as the care and feeding of animals in general.
- Arrange a demonstration of leather tooling (belts and boots).
- Invite visitors to the classroom (e.g., cowboy, farmer, rancher, blacksmith, ferrier, square dancer or caller, auctioneer, horse owner).
- Arrange a field trip to any of the following places.

farm/dairy	ranch
rodeo	horse show
horse show	square-dance festival
stockyard	feed grain and seed outlet
saddle and tack shop	stable
outlet for farm machinery	children's zoo

<u>Media</u>

"Hoedown"

"Collections"

There is the potential for developing a positive sense of self by showing a collection and being able to share information. The teacher can model acceptable ways to respond to presentations made by children and can encourage the other students to accept and express emotions in a similar manner. The children are given the opportunity to take turns. Children are encouraged to take pride in their accomplishments. They attach their names to the displays, answer questions the other children ask, and respond to the teacher's interest. Making collections and presenting information to the class encourages children to seek help and act independently in a simultaneous way. The activities related to collections are both enjoyable and interesting ways of fulfilling one's curiosity. Give children the opportunity to show their collections to the other children in the class or school.

The following activities are intended to foster development in the seven goals of the kindergarten curriculum.

Emotional Development and Well-Being

Give children the opportunity to show their collections to the other children in the class or the school. As children show and tell about their collection, they can gain self-esteem because they are able to make an interesting contribution to the program.

- Encourage children to make specific, positive comments about the collections of others. The teacher can model this kind of response by making comments such as, "I particularly liked the purple agate in Danny's rock collection and the way he spoke clearly when he told us about it."

Social Development

- Give children the opportunity to learn from others. The child who makes the collection can be considered "the expert." Direct questions about the collection to the person who compiled it. Encourage the children to show respect for the property of others and to demonstrate appropriate listening and audience behavior.
- Work co-operatively (as a class or in groups) to develop collections of materials.

Social Responsibility

- Take turns to discuss and consider factors implied by responsibility. The story "The Little Red Hen" illustrates this point.
- Collect stamps, dolls, or toys (or other items depicting a particular cultural group) to heighten the children's awareness and enhance their feelings of respect for their own cultural heritage and also that of others.
- Make collections of objects found in nature. Discuss the necessity of respecting the environment. Children can begin to understand the need to know about endangered species, to replace things where they were found, and so on.

Physical Development and Well-Being

Health and Safety

- Collect personal hygiene items (such as soap, comb and toothbrush) to facilitate discussions about care and respect for the body. Children could be encouraged to bring items to add to the class collection.
- Emphasize caution regarding the kinds of items collected (e.g., matches) or where to go to find items for collections.

Nutrition and Snack

- Collect dried beans, seeds, and nuts. Varieties of each could be incorporated into the cooking activities of the class.
- Make trail mix. Use nuts, seeds, dried fruit, oats, or whatever the children contribute.
- Collect fruit for a salad or vegetables to make soup.

Movement Education

- Make collections of different kinds of sports equipment or items used for playing games. Provide opportunities for the children to try the equipment.

Aesthetic and Artistic Development

Art

- Encourage the children to visualize the items from the collections in their original surroundings. Draw or paint pictures of the items in the natural environment.
- Explore, interpret, and respond aesthetically to individual items in the collection. Provide opportunities for the children to arrange their collections in a pleasing display.
- Encourage children to utilize their senses when observing the articles in collections.
- Create models or draw pictures of the items in a collection to represent what is known and understood about the items.

Music

- Invite a record or instrument collector to visit the class and share some recordings or instruments with the class.
- Encourage the children to sort the records in the class collection into groups.

Drama

- Collect new items for the prop boxes or the dramatic play centre.

Intellectual Development

Social Knowledge

- Examine collections of toys or artifacts to learn about dress, customs, celebrations, and traditions of other cultural groups.
- Take a trip to the museum. The children can learn that our society venerates knowledge of the past and that there are institutions for preserving relics and samples as collections.

Physical Knowledge

- Give children the opportunity to study the physical properties of a wide variety of objects. They use their senses to assist them in learning about the items and to describe them to others. In addition, the children are encouraged to expand their powers of observation.

Logical Knowledge

- Encourage children to compare and constrast the similarities and differences between collections or the individual items within a collection. Observation of individual characteristics can serve to provide the framework for organizing information on graphs.
- Count and compare the numbers of items in individual collections.

Representation

- Invite children to tell about their collections and to make illustrations of individual items or the entire collections. Label the items and make titles for the collections.
- Use clay or play dough to make models of the items in any of the collections.
- Help children predict what a particular item could be used for or where it could be found.

Language Development

Listening

- Instruct the audience to listen for specific information about the collection. Ask children to restate what the collector has said to the class.

Language

- Talk with the children about the items or the collections. As the dialogue is taking place, encourage the use of the appropriate vocabulary and sentence structure, and expand on what the children say, encouraging them to supply details and to reflect, reason, or predict as appropriate.
- Provide opportunities for the children to gain practice in asking questions, listening to the responses, stating further questions, or adding information of their own.
- Ensure that there is time for the children to observe and discuss the objects with one another in an informal way.

Emergent Reading and Writing

- Encourage the children to label the items in the collections, to attach their own name to collections, and to develop sentences that can be displayed close to the collection.
- Gather a wide variety of books (both fiction and non-fiction) to accompany the collections and stimulate further interest in any particular subject.
- Develop experience charts about the collections or the gathering of the materials to motivate students and to remind them of the sequence of events (even after the collections have been dismantled).

Resources

Books for Children (See the "Children's Books" section of this resource book.)

References for Teachers (including Field Trips/Visitors)

- Go to a museum (e.g., a transportation museum to view a collection)
- Have parents or visitors with special collections bring them in and talk about them.

Useful Toys and Equipment

- containers of all kinds
- sorting trays
- display tables
- cloth to cover tables
- classroom collections of shells, buttons, bottlecaps, or materials for construction
- costumes for the dramatic play centre (hats, purses, shoes, clothes, etc.)

"Collections"

"Fairy Tales"

Fairy tales are an important part of literature and our cultural heritage. Children enjoy fairy tales, and in-depth study can lead to a wide range of activities. The characters' experiences promote discussion of the children's own feelings and experiences. Discussion of the behavior of the characters provides an opportunity to evaluate how they acted and allows the children to consider other possibilities for solving problems. The following activities are intended to foster development in the seven goals of the kindergarten curriculum.

Emotional Development and Well-Being

- Discuss how the characters in stories solved problems. For example,
  Hansel and Gretel helped each other work out a solution;
  Ugly Duckling felt rejected initially but grew up to be beautiful;
  Sleeping Beauty experienced the jealousy of the evil fairy, but through her innocence and fate she triumphed at the end of the story.

Social Development

- Discuss how characters behaved in stories. Suggest other possibilities. For example, rewrite the ending of *The Three Billy Goats Gruff* so that the Goats negotiate with the Troll about crossing the bridge. Or rewrite *The Shoemaker and the Elves* so that they helped each other.

Social Responsibility

- Discuss the behavior of characters particularly in relation to the rights of others. For example,
  Goldilocks went uninvited into the bears' house;
  The woodcutter couldn't kill Snow White;
  In *The Three Little Pigs,* the third pig worked hard and helped protect the others.

Physical Development and Well-Being

Health and Safety

- Learn the song, "Beans in My Ears."
- Discuss Goldilocks going in the bears' house uninvited.
- Discuss concepts of real and unreal (e.g., Can Superman really fly? Can a pumpkin become a coach?)

Nutrition and Snack

- Make ambrosia (5-cup salad)
- Make snacks related to *Jack and the Beanstock* (bean salad, bean sprouts, baked beans)
- Make gingerbread to relate to *The Gingerbread Man.*
- Make porridge to relate to *The Three Bears.*

Movement Education

- Encourage the children to move like a king, a giant, a dragon, a princess, a queen, an elf, a bear, a duckling, a goat, or a troll.
- Play the "Princess Game" *(This Little Puffin)*.
- Climb an imaginary beanstalk.
- Lay out an obstacle course in the gym. Let the children enact the story of Hansel and Gretel, finding their way home.

Aesthetic and Artistic Development

Art

- Use a variety of media to create princesses, princes, kings, queens, crowns, magic wands, castles, bridges, houses, etc.
- Make puppets to depict characters in fairy tales or folktales.
- Make murals and backgrounds for puppet shows.
- Make beanstalks.

Music

- The following songs would be suitable for singing.
  - Elizabeth Matterson   "Oats and Beans"
  - *This Little Puffin*   "Princess Game"
- Listening to music about fantasy stories provides an avenue for appreciation (e.g., Walt Disney's *Fantasia*).

Drama

- Dramatize stories that are very familiar to the children. The teacher can facilitate and encourage this by helping to find props, making labels and costumes, and taking the role of the narrator. The following would be suitable choices.
  - *The Three Billy Goats Gruff*
  - *The Three Little Pigs*
  - *Cinderella*
  - *Sleeping Beauty*
  - *Goldilocks and the Three Bears*

Intellectual Development

Social Knowledge

- Focus the children's attention on traditions and social conventions as described in fairy tales. Discuss the differences between our behavior today and that illustrated in stories.

Physical Knowledge

- Use a projector in the gym to reveal children's shadows. Measure the height of shadows and then measure the actual heights of the children.
- Sprout beans. Name parts of the bean plant. Experiment with the growing conditions by comparing amounts of light and water given to plants.

Logical Knowledge

- Classify beans by color, size, shape, kind, weight, etc.
- Use beans to make bean sticks. Glue ten beans on a popsicle stick and use them as counters for counting by ten's.
- Classify foods according to smell. Use pairs of colored bottles with perforated tops. Put in a small quantity of spice (e.g., ginger or cinnamon). The children can match foods by smell.

Representation

- Talk about characters and events in stories.
- Provide gowns, crowns, capes, and other props at the dramatic play centre to encourage and stimulate play.
- Build castles using different kinds of blocks. Model dragons, castles, or fantasy characters using clay or play dough to enhance dramatic play.
- Make a co-operative dragon using papier-mâché or blocks.

Language Development

Language

- Read and discuss fairy tales. Invite children to bring things that relate to the theme and to tell about them. For example, puppets, stuffed animals, records, or costumes could be brought from home.

Listening

- Use commercial books, records, or tape sets of fairy tales, or tape record your own reading of various fairy tales.
- Have older students or parents read fairy tales to the children.

Emergent Reading and Writing

- "Read" and discuss the stories independently.
- Make a big book or retell a favorite fairy tale to a scribe. Illustrate written work.
- Dramatize a story by creating role dramas or through the use of puppets. Make labels and costumes for characters.
- Draw the sequence of events in a particular story. The teacher or some other scribe can record the child's words to accompany the pictures.
- Create flannelboard stories or enact tales using flannelboard shapes.
- Use the pattern of a familiar song such as "London Bridge" to create the framework for the development of poems. For example,
      Cinderella sits and weeps,
      Sits and weeps, sits and weeps;
      Cinderella sits and weeps,
      Because she's left at home.

Vocabulary

- sprout
- vine
- tendrils
- roots
- king
- queen
- prince
- princess
- spice
- invitation
- imaginary
- fantasy
- fairy talk
- magic
- work
- giants
- elf
- gnome

"Fairy Tales"

Resources

Books for Children (See the "Children's Books" section of this resource book.)

References for Teachers (including Field Trips/Visitors)

- Have a visit from a story teller or puppeteer.
- Attend a play, puppet theatre performance of a fairy tale.
- Go to the public library for storytime and for taking books out.

Media

- See Quees sequence puzzles
- Sifto castle puzzle
- Playschool Puzzles (e.g., Cinderella, Three Bears, Rumpelstiltskin, Hansel and Gretel, Little Red Riding Hood)
- flannelboard aids
- Trend bulletin board sets
- records
- puppets
- Fisher Price castle
- things to collect (e.g., gowns, capes, crowns, magic wands, deely boppers, aluminum foil, shampoo caps for turret tops for block castles, jewelry, fur or fake fur for animals, chair decorated as a throne, gold and silver paint, glitter)
- games (e.g., *Cinderella; Three Bears:* CADCO Games; *Sleeping Grump:* Comp. Leisure Time Promotions.

"Machines"

The "machines" theme has been developed to help children understand and appreciate some of the features of the man-made world. Despite the fact that machines are in abundance in the environment, many children are not aware that the general classification of "machines" can be applied to many objects that are part of their daily lives. Teachers are encouraged to help children make the distinction between those things that are machines and those that are not. Teachers and children can begin to explore the uses of machines and the impact of ever-increasing technology. Children should be given the opportunity to expand vocabulary and to extend their knowledge through experiences with machines that are found in the home, the school, and the surrounding environment.

The following activities are intended to foster development in the seven goals of the kindergarten curriculum.

Emotional Development and Well-Being

- Discussions about machines can focus on topics such as
    how people make machines work;
    how people repair machines;
    how people invent machines;
    one's pride in being able to run and care for machines doing a job;
    being an inventor.

Social Development

- Discuss and provide activities to focus on the implications for social interaction as presented through machines. Include such topics as
    What machines can be shared?
    What machines do jobs that give us time to do other things?
    What can people do to get machines?

Social Responsibility

- Discuss and present activities focused on our changing world and on the role and development of new machines to reflect those changes. Include topics such as
    What happens to old machines?
    What can people do about machines that pollute or make noise?
    What do machines use to run? (e.g., electricity)
    What machines can hurt others?

Physical Development and Well-Being

Health and Safety

- Focus discussions on health and safety measures to be taken around machines. For example, topics might include
    What machines should not be touched?
    What machines need protective gear? (e.g., ear plugs, goggles)
    What machines need trained operators?

What machines have byproducts that can hurt? (e.g., fumes)
Pollution from machines.
What machine noises mean danger? (sirens)
Recognition of symbols and signs warning of danger.

Nutrition and Snacks

- Make snacks using a variety of machines designed specifically to aid food preparation. Examples might include
  Ice cream made with an ice-cream freezer
  Peanut butter made with a food processor
  Apple juice made with a juicer
  Cranberry relish made with a grinder
  Popcorn made in a popper

Movement Education

- Encourage children to move like machines or to pantomime situations where they would be the operators of machines.
- Work in groups or with partners to recreate the movement of a machine. For example, several children could "make" a train.

Aesthetic and Artistic Development

Art

- Use any media to create pictures of machines, pictures of people using machines, or pictures of fantasy machines.
- Use machine parts for print making. Wheels, cogs, nuts, bolts, and gears could be dipped in paint and printed in repeated patterns.
- Make box sculptures of machines.
- Make an air-powered machine such as a pinwheel.
- Plan and draw a design for a machine. Try to make the machine using objects available in the classroom.

Music

- The children might enjoy learning and singing the following songs

This is Music for Today	"The Wheels on the Bus" (page 63)
	"Down by the Station the Train Is a Coming" (page 63)
	"Elevator Going Up" (page 155)
	"Trucks" (page 64)
	"I Went for a Ride" (page 125)
Sharon, Lois, and Bram	"I Am Slowly Going Crazy (Elephant Jam)
	"One Finger, One Thumb" (Elephant Jam)

"Machines"

Drama

- Pantomime the actions of machine operators or the actions of repairing a machine.
- Convert the dramatic play centre to a garage, railway station, factory, or cockpit of an airplane.

Intellectual Development

Social Knowledge

- Bring pictures of machines to school. These could be displayed in groups to illustrate where machines can be found and who operates them.
- Go on a search for machines at school.
- Discuss questions such as Why are certain machines, like a fire truck, ambulance, or police car, a special color? What kinds of noises do machines make?

Physical Knowledge

- Set up a simple pulley system for children to experiment with.
- Create a centre where children can experiment with simple household machines. For example, they may enjoy observing the movement of machines such as an egg beater, a potter's wheel, a food mill, and so on.
- Determine which machines have wheels. Used sewing machines, egg beaters, and vacuums could be dismantled and examined.
- Encourage children to try to recognize a variety of kinds of tracks left in mud, dirt, or sand (e.g, the tire tracks of tractors and trucks, animal tracks, or the impressions made by various kinds of footwear).
- Discuss with the children, "How does the shape of a machine help it do its work?"
- Arrange for demonstrations of levers, bottle cappers, windmills, grinders, and pulleys.

Logical Knowledge

- Classify pictures, plastic models, or toy representations of a variety of machines by characteristics such as size, shape, or number of wheels.
- Look at pictures of machines to identify parts by name and to learn the functions of each (e.g., "Wheels are round and they turn or roll").
- Encourage children to try to name the machine by looking at only a part of a picture.
- Compare sizes, shapes, colors, and functions of machines.
- Graph the locations of machines using the titles "Machines Found at Home" and "Machines Found in Industry."
- Count and record the numbers of machines found in the house, in the school, or in the grocery store or that can be observed from a particular place at the edge of the schoolyard.

Representation

- Transform the dramatic play centre into a garage, factory, or computer room. Collect a variety of suitable props and costumes to encourage play.
- Construct machines at the block centre. Many of the building toys have complementary pieces that include wheels, pulleys, cogs, and so on. Encourage children to reason and solve problems as they proceed. Help children predict details about what their machines will be able to do.
- Make plans and build machines at the woodworking or construction centres.
- Read *Children Solve Problems* by Edward de Bono. Choose activities appropriate for the children in your class.

Language Development

Listening

- Make a tape recording of machine sounds the children are familiar with. Have the children listen to determine the name of the machine or to describe what the machine sounds like.
- Have one child imitate the sound of a machine while the other children try to guess what the machine is.
- Bring a "hurdy gurdy" to school.

Language

- Bring pictures of real machines to school. Have the children name and describe as many of the machines and parts as possible. Practise using new vocabulary in descriptions. Help children recall where the machines are used and describe how they function.
- Encourage children to talk about the machines they are aware of and to describe not only the appearance of the machine, but also how each functions. Assist the children to project into the experiences of those who operate machines.

Emergent Reading and Writing

- Label pictures and models of machines, machine parts, and operators.
- Develop lists to describe tasks machines accomplish, places machines are found, kind of machines, and so on.
- Record children's talk about machines and have the children illustrate their own statements.
- Make booklets about what machines can do.
- Cut and paste to make a catalogue of machines and tools. Label and develop sentences or titles for each page. Store the class catalogue in the book centre.

Vocabulary

- machine
- vehicle
- car
- truck
- train
- bus
- boat
- plane
- jet
- crane
- tractor
- fork lift
- typewriter
- computer
- wheelbarrow
- food processor
- robot

Resources

Books for Children (See the "Children's Books" section of this resource book.)

References for Teachers (including Field Trips/Visitors)

- the janitor's room in the school
- service station
- large equipment factory
- pizza restaurant
- hardware store
- sales office for copiers or computers
- ride as many vehicles as possible
- construction sites
- street corner observation
- a bakery
- fast food restaurant
- business offices
- museum (old machines)

Media

- pictures and plastic models of machines
- parts of actual machines or tools
- puzzles about machines

"Machines"

"Space"

Many of the children in today's kindergarten have been saturated with both the real and fantasy aspects of the exploration of space. They have seen the television coverage of rocket and shuttle launchings, are familiar with the appearance and vocabulary of control centres, and have come under the influence of the impact space exploration is having on our lives. In addition, they have gone to space movies, have toys that replicate characters and machinery from the movies, and engage in their own dramatizations of space travel. The following activities are intended to foster development in the seven goals of the kindergarten curriculum.

Emotional Development and Well-Being

- Encourage children to take part in group activities and to derive pleasure and pride from their participation and accomplishments.
- Provide many opportunities to discuss feelings and fears about the unknown. Children need to know that astronauts and the adults involved with space programs experience the same range of emotions children do.

Social Development

- Discuss and encourage dramatic play activities that facilitate awareness of the need to work co-operatively in confined spaces. Activities could focus on locations such as a space centre or a space capsule.
- Provide opportunities to practise co-operation, teamwork, planning, solving problems, sharing, and thinking of the rights and needs of others.

Social Responsibility

- Discuss questions such as "Who owns the territory of outer space?" and "What should be done about debris abandoned in space?" Provide children with the opportunity to express their opinions, to listen to the opinions of others, to seek facts, and to examine their original position as part of the discussion and activities.
- Collect pictures, show films, and discuss how space technology influences our lives. Topics such as the use of technology in improving communications, or in seeking other forms of life in the universe, or in exploring space and the terrain of the planets could provide the focus for extended dialogue with the children.

Physical Development and Well-Being

Health and Safety

- Research to find out about the training of astronauts. What kinds of tests must they go through? What kinds of health habits are they expected to observe? What kinds of safety precautions must they practise?
- Show pictures of the protective clothing and emergency safety supplies necessary to support life in space. Find out about this apparatus and the functions of each piece.

Nutrition and Snack

- Make snacks in the shapes of objects related to space study. Examples might include
  "Frozen Banana Rockets" (½ banana frozen on a stick)
  "Jupiter Jumbo Juices" (combines fruit juices and soda water)
  "Popcorn Planets" (popcorn sprinkled with cheese)
  "Meteors" (frozen grapes or cherries)
- Prepare and eat food that simulates the kinds of food astronauts must eat in space. All "space foods" can be packaged in zip-lock bags to prevent losses due to zero gravity. Drinks will need to be capped and taken through a straw. Some examples might be dehydrated fruit in bags, granola bars in packages, and vacuum-packed cartons of milk or juice.

Movement Education

- Encourage children to move like objects in space, like astronauts in a cabin, like space creatures, or like robots. This activity could include the use of appropriate space music.
- Practise throwing and catching "flying saucers" (frisbees).

Aesthetic and Artistic Appreciation

Art

- Create space landscapes using boxes and scraps of "found" materials glued to heavy paper or to a lightweight board. Once completed, the teacher can spray paint these silver. An alternative to this activity would be to create spacescapes using Polyfilla applied to the surfaces of the box sculpture.
- Create box sculptures of spacecraft, landing gear, robots, and space creatures. This activity could be completed individually or as a group project.
- Work in groups or as a class to plan, organize, and compose a class mural. Drawings, paintings, and constructions can be attached to a large background.
- Construct individual spacecraft using Styrofoam meat trays, yogurt containers, and "found" objects.
- Create space scene dioramas. As the viewer looks into the box, he or she should get the impression of looking out into space.
- Make "planets" of papier-mâché by gluing strips of paper onto an inflated balloon. Once the mâché has hardened, the balloon is popped and the "planets" can be displayed.
- Use fine wire to create sculptures of rockets, spacecraft, or creatures.
- Create costumes and props by using donated materials. Space capes can be created by using fabric crayons and old sheets. The decorated cape is then sewn onto an old shirt collar. Space helmets can be made from old bleach bottles that have been well washed. Remove the bottom and cut holes for eyes.

Music

- Listen to theme music from movies (e.g., *Star Wars, The Empire Strikes Back, Return of the Jedi, 2001: A Space Odyssey, E.T.* or *Star Trek*).
- Make fantasy space instruments. Create and record the music the students make.
- Any of the following songs would serve to incorporate music with the other activities of the space theme

Raffi	"Big Beautiful Planet"
Sally Go Round the Sun	"Sally Go Round the Moon"
Traditional	"Twinkle, Twinkle, Little Star"
_____	"Five Little Spacemen" (Adaptation of "Five Little Pumpkins")

Drama

- Turn a table on its side, throw a cover over it, and make some windows out of cellophane to create a space capsule. A large box such as a refridgerator carton would work as well.
- Collect props and costumes for astronauts. Helmets, a piece of vacuum hose, a snowsuit, and boots would work well. If the props belong to the kindergarten, spray paint white, gold, or silver to add an authentic touch.
- Project a space film on the wall of the gymnasium. Children move as indicated by the music or action in the film.

Intellectual Development

Social Knowledge

- Talk with the children about the Apollo space flights and the fact that people have walked and driven on the moon. Do the children know that there have been female astronauts and cosmonauts? Or that there have been animals in space? Discuss.
- Discuss the need to co-operate — one astronaut with another, the astronauts with the command centre, and one country with another.

Physical Knowledge

- Explore the distinctions between real and fantasy. For example, the Space Shuttle, Apollo, Sputnik, and rockets are all real. The equipment and characters in *E.T., Star Wars, Flash Gordon,* and *Tron* are fantasy.
- Create "Constellation Viewers." The teacher can cover one end of a paper tube with black paper. Use a pin to poke holes to follow the pattern of various constellations. Children hold the "viewer" up to the light and look through the other end. The outside of the tube could be labelled with the name of the constellation. Encourage the children to invite their parents to do some star watching.
- Compare and talk about what is seen in the day sky with what can be observed at night.

- Explore the phenomenon of friction. Take children down the slide. After a number of children have gone down the slide, feel it. Ask, "Why is it warm?" Have the children rub their hands together or over the top of the table to experience the warmth created through friction.
- Investigate what happens when water is placed in a bucket with a string attached to the handle. As it is swung around in the air, centrifugal force keeps the water from spilling out of the bucket. Discuss how this physical phenomenon is related to what happens at the time of lift-off.
- Play with helium-filled baloons. Demonstrate how something can be "lighter than air."
- Make paper or Styrofoam airplanes to discuss lift and thrust. What happens as the shape, size, or style of the airplane is changed?

Logical Knowledge

- Practise counting forward (gradually increasing speed to simulate take off) or backward (as in the countdown) with the children.
- Use *E.T.* or *Star Wars* cards for games of matching, classification, recognition of parts and wholes, and so on (e.g., "Who's Missing").

Representation

- Transform the dramatic play centre to become the place where the children can dress up as astronauts, space creatures, movie characters, or command centre scientists. The children can collect props to enable them to dramatize a space flight, a space walk, life in a command module, or life on another planet.
- Challenge the children at the block centre with the following types of questions.
    "Can you build a spaceship using only rectangular blocks?"
    "Can you build a rocket ship using only yellow Lego?"
    "How many different kinds of spaceships can your group make?"
- Use Plasticine, play dough, or clay to create the landscape of the moon or a planet. Space creatures or movie characters could be added to the scene.

Language Development

Listening

- Use music, colored lights, and a narrative to simulate a space journey. After the experience, question the children as to how they felt when . . . or when they heard . . .
- Listen and respond to sound tracks from space movies.
- Display the *Star Wars* books and tapes for use at the listening centre.

Vocabulary

- radio
- Milky Way
- Big Dipper
- North Star
- star
- names of planets
- moon
- earth
- galaxy
- black hole
- space shuttle
- NASA
- gravity
- oxygen
- eclipse
- sun
- atmosphere
- nebula

Language

- Name and describe imaginary space creatures. Encourage the children to describe not only the physical characteristics but also habits and habitat.
- Invite children to describe their imaginary space journeys to each other. This activity could accompany the painting of space pictures.
- Name the different spacecraft and begin to use the correct terminology for the parts of the craft or the equipment needed by the astronauts.

Emergent Reading and Writing

- Make lists of things to take on a journey into space.
- Label articles, pictures, and models that the children make. Where possible, encourage the use of new vocabulary by expanding the key words into sentences or titles.
- Make booklets in shapes to reflect the contents. As each child completes his or her page for the class booklet, record what the child has to say about the picture. Staple the books together; share them with the class; and store them in the book centre.
- Make a big book called "Spaceman, Spaceman" following the pattern in Bill Martin Jr.'s, *Brown Bear, Brown Bear*.
- Make invitations to parents to come to a reading of "Spaceman, Spaceman" or to a "Dance of the Planets."
- Have scribes record stories about real or imagined trips into space.
- Make experience charts about things that would be found in space (the surface of the moon, the planets, and so on).

Resources

Books for Children (See the "Children's Books" section of this resource book.)

- technician
- satellite
- "dish"
- comet
- telescopes
- planet
- observatory
- telecommunication
- T.V.
- planetarium
- the language of the movies (land speeder, Jedi Knight, light sabre)

Useful Toys and Equipment

- *Star Wars* toys and books
- rocket ship models
- spacecraft models
- models of planets, earth
- viewmaster (space reels)
- bleach bottles (helmets)
- snow suit
- boots
- fabric
- foil

References for Teachers (including Field Trips/Visitors)

- Preview films. While some of the dialogue in the films or filmstrips about space may be too sophisticated for the children in the kindergarten, much of the visual material is most suitable. Screen without the sound.
- Talk to the people at the planetarium. Ask for kits, posters, or information they may have available on loan.
- Invite an astronomer to bring a telescope to school and have the children return after dinner to watch the sky with their parents in the school yard.
- Invite a person who has a collection of books on space, an amateur radio operator, or a pilot to speak to the class.
- Go to an observatory or planetarium.
- Go to a space movie.
- Go to a T.V. or radio station.

Media

"Space"

"Whales"

The mystery associated with whales has always held fascination for young children. This theme permits transition from other themes or further development of other units of study such as sealife, animals, or an aquarium field trip. The topic is suitable for this kind of integration in that it deals with both the affective and cognitive domains. The theme has general appeal to children and can be used to motivate awareness of environmental and cultural issues. Many of the activities described could be adapted to and modified to focus on an animal of local interst. The following activities are intended to foster development in the seven goals of the kindergarten curriculum.

Emotional Development and Well-Being

- Discuss how people often fear things that are much larger than themselves. Much of this fear can be dispelled by providing children with information. Discussions could focus on comparisons between whales and humans — how are they alike or different?

Social Development

- Focus on group planning and co-operation during projects and activities.
- Talk with the children about the label "killer whale." Is it really a killer? Animals need to eat, just as humans do. Some humans eat meat and fish, as does the killer whale. Talk with the children about the fact that the whale has to kill in order to survive. Humans (for the most part) are exempt from this necessity.
- Make an experience chart of group names for other animals. For example, whales live in pods; bees live in swarms; fish live in schools; hoofed animals live in herds; and so on. Talk about the similarities and differences between animal and human families and social groupings.

Social Responsibility

- Discuss the enemies of the whale and the fact that some whales are listed as "endangered species." The topic "Whales" would provide an appropriate bridge to discussions about extinction and other environmental issues.
- Discuss with the children the uses of whale products in our homes. For example, by-products such as food, oil, floor wax, shoe polish, and perfume result from the killing of whales.

Physical Development and Well-Being

Health and Safety

- Discuss safety precautions to be taken when out in a boat or swimming. Whales live in the water and don't need to consider safety factors in the same way humans do.

Nutrition and Snack

- Encourage the children to try tasting dulse (a reddish-brown seaweed from the Atlantic Coast).
- Prepare fish sticks or tuna fish sandwiches, or taste a number of different kinds of smoked, barbecued, or canned fish (e.g., shrimp or prawns).

Movement Education

- Use dance and drama techniques to have the children act out some aspects of whale behaviour such as spouting, blowing, diving, swimming, fluking, feeding, sleeping, and fleeing from predators.
- Help the children to create a dance drama about whales. Examples of story parts could include the life of a whale from birth to death, a day in the life of a whale, the enemy approaching, and the ensuing battle or escape.

Aesthetic and Artistic Development

Art

- Introduce the children to mono and block printing by having them make Styrofoam outlines of whales and print them onto large mural paper.
- Use crayon resist techniques to create underwater effects. Paint a wash of water color over crayon, felt pen, or ink drawings.
- Make torn paper outlines of whales. Assemble the pieces to create a collage.
- Model different species of whales using clay, Plasticine, papier-mâché, or play dough. Bake, glaze, paint, or shellac the models as appropriate.
- Create a life-sized baby whale as a class project. Large paper outlines could be stuffed and painted, or the children could make a diorama or box sculpture, which is then covered and decorated.
- Explore the possibilities of a "whale's-eye view" of the world. Encourage the children to imagine that they are whales. Have the children draw or paint what they would see.
- Examine the stylized versions of depictions of whales by looking at the artwork of various groups of West Coast Indians. Encourage the children to try to copy some of the designs or create their own in this style.

Music

- The children might enjoy the following pieces of music about whales.
Paul Horn (and Haida!)	*Flute and Whale Sounds*
Raffi	"Baby Beluga"
Gordon Lightfoot	"Ode to Big Blue"
Nash and Young	"Mass-Critical"
Roger Payne	*Songs of the Humpback Whales*
- Compose songs about whales using the pattern of a traditional song.
- Write the words to songs the children have heard onto large chart paper. The children can illustrate the song and "read" the words as they sing.
- Encourage the children to provide verbal interpretations of the whale songs or of the music of whale songs. What does the recording make them think of? How do they feel? What kinds of patterns, rhythms, or messages do they think they hear.

Drama

- Make whale costumes. Perform the dance drama (see "Movement Education").
- Predict and dramatize what it would be like to live in a rough sea as compared to a calm sea.

Intellectual Development

Social Knowledge

- View films and videotapes. Go on a field trip to an aquarium or go out on a boat to observe real whales.
- Ask if children have seen a whale. Invite a guest to tell when and where children can expect to see whales in British Columbia waters.
- Discuss the life cycle of the whale and the names for the whale at different stages of develpment (bull, cow, calf).
- Set up an aquarium in the classroom. Make frequent comments on the habits and needs of fish as compared to whales.

Physical Knowledge

- Identify and name different kinds of whales

Sperm	Blue	Fin
California Gray	Right	Humpback
Killer Whale	Dolphin	Bowhead
Porpoise		Narwhal

- Identify and name different body structures and parts

rostrum	blowhole	flukes
grooves	snout	knuckles
eyes	ears	

- Become familiar with some of the behavior and characteristics of all whales

moving	fluking, breaching, blowing, rolling, diving, travelling in pods
eating	krill, shrimp, plankton, fish, seals, octopus, squid
breathing	blowholes, (baleen whales have two blowholes; toothed whales have only one. When the whale is sleeping, the blowhole is out of the water)

- Graph pictures of the various species of whales according to whether they are toothed or baleen.
- Develop concepts of size by comparing a person to a whale. Take the children onto the playground and outline the shape of the whale (using field lime) in actual measurement. Locate and illustrate placement of various parts of the body. Have the children "measure" the outline using hand spans or footsteps.

Logical Knowledge

- Order or seriate pictures or models of whale species according to the size of the whale they depict.
- Classify pictures of whales into groups according to color, shape, size, number of blowholes, where they live, what they eat, and so on.

- Obtain vertebrae, rib bones, or whale teeth and discuss the features of each with the children. How do they compare to those of humans or other mammals?

Representation

- Provide or make puppets for children to dramatize stories or songs.
- Invite children to tell what they know about whales.
- Encourage the children to pretend that they are trainers or caretakers at an aquarium or the zoo.
- Provide Plasticine, play dough, or clay for making whales. Encourage the children to use photographs of whales for reference.
- Children can be given the opportunity to act out some of the behavior that mother whales and young whales exhibit.
- Use blocks or masking tape on the floor to outline the shape of a whale's body.

Language Development

Language

- Compare the similarities and differences among whales.
- Ask children to bring photos or items related to whales. Discuss these with the children.
- Develop word "banks" or lists to use when making language-experience-chart stories, charts, and poems. Display these prominently where the children can see them.

Listening

- Listen to stories and poetry about whales. Encourage the children to interpret the author's regard for whales from the words used.
- Listen to recordings of the sounds made by whales. Can the children reproduce the sounds? What other sounds would normally be a part of the whale's environment?

Emergent Reading and Writing

- Use scribes to assist with the writing of stories about whales or captions for the children's artwork.
- Make booklets using the shapes of whales. The children can complete the booklets individually or as a class, each student completing a page and compiling the booklets at the end of the activity.
- Find and display information about whales from books and magazines. Encourage the children to draw their own pictures and print captions to accompany the pictures.
- Develop class letters that express interest and request information of conservation organizations.

Vocabulary

- pod
- toothed
- environment
- harpoon
- plankton
- rolling
- diving
- baleen
- migration
- extinct
- krill
- fluking
- blowing

Resources

Books for Children (See the "Children's Books" section of this resource book.)

References for Teachers (including Field Trips/Visitors)

- Defenders of Wildlife
  1244 - 19th Street NW.
  Washington, DC   20036

- The Fund for Animals
  1765 P Street NW.
  Washington, DC   20036

- General Whale
  P.O. Save the Whale
  Alemeda, CA   94501

- Greenpeace Foundation
  240 Fort Mason
  San Francisco, CA   94123

- Project Jonah
  Box 476
  Bolinas, CA   94924

- Animal Welfare Institute
  P.O. Box 3650
  Washington, DC   20007

- The Cousteau Society
  Box 1881
  New York, NY   10017

- World Wildlife Fund
  1319 — 18th Street NW.
  Washington, DC   20036

- Humane Society of United
  States
  2100 L Street NW.
  Washington, DC   20037

- The Whale Protection Fund
  c/o Centre for Environmental
  Education
  2100 M Street NW.
  Washington, DC   20037

- The Oceanic Society
  Stamford Marine Centre
  Magee Avenue
  Stamford, CT   06902

- Rare Animal Relief Effort
  National Audubon Society
  950 Third Avenue
  New York, NY   10022

- "whalewatching" from B.C. ferry or fishing boat
- Stanley Park Aquarium, Vancouver, B.C.
- Sealand, Victoria, B.C.
- Greenpeace Offices, Vancouver, B.C.
- International Whaling Commission, London, England
- Ocean Sciences Institute, Patricia Bay, Victoria, B.C.
- oceanographer
- fisherman
- botanist
- person with slides or photos of whales

Useful Toys and Equipment

- aquarium
- plastic models of whales
- pamphlet and picture collections
- baleen
- whale vertebrae or tooth
- dried krill (available from a pet store)

Media

"Whales"

"Bears"

Stuffed animals in general, and teddy bears in particular, have long been recognized to provide emotional security for young children. Children "talk" to their bears, confide in them, and often express a wish to "take teddy, too." Many children are aware of the special nature of this relationship, but few have been given the opportunity to discuss their needs or concerns with adult sanctioning. The following activities are intended to foster development in the seven goals of the kindergarten curriculum.

Emotional Development and Well-Being

- Discuss the following kinds of statements with the children.
  My teddy loves me no matter what I do.
  My teddy will do anything I tell him to.
  I can tell my teddy secrets. He won't tell.
  My teddy goes everywhere with me.

Social Development

- Role play parts of the story *Goldilocks and The Three Bears* and discuss the following situations with the class or with small groups of children.
  How do you think Goldilocks would feel when . . .?
  How do you think the baby bear would feel when . . .?
- Ask the children to imagine they have been hibernating. What would they do when they first woke up?

Social Responsibility

- The following topics could be useful stimuli for decision-making activities.
  Bears in the wild are a precious part of the environment. How can we protect them?
  How should we protect their homes?
  How do we treat bears?
  How should we behave in bears' territory?

Physical Development and Well-Being

Health and Safety

- Introduce the breads and cereal food group by making "The Three Bears' Porridge." In particular, focus on the value these foods have for good health.
- What do you do if you are hiking in the woods and you know that bears live there too? How do you behave and protect yourself and the bear? Children need to know that they shouldn't feed wild animals.

Nutrition and Snack

- Sample or prepare any of the following
nuts and seeds	orange marmalade
berries	animal crackers
porridge	salmon
fish	blueberries
- Introduce the breads and cereals food group. Use nuts and seeds when baking granola, porridge, and cookies.

Movement Education

- Use the "Teddy Bear, Teddy Bear" song as the basis for creating movement sequences that the children make up.
- Encourage the children to simulate the actions of bears by
  walking on two feet or four feet;
  climbing up trees
  pushing things over (logs, garbage cans);
  digging in the ground;
  swimming;
  catching fish;
  eating berries.

Aesthetic and Artistic Development

Art

- Collect brown "fun" fur (to make bear shapes).
- Use corks to create "cork-print" bears.
- Paint and model bears using the materials available in the centres.
- Make circle teddy bears or drawings of teddys.
- Make bear bag puppets. Add clothes to depict Papa, Mamma, and Baby Bear.
- Make a magazine picture collage for the breads and cereals food group.
- Ask the children to bring their own teddies. Trace them and fill in the features and details.

Music

- Listen to, chant, or sing any of the following
  "The Bear Went Over the Mountain"
  "Teddy Bear, Teddy Bear, Turn Around"
  "Teddy Bears Picnic"
  "The Three Bears Chant"
  "The Bear Hunt"
  "Daddy Loves the Bear"
  "Shaggy Bear"
  "Winnie the Pooh"
  "Fuzzy Wuzzy Wuz a Bear"
  "Hairy Bear, Beary Bear"

The Three Bears Chant

Snap your fingers as you chant this.

Once upon a time
In a nursery rhyme
There were Three Bears.
REPEAT
Three Bears.

One was the Mama Bear
One was the Papa Bear
And one was the Wee Bear.
REPEAT
Wee Bear.

Well, they all went a walkin'
   in the deep woods a stalkin'
When along came a girl with
   long flowing hair.
Her name was Goldilocks and up
   on the door knocked.
But no one was there.
REPEAT
No one was there.

So she went inside, had herself
   a ball
She didn't care 'cause no one
   was there.

Home came the Mama Bear, came
   the Mama Bear.
Home came the Papa Bear, came
   the Papa Bear.
Home came the Wee Bear.
"My, my, my!" said the Mama
   Bear, said the Mama Bear.

"Bears"

Drama

- Make puppets and re-enact the story *The Three Bears*.
- Have the children demonstrate characterizations of different bears.
  - Yogi Bear
  - Winnie the Pooh
  - Smokey the Bear
  - Paddington Bear
  - Berenstein's Bears
  - Care Bears
- Add a blanket and picnic basket to the dramatic play centre.

Intellectual Development

Social Knowledge

- Visit the children's zoo or a museum to see a live bear.
- Visit a museum or toy store to see collections of stuffed bears. Talk about the characters developed. For example, Paddington is a pretend bear. He acts like a bear and a person. Talk about the many stuffed bears represented in literature.
- Classify bears into two groups: real and pretend. Discuss the similarities and differences between real and pretend bears and among bears within each category.

Physical Knowledge

- Use masking tape on the floor or butcher roll paper to draw a life-sized bear.
- Observe "artifacts" such as bearskin, bear's teeth, piece of honeycomb, and so on.
- Learn about real bears.

  A bear is a wild animal. There are several varieties of real bears. These include polar bears, grizzly bears, black bears, brown bears, and panda bears.

  Bears have different habitats. Guide discussions to develop an awareness of the need to preserve the environment so that all creatures can live in the habitat necessary for their preservation.

  Bears eat different foods.
  - polar bears — fish, seals, etc.
  - black, brown, and grizzly bears — insects, small animals, fish, honey
  - panda bears — bamboo
  - koala bears — eucalyptus leaves.

  Some bears hibernate during the winter.

  Some bears climb trees.

  Bears have distinctive physical characteristics.
  - They are mammals.
  - They have fur.
  - They walk on all four feet most of the time.
  - They have claws.
  - Their teeth are suited to the food they eat.
  - They have a keen sense of smell.

"My, my, my, my, my!" said the Papa Bear, said the Papa Bear.
"Oh dear," said the Wee Bear, "someone has broken by chair!"
Just then Goldilocks woke up — and broke up — the party
And beat it out of there!

"Bye, bye, bye," said the Mama Bear, said the Mama Bear.
"Bye, bye, bye, bye, bye," said the Papa Bear, said the Papa Bear.
"Hey-bop-a-re-bop," said the Wee Bear.
And so ends the story of The Three Bears.
REPEAT
The Three Bears.
  (Traditional)

"Bears"

A bear can be dangerous.

Learn about real bears living in captivity.

A bear in a zoo is still a wild animal, not a pet.

Some bears have been partially tamed and taught tricks (dancing bears in circuses).

Compare the different attributes of, and be able to differentiate between, a real bear and a "pretend" bear. This point is particularly important in discussing children's books about bears — some are about real bears, some are about teddy bears, and some are about anthropomorphic bears.

Learn about some "famous" bears now a part of our cultural heritage.

Winnie the Pooh	Root Bear
Paddington Bear	Punkinhead
Smokey the Bear	Rupert Bear
Yogi Bear	
Safety Bear (used by the police to teach safety rules)	

Logical Knowledge

- Put picture cards of *Goldilocks and the Three Bears* story into correct sequence. Compare a bear family to your own family.
- Classify, sort, and graph
  Papa Bear, Mama Bear, and Baby Bear.
  Match bowls, chairs, and beds to each one by size;
  real bears and teddy bears;
  wild animals and pets.
- Make patterns and designs using seeds and grains.
- Invite children to bring their teddies to school. Compare, classify, seriate, and describe them.
- Encourage children to try set-to-set matching and set-to-numeral matching. Prepare the following.
  Make teddy bears, each with a different number of buttons on. Match the bears' bow ties with numerals corresponding to the number of buttons on each bear.
  Put a set of bears in order from smallest to largest (prepared by the teacher from felt for use on a flannelboard).
  Compare, group, seriate, and describe photographs of *real* bears.

Representation

- Encourage children to tell what they know about bears.
- Re-enact the story of *Goldilocks and the Three Bears*. Provide bowls, chairs, beds, a blond wig, and sets of ears for three bears. Encourage children to recall the sequence of events as they enact the drama.
- Add plastic bears for use at the block centre. Use large building blocks as chairs. Use blocks to build a life-sized "bear."
- Put blocks out to represent how large a real bear is. Give the children one piece of string to show how long the form should be and another piece to show how high it should be. Develop measurement and comparison vocabulary (e.g., metres, centimetres, taller, wider, etc.).
- Provide Plasticine, play dough, or clay for making bears.

- Make the Three Bears and Goldilocks to use for puppet plays and flannelboard stories.
- Provide bear puppets (and appropriate name cards), a variety of "people," and other animal puppets so that children can dramatize stories they have heard.

Language Development

Language

- Take the poem "Teddy Bear, Teddy Bear" and make up new verses to accompany it.
- Ask the children to describe and draw their teddy bears and tell how they like to play with them.
- Discuss parts of the bear's body and discuss parts of human bodies. (How are they the same? How are they different?)

Listening

- Listen to records or tapes of songs about bears.
- Collect tapes and books of bear stories (e.g., *Winnie the Pooh* and *Paddington*) for the children to listen to.

Emergent Reading and Writing

- Provide paper shaped like teddy bears for the children's use at various centres.
- Make a big book modelled on the patterning found in *Brown Bear, Brown Bear,* using the children's names and self-portraits.
- Write invitations to teddy bears to come to school. Plan and organize a "Teddy Bear's Picnic."
- List words that rhyme with bear.
- Brainstorm words and ideas. Use the words and ideas to stimulate the writing of group poems and stories.
- Create language experience charts about real bears. Record the information provided by the children.

Vocabulary

- bear
- teddy
- grizzly
- black bear
- brown bear
- Pooh
- honey
- honey pot
- fur
- Mama Bear
- Papa Bear
- Baby Bear
- Goldilocks
- porridge
- bed
- chair
- hibernation
- bear caves
- salmon
- blueberries

"Bears"

Resources

Books for Children (See the "Children's Books" section of this resource book.)

References for Teachers (including Field Trips/Visitors)

- zookeeper
- librarian bringing "bear books" to school
- park naturalist to tell about bears
- person who has slides of bears
- person who has teddy bear or stuffed animal collection
- circus trainer
- beekeeper
- Stanley Park Zoo
- Okanagan or Vancouver Game Farm
- Child's World Zoo in Duncan
- toy store to compare different stuffed toys
- museum to look at old toys
- honey processing

Media

Useful Toys and Equipment

- teddy bears
- pictures of bears
- fake fur

"Chinese New Year"

There are large Chinese communities in many centres in British Columbia, and the influence of Chinese people is reflected in the history and cultural activity of the province. By developing a theme such as the celebration of the Chinese New Year, the teacher provides the opportunity to build an understanding of the similarities and differences between cultural groups. Through activities such as the following, information is gained and true understanding and respect for others can be developed. These activities are intended to foster development in the seven goals of the kindergarten curriculum.

Emotional Development and Well-Being

- An opportunity is provided for Chinese children to feel that this special time of year is acknowledged, understood, and appreciated.
- "Buddy" relationships with older Chinese or E.S.L. students can be developed. Such children can provide resources for stories, language, and interpretation.

Social Development

- Children can be encouraged to develop an appreciation of their own or others' cultural identity and heritage by showing things and telling about customs from their own cultures.
- Discuss with the children the things we have learned or acquired from the Chinese culture that are now an everyday part of our lives.

Social Responsibility

- Every culture or group of people has a special festival or time of year. These special times and festivals are different for different groups of people. Chinese New Year is the special festival for Chinese people. How does it compare with other festivals or special times such as Divali, Hanukkah, Thanksgiving, Christmas, New Year's Eve, etc.?

Physical Development and Well-Being

Health and Safety

- The use of fire crackers takes supervision and care. Discuss the potential hazards and encourage children to recognize the need for extreme caution.

Nutrition and Snack

- Prepare and sample any of the following foods
  fortune cookies (children can write their own fortunes)
  stir fried vegetables
  steamed rice
  shrimp chips
  won ton soup
  soya sauce
  chow mein
  tea

171

Movement Education

- Create a Chinese Ribbon Dance to oriental music. First, make ribbons by attaching red, white, and black streamers to rhythm sticks. Using Chinese music, have children compose their own sequences and patterns by beating sticks on the floor, circling and stepping, and twirling and swishing the "ribbons." Children face each other in pairs, taking turns with one leading and the other mimicking the patterns and sequences, and then changing roles.
- Have the children dance the Lion Dance. Wearing the lion heads made in the construction centre, the children follow a pattern in which they search for lettuces (that are traditionally hung in shop doorways), and when they find them they jump for them and eat them. If the "lion" devours the lettuce, the shop owners will have good luck throughout the New Year.
- Have the children dance the Dragon Dance. Wearing the dragon costume, the children hold the body over their heads, swaying from side to side and following the leader (head). This procession can include a drum beater, cymbol and xylophone players, and children carrying streamers.

Aesthetic and Artistic Development

Art

- Make scrolls that say *Gung Hay Fat Choy* (Happy New Year) on red paper. Hang the scrolls in pairs, and use brushes with black or gold paint.
- Make Plasticine or clay dragons and lions.
- Make a lion mask for the dance and parade. Use a large brown paper bag. Paint the bag and decorate it with eyes, mouth, nose, and feathers or hair (curled paper). Cover it with colored shapes. Add a tail to the bag, and decorate it with stripes made from print making shapes. Cotton balls and cupcake papers add realistic detail.
- Make red paper lanterns.
- Have the children make puzzles out of the Chinese zodiac, which they try to match together by placing an extra set of pictures of animals, and names of the animals, on to the format. (Restaurants will often supply paper place mats illustrating the zodiac).

Music

- Provide lots of opportunity for children to use rhythm instruments in time to recorded Chinese music.
- Ask people from the Chinese community to demonstrate traditional instruments or to teach a simple song.
- Use a big drum, cymbols, and a xylophone to create an oriental sound to accompany songs.

Drama

- Research customs and provide children with enough background information to role play situations such as going to the homes of others, eating, and giving lucky money.
- Perform the Dragon and Lion Dances. These are essentially the same except that the dragon costume is a more elaborate costume and requires many people to carry it.

Intellectual Development

Social Knowledge

- Compare "oriental" cultures. "How are they the same? How are they different?"
- Make, a field trip to Chinese grocery store to buy foods for a New Year's celebration.
- Ask someone to come and tell about the celebration of Chinese New Year.
- Go to a Chinese restaurant for tea and *dim sum*.
- Research the special customs, songs, dances, colors, clothes, food, stories, and language associated with Chinese traditions. The scrolls and lucky money envelopes are part of the special traditions. Scrolls are placed in every room in the house. Money envelopes are given to people who visit your home to wish you Happy New Year.
- Invite someone to show the envelopes and tell about the custom. Invite children to bring their grandparents to visit the kindergarten. Discuss aspects of life in extended families.
- Investigate the eating utensils and foods used by Chinese families. How are the dishes the same or different from the ones used at home? At snack time, the children can experience Chinese foods and try using different utensils for both food preparation and eating.

Physical Knowledge

- Observe and discuss changes in foods during cooking experiences. For example, what happens to shrimp chips when they are deep fried? What makes them puff up? What happens to won ton when it is deep fried? How does it change? Seriate the steps in the process of cooking foods.
- Classify, sort, describe, and group collections of Chinese items and artifacts.

Logical Knowledge

- Count the pennies in the lucky money envelopes.
- Make graphs (e.g., "Which do you like the best?"). List the kinds of Chinese foods the children have tried and collect information regarding their preferences.
- Seriate sets of Chinese lanterns.
- Recognize and repeat the patterns and rhythms or movements in the Dragon or Lion Dances. For example, search, find, jump, and eat.

Representation

- Talk about some of the customs and traditions of China.
- Prepare the dramatic play centre for Chinese New Year with lanterns, scrolls, lucky money envelopes, chopsticks, bowls, newspapers, clothes, and wrappers and boxes from Chinese foods.
- Make zodiac animals using modelling media. Classify the collection; match to the zodiac, and graph.
- Look at pictures of Chinese architecture in story books and references. Try to build these sorts of structures with the blocks.
- Dramatize the lion dancing up to the doorways for the lucky money or the dragon parading down the street.
- Paint Chinese characters and symbols. Some "chops" look like the objects they are intended to portray.
- Model Plasticine or clay dragons or lions.

Language Development

Language

- Provide opportunities for discussion and observation of cooking processes involved in making shrimp chips and won ton soup recorded on language experience charts.
- Brainstorm to develop a list of descriptive words and compose a class poem about the Lion or Dragon Dance or some event the children have observed.
- Use a zodiac chart as a basis upon which to discuss which year each child is born on the Chinese zodiac.
- Discuss special items brought to class by the children.
- Discuss processes involved in making and eating snacks.
- Make and record plans for the celebration.

Listening

- Listen to Chinese words and the rhythms and patterns in the language.
- Listen to Chinese music.

Emergent Reading and Writing

- Use language experience charts to record recipes and observations.
- Record changes (e.g., "before and after") on picture graphs to help children articulate comparisons.
- Generate labels and headings for objects, artifacts, and artwork.
- Dictate a story about Chinese New Year to a scribe. Illustrate the story after it has been recorded.
- Look at Chinese New Year cards. Make and exchange cards.
- Bring in a Chinese newspaper, book, or magazine for the children to examine. Encourage children to look at and discuss the similarities and differences between books.
- Encourage the children to replicate Chinese symbols at the painting centre or at the drawing and writing centre. Use black paint on red paper.
- Invite a guest to tell some Chinese stories and fairy tales.

Vocabulary

- China
- dragon
- lion
- chopsticks
- gong
- sampan
- rice
- rickshaw
- bicycles
- scroll
- t'ai chi
- fortune
- silk
- wok
- won ton
- soya sauce

"Chinese New Year"

Resources

References for Teachers (including Field Trips/Visitors)

- This theme provides a wonderful link to fairy tales and fantasy; dragons and magic.
- Visit from T'ai Chi artist, Tai Kwon Do artist, Chinese painter, or calligrapher, or parent who will demonstrate cooking for snack.
- Visit from Lion or Dragon Dancers or from person who has slides or photographs of China.
- Demonstration from Kung Fu expert.
- Visit Chinatown for a meal, shopping, or just observing.
- Visit a local Chinese food market to purchase food for snack time.
- Visit to watch the Chinese New Year Parade in Chinatown, February 1.

Media

Useful Toys and Equipment

- plastic replicas of Chinese eating utensils and dishes
- chopsticks
- wok
- bamboo steamer
- pictures of Chinese cycle of years
- rice paper
- traditional costumes and clothing
- collection of lanterns
- lucky money envelopes

"Chinese New Year"

"Unique"

Using the concept of uniqueness as a theme invites the children to personalize the experience with their contributions of unique items. The theme will be unique to each class because of the varying backgrounds and resources of the children. The teacher can use this time to introduce new or different experiences and activities. The unique theme works well for a short period of time between major themes. The following activities are intended to foster development in the seven goals of the kindergarten curriculum.

Emotional Development and Well-Being

- Reinforce the concept of specialness. Display photographs and discuss how each person is unique.
- Invite children to demonstrate or tell about talents (e.g., dance, sing, show skates, swimsuits, tell about a trip).

Social Development

- Discuss with children how each of us is unique *and* how we have things in common.
- Have children bring costumes and artifacts from their homes, or invite guests to demonstrate language or customs, to familiarize children with the uniqueness of each culture.

Social Responsibility

- Discuss the necessity for uniqueness. If things are altered to be the same as everything else, they may not be as useful or effective.

Aesthetic and Artistic Development

Art

- Make finger- or thumb-print creatures by pressing on ink stamp pad and adding details.
- Create handprint or footprint wrapping paper.
- Use clay to make unique (handmade) containers.
- Make play dough finger puppets.

Music

- Sing "Madelina Catelina." Draw Madelina's picture.
- Bring in different instruments. Invite people who can play instruments to demonstrate.

Drama

- Use play dough finger puppets to tell stories made up by the children.
- Encourage children to use dramatic play props to create new characters. Provide wigs, glasses, hats, and clothing.

Physical Development and Well-Being

Health and Safety

- Talk about people who have special needs. Collect pictures and invite children or parents to tell about their unique needs (e.g., wheelchair, allergies, glasses, medication).
- Talk about stunt performers and how can they do tricks that would harm most of us.

Nutrition and Snack

- Make personalized pizzas. Prepare a variety of toppings and encourage the children to create their own pizza by choosing the toppings they like or would like to try.
- Make shape pancakes.
- Set up a simple salad bar. Let each child select salad ingredients and dressing.

Movement Education

- Take children into the gym. Use a projector for light source. Encourage them to experiment with their shadows.
- Invite each child to select two pieces of equipment to create a game.
- Invite each child to explore and demonstrate ways of moving.

Intellectual Development

Social Knowledge

- Invite children to bring and tell about unique items. Prepare space for the children to display, observe, and examine unique items.
- Invite an artist to visit and tell the children about his or her work.

Physical Knowledge

- Set up a table for unique items. Encourage children to handle the items and describe their physical features.
- Put some unique items in the exploration centre. For example, children could investigate lava pieces in water (the rocks float).

Logical Knowledge

- Encourage children to classify the unique items by setting up categories ahead of time. Ask, "Who can bring something that shows us how to do something differently?"
- Count and classify unique items by color, material, and size.

Representation

- Talk about things that the children bring. What makes the item unique? (Because they have one attribute that is different, a four-leaf clover or six-toed cat are considered unique.)
- Make pictures of unique items or unique creations using various art media at the woodworking centre.
- Make a big book about the song "Down By The Bay." Have children illustrate the different verses.

Language Development

Language

- Discuss with the children things that are unique, different, or special. Why are they unique? Where might they be found? What might they be used for?
- Use selected children's literature to help children to project into the experiences, feelings, and situations of others.

Listening

- Listen to a tape of children's voices and have children predict who is speaking. Encourage the children to identify what allowed them to differentiate one voice from another?
- Record the voices of T.V. stars and have the children try to recognize who is speaking.
- Bring in recordings of original or different musical instruments (e.g., sitar, balilika) and discuss the difference in sound between these and more familiar instruments.

Emergent Reading and Writing

- Make a big book using the pattern illustrated in *And Rain Makes Apple Sauce.*
- Make a chart "These Things Are Unique."
- Label collections of unique items.
- Collect and record names that are unique.

Resources

Books for Children (See the "Children's Books" section of this resource book.)

- special
- different
- flaw
- characteristic
- unusual

Useful Toys and Equipment

- magnifying glass
- microscope
- stamp pad
- table for displaying
- four-leaf clover

References for Teachers (including Field Trips/Visitors)

- museum
- worm farm
- X-ray technician
- fingerprint expert
- artist, weaver, or potter

Media

"Unique"

"Change"

This theme captivates children because they can see things changing around them. It provides the teacher with an opportunity to help the children talk about their feelings when things change. "Change" as a theme can direct attention to changes in the environment and changes in one's self as well as to what changes can be controlled and what changes are inevitable. The following activities are intended to foster development in the seven goals of the kindergarten curriculum.

Emotional Development and Well-Being

- People change as they grow. These changes can be observed and discussed with the children. Encourage the children to bring baby pictures and pictures of their brothers and sisters for this purpose.
- Some changes can be controlled; some can not. Talk about incidents such as the death of a pet, moving, separation, and illness. Encourage children to name their emotions and discuss their feelings.
- Read *The Tenth Good Thing About Barney* by Judith Viorst or *The Dead Bird* by Margaret Wise Brown. Talk about death and the children's feelings.

Social Development

- Make a "Who Has Lost a Tooth?" chart.
- Talk about changes in feelings about kindergarten. For example, children may have been nervous in the fall but have now made new friends.
- Read *The Ugly Duckling* by Hans Christian Andersen or *Rich Cat, Poor Cat* by B. Waber. Talk about experiences and subsequent feelings.

Social Responsibility

- Discuss the differences in family compositions (e.g., children living with both parents, with one parent, with grandparents, or with guardians).
- Encourage children to bring items, to take part in discussions about change, and to provide experiences for the whole class to share.
- Plan some changes in the arrangement of the classroom. Talk about the need to consult others before making changes and to work co-operatively to effect the change.

Physical Development and Well-Being

Health and Safety

- Talk about changes in weather. What kinds of protective clothing do we need to use to be safe and healthy?
- Talk about how food, exercise, and rest make people change and grow.
- Discuss how fire changes things. Expand the discussion to include activities that stress fire safety.

Nutrition and Snack

- Talk about what foods make us grow, give us energy, and repair tissues in our bodies.
- Observe and talk about how food changes as it is prepared. Make popcorn, applesauce, ice cream, or melted cheese on toast.
- Have a tasting party. Compare the taste and appearance of foods that have been prepared in a variety of ways (raw, cooked, frozen, canned, sweetened, etc.)

Movement Education

- Experiment with body movement. Change places and changing kinds of movement (using space vertically and horizontally).
- Blow up balloons and use them in the gym in place of balls.
- Encourage the children to pretend to be balloons, seeds growing, or leaves in the wind.
- Use scarves or ribbons with music. Have children move to make the shapes of the scarves change.

Aesthetic and Artistic Development

Art

- Mix paints to show how colors change when they are combined.
- Make and fire clay objects. Observe and discuss the changes.
- Have children arrange crayon shavings on wax paper. Cover the shavings with wax paper and have an adult iron it. Encourage the children to observe and discuss the changes.
- Challenge children to make a picture that changes. Facilitate this by supplying plenty of tape, scissors, staplers, and paper punches.

Music

- Examine and compare differences in sounds made by changing where strings on stringed instruments are touched.
- Have children move to various tempos and adapt their speed of movement to reflect the tempo.
- Provide tumblers and a mallet and let the children experiment with changing pitch by changing water level (see Leon Burton and William Hughes, Music Play).

Drama

- Bring some wash-off make up for children to try (with adult supervision).
- Supply props, wigs, hats, and glasses so that children can change their appearances.
- Describe an activity and have the children dramatize the action. Examples could include seeds growing into plants or balloons expanding.

Intellectual Development

Social Knowledge

- Observe and discuss differences in traditional and modern dress in various cultures. Invite guests to share examples of traditional and modern clothing.
- Collect objects or pictures of things that illustrate technological changes. For example, egg beaters, mix masters, food processors, and old irons and modern irons could be observed and discussed. Ask children to suggest the reasons for the changes.
- Invite grandparents and senior citizens to come and tell the children about how they lived when they were children. Discuss changes.

Physical Knowledge

- Measure the children's heights at different periods during year. Compare and discuss changes.
- Bring ice or snow into the classroom. Observe and discuss changes that occur.
- Set up a chrysalis in a jar. Observe as it changes into a butterfly.
- Bring in an ant farm. Observe and discuss how ants change the environment.
- Leave a piece of bread on a plate. Observe stages of change from fresh to stale to mouldy.
- Visit a favorite park or tree at different times of the year and record the changes.

Logical Knowledge

- Set up a balance scale. Encourage the children to experiment with adding and removing articles to affect change.
- Include several shapes and sizes of containers at the water centre. Discuss the capacity of the various containers with the children and encourage them to note how water assumes the shape of the container.
- Give children opportunities to play with clay or Plasticine. Discuss the changes that occur as they handle the material.

Representation

- Discuss things that change. Create a "What Makes Them Change?" list.
- Make a weather chart. Observe, discuss, and record changes in weather.
- As children create, the object they are representing may change once or many times before the "creation" is complete. Encourage the children to try to describe the changes.

Language Development

Language

- Talk with the children as they experiment with materials you have supplied to stimulate their thinking about change. For example, pour water on sand, make peanut butter, or observe tadpoles.

Vocabulary

- observe
- notice
- experiment
- alter
- materials
- result

- Invite children to tell about changes that have happened to them.
- Ask children to bring objects that show change and to tell the others how these things change.

Listening

- Put on a recording at the listening centre with music that changes. Children who choose the centre can indicate the change by waving to each other at each change.
- Play games that allow children to try changing their voices to attempt to conceal their identity.
- Play the "Whisper" game. The first child whispers a word or message to the next person. This follows around a circle and the last person tells the word. Did it change?

Emergent Reading and Writing

- Make lists of things that change.
- Make a "How We Have Changed" chart.
- Share the picture book *Changes* by Pat Huchins. Ask the children to supply a text. Record their suggestions.
- Make a chart of seasonal changes apparent on the school grounds in the neighborhood.
- Describe and record the changes that occur as food is prepared (e.g., peanut butter, pancakes, butter).
- Introduce the children to "kaleidescope" books. By moving a tab, the entire illustration is changed (e.g., Larry Shapiro, *Baby Animals*).

Resources

Books for Children (See the "Children's Books" section of this resource book.)

- compare
- similar
- different
- conditions
- describe
- cause
- examine
- explore

Useful Toys and Equipment

- sequence puzzles
- tangram puzzles
- Parquetry blocks
- Lego
- blocks
- dramatic play props
- water table
- sand table
- balloons
- bubble mix
- popcorn popper
- blender
- dehydrator

References for Teachers (including Field Trips/Visitors)

- Visit a stream to observe salmon spawning.
- Visit a building site on several occasions.
- Pick a tree on or near the school grounds. Visit, observe, and record changes.
- If safe conditions are insured, visit a mill or factory to see how raw materials change.

Media

"Change"

SAMPLE ACTIVITIES

Fostering Emotional Development and Well-Being

Beginning with the knowledge that how children view themselves will contribute to the way they feel, think, and learn, the kindergarten curriculum recognizes the need to develop positive feelings of self-worth in each child. Learning to name, understand, and express feelings in socially acceptable ways is a part of this process. The emotional security that results from a positive (yet realistic) self-concept can enable children to accept challenges, enjoy learning, and develop independence. In this section, suggestions are provided to assist the teacher with the planning and preparation of experiences that are intended to foster emotional development.

The ideas in this section have been extracted and adapted from Jack Canfield and Harold C. Wells, *One Hundred Ways to Enhance Self-Concept in the Classroom*, (Englewood Cliffs, N.J.: Prentice-Hall, 1976).

Suggested Activities for Fostering the Development of a Positive and Realistic Self-Concept

- Help children feel secure and comfortable in the school setting. Notice them as individuals; recognize their concerns and accomplishments; and listen to their problems.
- Make a "magic box" (any box with a mirror fastened to the bottom so that when a child peers in he or she sees his or her own reflection). Have a class discussion about special people. Every child has an opportunity to name special people. Bring out the magic box and explain that when the child looks into the box, he or she will see a very special person. The children must keep the special person a secret until everyone has had a turn. A discussion follows where the question of who the special person is answered (i.e., each child saying "me"). Discuss how it is possible for everyone to be a special person.
- Draw self-portraits, using mirrors when necessary. The portraits may be drawn on many occasions throughout the year, be signed by each child, and be displayed in the classroom. Teachers can draw and display self-portraits, too.
- Trace a silhouette of each child's head. Then ask the children to cut out from magazines pictures of things they like or like to do. Glue these pictures on the outline shape. The group can discuss the activities that many children enjoy and the things that are unique to a few children.
- Whole group or small group sharing sessions of personal achievements encourages feelings of self-worth and helps children focus on the positive aspects of themselves. At first, some children may not be able to remember their successes. Accomplishments can be those prior to school and those achieved after coming to school. For children unable to think of any such accomplishments, the teacher can ask questions such as "You've been helping your dad feed the dog. Didn't you feed your dog all by yourself last week? I'd consider that an accomplishment," Or "Didn't you walk home all by yourself yesterday? How do you feel about that achievement?"
- Share warmth and humor with individuals. Help each child feel like a valuable member of the group.
- Notice and develop children's ideas and contributions wherever possible. These can often work together with the teacher's plans.

Suggested Activities for Fostering the Expression of Emotions in Socially Appropriate Ways

- Have children bring and share objects that have special meaning (e.g., teddy bears, toys, etc.). Help children to share and take turns during discussions.
- Help children discover that it is acceptable to have feelings of anger, frustration, etc. To explore negative feelings, have the children talk about their experience with some of the following types of common childhood problems. Maintain an open and accepting environment of trust and empathy as you ask such questions as
  How many of you are afraid of ghosts?
  How many of you ever get scared?
  How many of you like to get angry?
  How many of you are afraid when your parents get angry?
  How many of you get so mad you could hit someone?
- Use situations that arise in the classroom to help children identify and express their feelings (e.g., "How does it make you feel when someone knocks over your blocks like that?").

Suggested Activities for Fostering the Acceptance and Demonstration of Empathy

- Use situations that naturally arise in the class to point out to children how their behavior affects the activities and feelings of others (e.g., "You make it hard for us to enjoy the story when you whistle like that.").
- Use selected children's literature as a basis for encouraging children to project into the feelings, reactions, experiences, and situations of characters in the books.
- Take the class into your confidence. Solicit their help when dealing with problems (e.g., "Tom is very upset right now. You can help me by sitting and talking softly to your friends while I look after him. Tom, could you bring a tissue?").
- Pay attention to individual concerns and problems, and demonstrate empathy in your responses. Children will model this behavior.

Suggested Activities for Fostering the Willingness to Accept Challenges

- Plan activities that appeal to children with a wide range of abilities and interests. Many children need to feel secure about their ability to participate in the most non-threatening and familiar activities before they will build the confidence to try new things. Play dough, water play, crayons, familiar stories, etc., should be available alongside more challenging teacher-directed or theme-related projects.
- Encourage children to broaden their interests by being an active and interested participant yourself. Children like to be near the teacher and will emulate that behavior.
- Do things together as a group (e.g., songs, chants, readings, drama, dancing). This protects the less-confident individuals and allows them to try without being singled out or ridiculed.
- Prepare challenging and interesting activities. Introduce them carefully and encourage children to take part.

Fostering Emotional Development and Well-Being

Suggested Activities for Fostering the Feeling of Pride Through Accomplishment

- At the end of each day, have the children briefly share with the rest of the class the successes they have experienced during the day. A variation is to have the children share what they feel they have learned that day. Once the children are used to sharing successes, the rest of the class will help remember the successes of the child who thinks he or she has none (i.e., "Remember Billy? You made the tower of big blocks").
- Encourage children to reflect on topics such as "things you've done for your parents," "how you spend your free time," "something you own," and "something you've learned to do all by yourself."
- Display a large sign with the words: "Today is _____ Day!" Each day a different child has a turn. This entitles the child to do all the classroom chores. The other children are encouraged to do all they can to make the chosen child's day a good one.

Suggested Activities for Fostering the Development of Independence

- Mount photographs of children to illustrate their growth and development. Discuss changes that have occurred and future expectations (e.g., as a baby, now, imagined adult appearance).
- Encourage the children to take care of the classroom and to take part in routines such as pouring milk, sweeping sand, and wiping tables.
- Let the children do as much as they can for themselves. For example, the teacher may need to "start" the zipper, but the children can often do the zipping themselves.
- Help the children become familiar with the whole school so they can move around with confidence.
- Set up most activities and centres in such a way that children can manage independently.
- Encourage children to assist each other rather than always turning to an adult for help.

Suggested Activities for Fostering the Enjoyment of Living and Learning

- Trace the children's bodies on large sheets of paper. The children can paint or color their clothing or glue cloth on the outline to represent their clothes. A label showing the child's name (and other information such as the child's height or child's favorite toy) can be attached to each tracing.
- Sing "If You're Happy and You Know It" or read *Happiness Is . . .* by Charles Schultz. Talk about reasons for being happy. Make happiness booklets.
- Do things "just because . . . " For example, play outside "just because" it's a nice day; sing "just because" you feel like singing; read a story "just because" someone brought a favorite book; or extend activity time "just because" no one wants to stop.
- Share in the young child's humor.
- Enjoy books filled with humor and nonsense.
- Model enjoyment or living and learning in the kindergarten environment.
- Plan activities that are at the level of the children, and meet their need for alternating quiet and active times.

191

Fostering Social Development

The kindergarten environment provides many opportunities for the children to socialize with their peers and a variety of adults. They interact in pairs, in groups and as members of the entire class. This process is necessary as positive interactions permit the smooth functioning of experiences and activities. Further, encouraging positive interaction is socializing in preparation for experiences outside of the classroom. This section is intended to provide suggestions to assist the teacher in the planning and preparation of experiences intended to foster social development.

Suggested Activities for Encouraging Sharing and Co-operation

- Take photographs of children playing and working together. Show the prints or slides to the children and comment on the positive aspects of their interaction. Encourage the children to add comments of their own when discussing the photos. Place these photographs in an album; add simple captions; and put the album in the class library for reading at book time or for taking home.
- Organize activities and games in such a way that co-operation results in success for all members. Co-operative games or problem-solving experiences highlight the need for input from all members of a group. Following any experience of this nature, encourage the children to identify why the game was fun, how the problem was solved, or how a project was completed.
- Plan small group projects that necessitate co-operation (e.g., murals, sorting tasks, mapping).

Suggested Activities for Encouraging Acceptance of and Respect for Others

- While it is important to recognize, accept, and respect individual differences, true understanding occurs only when the children know or can empathize with another person's experience. By first focussing on universal similarities, children are then more open to attitudinal changes. Some examples of this kind of experience would be discussion of any of the following.

All people have bodies.	Our bodies are different.
All people need foods.	The foods we eat may be different.
All people need housing.	Our homes may be different.
All people have families.	The size and composition of our families may differ.
All people have feelings.	The ways we express our feelings may differ.

- Provide opportunities for parents and other family or community members to participate in the activities of the classroom. Much information with regard to cultural values, family life, and heritage can be shared with a member of the kindergarten group in an informal way.
- Use situations that arise at school to focus on the need to respect the wishes and interests of others (e.g., selecting activities, taking turns).

Suggested Activities for Encouraging Learning From Others

- Organize a "buddy system" whereby the kindergarten child is partnered with an older student. The kindergarten teacher and the teacher of the other class can co-operate to plan varied learning experiences for both groups of children.
- Request that children report to the group or share specific information in order to impart what they know and for others to learn from them. Much of this kind of activity can be arranged informally.
- Role play situations that enable children to develop some sense of the experience and feelings of others. This involves the children in being required to recall from their own experiences and observations as well as being able to predict how they think events might take place.
- Provide opportunities to work in groups during centre time. The teacher can encourage children to learn from others by making positive comments regarding the ideas children share (e.g., "Tom found a great way to make a block boat. He showed Susan how he did it. He said he would be glad to show other people, too.").
- Visit another kindergarten. Learn about the new classroom from the "host" children. Later, compare this classroom and the ways things are done there with your own classroom.

Suggested Activities for Encouraging Children to Seek and Offer Companionship

- Establishing the practice of encouraging children to accept the offer of the first person who asks for companionship helps make asking and risk-taking less painful. The teacher can help avoid having children left out by saying, "If you don't have a partner, come to me." Then, as the children come forward, match them in pairs (e.g., "Sam, will you please choose a friend to sit with"). Often choose first the children who struggle with this.
- Play the singing game "Rig a Jig Jig" (Mary Helen Richards). This game involves choosing a partner.
- Play traditional games (e.g., "Farmer in the Dell") in such a way that the game does the choosing. As each verse is completed and the music stops, the children stop and ask the person closest to them to join the game.
- Encourage a "sharing a book" time.
- Encourage children to go to a centre with a new or different friend. Ask classmates to volunteer to help each other tidy a centre after use.
- Send "get well" cards and birthday cards, and "write" letters to children in the class.
- Invite children to take on the responsibility of acting as "host" to a new child in the class. This special job may involve showing the new classmate where belongings are kept and where the washrooms are and playing together throughout the day.
- Spend time informally in the playground (autumn is a good time to do this). This enables the children to get to know each other in a natural way.

Suggested Activities for Developing the Ability to Anticipate the Consequences of Actions

- Establish a policy whereby the person who hurts someone must take part in the first aid (e.g., if Bob turns quickly and accidently hits Sam with a block, Bob gets the Kleenex and wet paper towels). The teacher can facilitate this and give support to both children.
- Describe situations with two or three possible conclusions. After role-playing each variation, discuss how the characters felt in each circumstance, and encourage the children to identify the path and consequences of each action.
- Challenge the children to consider what might happen if they

    dash across the parking lot,
    run in the classroom,
    build the blocks too high,
    don't share the scissors,
    strike a classmate,
    touch the hot corn popper,
    take an unfair share of the snack,
    go to a centre when it is "full,"
    forget to clean up,
    spill water on the floor,
    leave the gerbil cage open, or
    do not give water to the plants.

Fostering Social Responsibility

Social responsibility is understood to be the development of attitudes that will enable children to recognize personal responsibility for working co-operatively to find solutions to social problems. Children are encouraged to develop friendships, participate effectively in groups, and demonstrate responsible actions. Through experiences, children will gain information that enables them to recognize cultural similarities and respect cultural differences. To the degree that maturation levels permit, and through everyday occurrences, social issues are explored in kindergarten. This section provides suggestions that can assist the teacher in planning and facilitating experiences intended to foster social responsibility.

Suggested Activities for Fostering the Development of Friendships

- Observe and note the social patterns as they emerge among the children. By commenting to the children who are playing together as friends, the teacher reinforces the behavior that supports and encourages friendship. When the class gathers together at the carpet for group time, friends can tell what they were doing together and how they shared in their play.
- Develop a puppet play with the children to illustrate social interaction. Behavior that discourages friendships, as well as positive behavior, should be discussed as they appear. The puppets should focus on an activity such as building with small blocks, looking at a book, etc., to enable the audience and actors to observe interactions.
- Make big books such as "I Like Friends" or "A Friend Is Someone Who _____."
- Create a "How to Make Friends" chart.

Suggested Activities for Enhancing Participation in Groups

- Encourage experiences in which small, independent groups of children work on projects. Centres where children have chosen to work together provide daily practice. However, not all children will choose the variety of situations offered, nor will they want to work in new groups each day.
- Establish situations in which children are channelled into groups for project work to provide new experiences in group behavior. The comments of the teacher reinforce acceptable group behavior and can clarify the child's understanding of how to behave in a group.
- Provide opportunities for teacher-directed discussion groups to provide experiences in group behavior with a structured format. Ground rules for behavior ensure that everyone (who wants to) gets a turn, that only one child speaks at a time, and that listeners are expected to display appropriate listening techniques.
- Make murals as group or class projects. Planning, carrying out the mural construction, and evaluation of the process and product are all group activities.
- Prepare food on a regular basis. Rotate the kinds and levels of participation. Collecting, planning, preparing, serving, and cleaning up after cooking are activities that require the co-operative efforts of individuals. Following such experiences, encourage children to evaluate their participation as a group member.

Suggested Activities for Facilitating Responsible Citizenship

- Use group meetings to determine what the children can be responsible for during centre time. Discussion should occur just before the children choose their centres. Upon completion of activities, a discussion can be held to evaluate how each job was done.
- Discuss and determine ways in which to share classroom duties. A class list with a clothes peg for each child can help to facilitate this process. As the child has a turn, the clothes peg is moved to the other side of the list. Any visible means such as a "Helping Hands" chart lets the children see that their turn will not be missed. The opportunity to be "Teacher for the Day" on a rotating basis allows children a chance to carry out these tasks and to feel that they are making a special contribution.
- Develop picture and photograph collections. The children can be encouraged to bring photos or pictures depicting people assuming responsibilities such as helping someone cross the street, picking up litter, using the crosswalk to cross the street, etc. Photographs of children (taken by the teacher or the parent helper) can be included in the collection. The pictures and photos can be placed in a photo album or big book or on a wall display labelled "Responsible Citizens."
- Encourage children to become responsible for their own belongings (e.g., clothing, dressing and undressing; bringing things from home, taking things home, etc.).

Suggested Activities for Developing the Ability to Cope With Change

- Discuss change as a natural part of life. Long and short term graphs that show children's height, tooth loss, age, number of family members or siblings, etc., depict changes that have occurred in the child's life. After a graph has been constructed, the teacher and children can analyse the visual representation and record statements that reflect information gained through analysis on charts to accompany the graph.
- Initiate class discussions when a change of the classroom environment is needed (e.g., "Does the water centre have to be put away to allow room for the rice centre?" or "Where can the new egg-hatching equipment be placed so the incubator can be plugged in?"). Children who are consulted about changes that need to occur in the classroom feel in control. Arriving at school one day and finding a new centre, for example, may be exciting to some but can be disorienting or confusing to others.
- Explore reaction to change through drama. Each child can use three stick puppets with "happy," "neutral," and "sad" faces. As events arise in the classroom, outside the classroom, or in the neighborhood, the kindergarten group can discuss them. A change (e.g., the school carpenter coming to build a new sandbox, no playground balls allowed outside for a week, snow that is turned to slush, a field trip to the zoo, etc.) can be announced by a child or teacher. The children hold up their puppets to signify how they feel about the change. Children can then give a reason why they feel sad, happy, or indifferent.
- Discuss situations that create emotional outbursts. For example, talk about spilled paint and knocked-down block towers.

Suggested Activities for Encouraging the Acceptance of Cultural Identity and Heritage

- Invite parents of the children to the class, or have the teacher cook traditional foods that represent the countries of origin of the children in the class.
- Invite parents or relatives of the children to share information about customs and costumes with the class. Give the children time for personal contact with the resource person. In many areas, multicultural societies have lists of activities and speakers who are willing to share their culture with children. Groups such as these can be valuable sources of information to the teacher and the children.
- Create cultural displays or collect photographs, pictures, and books that depict traditions from all the cultural backgrounds represented in the classroom.
- Learn songs, dances, and games from the countries of origin of the children.
- Use holidays as a vehicle for sharing special cultural customs, artifacts, food, and clothing, from different countries.
- Read stories from other cultures to stimulate group discussions and role-playing situations. Children could take roles and dramatize the characters from the book.

Suggested Activities for Encouraging Respect for Cultural Similarities and Differences

- Explore the cultural backgrounds of the children and the teacher. Share customs and traditions associated with food, language, dress, dance, art, special days, etc.
- Help children generalize (e.g., "We all love to dance! There are many different kinds of dancing.").
- Do projects that can be shared with the principal or another class (e.g., a big book, a dance, a song, etc.).
- Use E.S.L. students where appropriate as resources (e.g., Japanese students could help with simple paper folding).
- Plan a cultural event or festival in which children share dress, dances, games, food, etc., that relate to their backgrounds. This event could be school-wide.

Suggested Activities for Fostering Respect for the Environment

- Help the children understand who is responsible for keeping the classroom clean and neat. Establishing guidelines for putting away material and having the room organized so every object has an easily recognizable place will help children contribute to the order and cleanliness of the room.
- Walking around the school, and later around the neighborhood, helps focus the children's attention on the outdoor environment and provides a basis for dialogue about how each child can participate in maintaining the quality of the environment. Discuss what would happen if the environment were mistreated, and discuss also how the children can help protect it.

Fostering Social Responsibility

- Invite resource people such as conservationists to provide information for children to begin to understand why the environment is important.
- Take field trips to a salmon spawning ground, a tree farm, a fish hatchery, etc., to provide the children with first-hand information and experiences in the natural environment.
- Plant trees, flower bulbs, and vegetable seeds to foster understanding and respect for a small part of our environment.
- Bringing small animals and plants into the classroom offers children the opportunity to observe, care for, form attachments to, and take responsibility for the growing and living part of their environment.

Fostering Social Responsibility

Fostering Physical Development and Well-Being

Physical growth and well-being are aspects of development that can be positively affected through information and through acquisition of the values associated with healthful living. Children are provided with information through experience and are encouraged to take responsibility for factors such as hygiene, safety, nutrition, movement skills, and physical fitness. In this section, suggestions are provided to assist the teacher with the planning and preparation of experiences intended to foster physical development.

Suggested Activities for Encouraging Care and Respect for the Body

- Be a good model. Comment on positive actions taken on the part of children.
- Provide easy access to soap, water, and washrooms so that children can take care of their needs.
- Stress the need for good food, activity, and rest with appropriate comments during activities. For example, by providing time for children to mimic the actions of rag dolls at the end of a session in the gym, the teacher could say, "This activity will help your heart get back to normal rate and help your body to cool off."

Suggested Activities for Enhancing the Learning and Practicing of Safety Procedures

- Model and stress positive safety attitudes as part of every kindergarten activity.
- Encourage the child to check conditions and thus prevent problems. For example, children can learn to move a chair from a traffic area.
- Talk with children about safety. Comment on good practices (e.g., say "Sam is carrying that chair with the legs pointed down. He's really thinking of others.")
- Go on a "Safety Search" around the school. The Red Cross supplies a free School Safety Checklist.
- Invite professionals to come and talk to the kindergarten class.
- Develop "Safety" as one theme. Involve children in planning the theme by starting with a co-operative list (e.g., "Places to Think About Safety").

Additional Resources
- I.C.B.C. Traffic Safety Education
  Room 151
  North Esplanade St.
  North Vancouver, B.C.
  V7M 3H9
- R.C.M.P. Community Relations Office
  (Safety Bear; Block Parent Program)
- Consumer and Corporate Affairs (Canada)
  ("Stop and Save a Life"; Hazardous Product Symbols)
- J. Colleen Politano, *Child Survival: Lost in the Woods*, (Sydney, B.C.: Porthole Press, 1984).
- Red Cross Catalogue of Programs
  Red Cross Youth
  4750 Oak St.
  Vancouver, B.C.
  V6H 2N9.
- Martin I. Green, *A Sigh of Relief*, (Toronto: Bantam, 1977). First-aid handbook for childhood emergencies.

Suggested Activities for Encouraging the Awareness and Practice of Good Nutritional Habits

- Make the preparation of nutritious food an integral part of the program.
- Prepare snacks to accompany a theme.
- Prepare nutritious snacks to celebrate holidays. For example, in place of cookies or cake for Valentine's Day, make "Raggedy Ann" salads.
- Invite children to bring food for the others to sample. For example, at Chinese New Year the children could bring homemade fortune cookies.

Additional Resources
- *Nifty Nibbles: An Ideas Book for Kindergarten Snack Program*, School District #57 (Prince George)
- *Kindergarten Integrated Cooking Program Developed for Special Little People*, School District #69 (Qualicum)
- *Big Ideas*, B.C. Dairy Foundation

- Use food as a theme. Have a food group day or party.
- Make a big book of "Food Groups."
- Read Dr. Zeuss' *Green Eggs and Ham* or Hoban's *Bread and Jam for Frances.*

Suggested Activities for Developing Physical Fitness

- Provide time, space, and equipment to permit children to play indoors and outside, explore and practise movement, experiment and practise with equipment, and experience expressive and rhythmic movement.
- Allow time during each activity for warming up, sustaining activity, and cooling down.
- Encourage children to evaluate their activity in terms of themselves rather than in comparision to others.

Suggested Activities for Developing Muscle Control and Co-ordination

- Encourage children to regulate the intensity of their activities to accommodate personal skills and confidence levels. For example, skipping ropes can be used for skipping or for merely stepping over. Provide an environment that invites children to feel comfortable to try different activities using similar equipment.
- Set challenges that encourage children to try new ways of moving both themselves and equipment (e.g., "Can you move along a line using both hands and one foot?").

Suggested Equipment and Materials

- balls of various sizes and materials (nerf, rubber, soccer, medicine)
- hoops
- skipping ropes
- scoop sets
- climbing apparatus
- benches
- trestles
- bean bags
- wooden block
- peg
- play bats
- mats for landing

Fostering Physical Development and Well-Being

Fostering Aesthetic and Artistic Development

As with other kinds of learning, aesthetic and artistic development is an ongoing process that occurs over a lifetime. Teachers are encouraged to provide the children in kindergarten with experiences that will enable them to explore, create, respond, interpret, and express their knowledge through a variety of forms. Sensory and artistic activities generated by the children and stimulated by the teacher can serve to provide opportunities, ideas, feelings, and images that are clarified and shared through the arts. This section provides the teacher with suggestions for planning and preparing experiences intended to foster aesthetic and artistic development.

Suggested Activities for Encouraging Children to Explore and Create

- Choose a color to find examples of in the classroom. As the children locate objects that are red, for example, display them on a table. Encourage the children to notice the differences in tints, shades, and intensity. Then provide each child with a dish of white powder paint and a dish containing a small amount of red. Have the children mix a drop of red with the white and test the results on a piece of paper. Challenge the children to find as many different tints of red as they can create. The same activity can be done using other colors, red and yellow for example. A great deal of paint can be saved if children learn to add drops of the dark color to the lighter one.

- Provide each child with an instrument from the rhythm instrument box. Group the children according to the kinds of instruments they are using (all bells together, drums together, etc.). Present a simple rhythm to the group and provide verbal assistance to help the children remember the pattern (e.g., "Loud Soft, Loud Soft" or "tap-tap, tap"). Ask each "section" to repeat the rhythm in turn. Then combine two groups and repeat the rhythm. Finally, ask the entire group to repeat the pattern. Tape record at different intervals throughout this process. Listen to the tape and ask the children to recall which groups are repeating the pattern. Then ask individual children to create a rhythm for the class to repeat. Follow the same process: record each group separately; record the combinations of "sections"; and finally, record the entire class. Once the children understand this process, the exercise can be repeated independent of the teacher. At the music centre, one child can become the "conductor," introducing and naming a pattern for other children to repeat.

- Provide a box of assorted props such as wigs, glasses, hats, fabric, etc. for the children to use. Discuss each prop with the children, and encourage them to imagine many different uses for each. For example, a piece of fabric could be tied as a kerchief for an old woman's head, a cape for a super hero, an apron for a cook, a blanket for a baby, etc. Ask the children to use only the props in the box to invent as many different kinds of costumes as they can think of. If time permits, have the children dress in the costumes and act out the characters they are representing.

Suggested Activities for Encouraging Children to Interpret and Respond

- Have the children sit in a circle. Explain to them that you are going to play a piece of music and that you want them to respond, using their bodies to show how the music makes them feel. Encourage them to respond to the music and the movement of the group. Play a recording of lyrical music. Encourage the children to join hands or close the circle by placing their hands on each others' shoulders. As the music dictates, children can sway or rock from side-to-side, move from the centre and back to sitting position, and so on. The actions of one child (such as hands on floor in front and then raised in the air) can be copied and sustained until there is a change in the music.

- Stimulate the children's thinking and future discussion by presenting slides or picture examples that emphasize lines. Ask the children to describe the kinds of lines they saw. For example, they may identify thin and thick lines, smooth and jagged lines, sharp and rounded lines, straight and wiggly lines, and so on. Once the children have identified kinds of lines, list instruments that could be used to make lines such as brushes, pencils, felt pens, crayons, string, and chalk. Provide a selection of instruments and media at tables for the children's use. Provide each child with a large piece of paper and have them fold it to make four distinct sections. Have one child select someone to describe the kind of lines. If the child identifies rounded lines, then all children select something with which to make rounded lines within one of the sections. Then have another child choose a different kind of line for the next section. Encourage children to exchange the tool used in the first exercise for a new instrument for making lines. When the pictures are completed, encourage the children to discuss the different sections and the kinds of images each evokes.

Suggested Activities for Encouraging Children to Imagine and Visualize

- Suggest to the children that they will be given the opportunity to create a mural backdrop for a scene from a fairy tale. Before they do so, however, it will be necessary to think of all the things that will be represented on the mural. Then read a passage from the tale that is to be depicted on the mural. The children will close their eyes, trying to see the picture in their minds. When they are finished, ask the children to identify and discuss the things they "saw" in their minds. For example, one child may say "castle"; another may say "made of grey rocks"; and someone else may say "with vines growing on it." Details such as thrones, candles, tables, carpets, suits of armor, and so on may all be discussed. Once the discussion has been concluded, children can begin to work on the mural. Encourage the children to represent the things they visualized. If a child said "with vines growing on it," talk about the vines — how they looked, how they twisted, whether they had leaves, and so on. If the backdrop is left on the wall, children can enact the scene as part of the activity period.
- Read an action story or create one of your own for use with the class. In a large, clear space in the classroom or gym, have the children act out the sequence of the story as it is read or recited. From time to time, stop the story and ask the children to look to their left. What do they "see"? Ask them to look to their right, in front, and behind themselves. What do they "see"? After this activity, the children may enjoy the opportunity to paint or draw their impressions of the experience.
- Play a short piece of music that represents a distinct mood or that evokes particularly strong images. Ask the children to relax by putting their heads down and closing their eyes. When the piece is finished, ask the children to recount their images to the others. Encourage the children to recognize that each person's visualization will be different. Have them compare the similarities and differences.

Suggested Activities for Facilitating Development of the Senses

Caution: Children should be made aware of the possible dangers of tasting unknown substances.

- Acquaint children with their senses on a conscious level by introducing and reinforcing vocabulary in association with everyday discussions and by providing a wide range of sensory experiences for them. When objects are brought into the classroom, encourage children to make observations related to the senses. Ask questions such as the following.
  "What does the object look like? Describe its appearance."
  "What does the object smell like? Describe the odor."
  "Can this object make a sound? Describe the sound."
  "How does this object feel? Tell us about it."
  "Does the object have a taste? How does it taste?"
- Provide opportunities for children to use their senses to match objects with the same texture (pairs of cards with scraps of fabric glued on); smell (pairs of pill bottles with spices, etc. inside); appearance (pairs of paint chips); sound (pairs of boxes with objects inside); and taste (supervised tasting game).
- Use media such as clay and play dough to provide a wide range of sensory experiences. The material feels wet, cold, damp, and sticky. It can be pinched, moulded, rolled, stretched, and patted. It has its own odor. As the material hardens, it will change in appearance and texture. It becomes firm and dry. It can be sanded, burnished, painted, varnished, or glazed. Once baked, the material is hard and may have a dull or shiny finish. When working with clay or play dough, the teacher is encouraged to discuss these physical changes with the children.

Suggested Activities for Facilitating the Development of Critical Awareness

- Following a movie, a play, or an art exhibit, adult observers often discuss the merits and faults in the show. The level of sophistication of criticism is largely dependent upon the degree of knowledge the participants have. Children, too, need to be given opportunities not only to increase their knowledge but also to express their individual preferences. Most kindergarten children are able to say whether they like something or not, and at times some children are able to identify those elements of a picture, a movie, or a puppet play that affect their feelings.
- Show the child a slide or a picture of a recognized artist's work. Encourage them to react to the picture by expressing what they like or dislike in the picture. Can the children recognize and respond to particular features of the picture? Can they identify the kinds of colors, the medium, and the choice of subject matter? Can they identify work done by a single artist from a group of pictures?
- Read the children different versions of a familiar story. Invite them to tell which version they prefer and to tell why that version has more appeal than the other(s). The same technique can be used as a basis for a discussion of a variety of formats for a particular story. Ask the children to express their feelings about the book story as compared to the puppet play or movie version.
- Introduce the children to two pieces of music that illustrate a particular phenomenon (e.g., "Did the music make you think of rain, a storm, a summer day, bumblebees, etc?" "How were the pieces the same or different?" "Which piece did you prefer? Why?").

Fostering Aesthetic and Artistic Development

Suggested Activities for Enhancing Expression and Representation in a Variety of Forms

The approach described in the "Themes" section of this book amplifies the means by which teachers can plan and present experiences that can be expressed and represented in a variety of forms. For example, if the theme is "Orange," the children could do the following kinds of activities.

- Paint pictures using various tints and shades of orange.
- Use oranges and sections of oranges to dip in paint or printing ink to make their own pictures.
- Create a bulletin board or table display labelled with the title "These Things are Orange."
- Find of listen to songs or poems about the color orange or about things that are orange. Decide which piece is preferred by the majority of children. Plan the staging of the song or poem by discussing the making of costumes, parts, and so on. Produce the "show" for other classes or the parents groups.

206

Fostering Intellectual Development

In the Curriculum Guide section of this book, intellectual development is defined as ". . . the process of acquiring, structuring, and restructuring knowledge." The stages of thinking, the influences on intellectual development, and the ways of providing for intellectual development are discussed at length. Teachers are encouraged to provide children with a multitude of first-hand experiences with their environment and to promote interaction among themselves and between children and adults. The kinds of knowledge are defined and explained. In this section, suggestions are provided to assist the teacher with the planning and preparation of activities that are intended to foster intellectual development.

Suggested Activities for Sustaining and Extending Natural Curiosity

- Provide each child with a hula hoop to take to the playground. Place the hoops on the ground and encourage the children to investigate the ground inside the boundaries of their hoop. Give the inquiry "status" by using terms such as "investigate," "examine," "experiment," and "observe." Point out the parallels to adult life. For example, the teacher could say, "A person who studies living things is called a biologist. You are working like a biologist when you watch the ants in the grass. Tell me what you see."
- Use the introduction of new materials and activities to stimulate curiosity. Encourage children to predict and reason, and, utilizing their contributions, to fill in the additional information required.
- Provide a stimulating environment to entice the children's curiosity. Encourage questioning and examination by providing enthusiastic responses such as, "I'm pleased you noticed that. I'm sure other people would be interested in your discovery. Let's share this information with the rest of the class."

Suggested Activities for Developing Thinking Processes

Thinking processes include observing, recalling, comparing, patterning, classifying, predicting, and generalizing.
- Take the children to a park or stand of trees to observe the changes of the trees in the fall, winter, and spring.
- Recall previous experiences. For example, ask the children to recall what they did in the gym yesterday. Or ask the children to recall the sequence of events in a cumulative story such as *Chicken Little*.
- Make comparisons about such things as the homes of animals, the uses for boxes, thick and thin things, hot and cold, smooth and rough, or things that sink and float. Whenever possible, incorporate concrete experiences with the discussions.
- Encourage children to make predictions. Ask the children to estimate how long it would take for jello to set, snow to melt, or water to evaporate. Ask them to predict which items will float and which will sink, or to predict what the Troll will do to the Biggest Goat. Once the event has occurred, refer back to the original predictions and compare.
- Once children have had shared experiences, they can be encouraged to make generalizations such as "some trees lose their leaves in the fall," "snow melts," or "we all enjoyed the snack."
- Classify the items in the collections boxes in many ways or by a single attribute such as color or shape.
- Encourage children to examine patterns and routines. For example, you might say, "Everyday a postal worker delivers the mail," or "Every morning we start our session with a song."

Suggested Activities for Developing the Ability to Identify, Solve, and Anticipate Problems

- Invite children to identify, solve, and anticipate problems in relation to everyday experiences in the program. Examples might include the following.
  - "How shall we serve the pineapple for snack?"
  - "What will we need to prepare for our field trip?"
  - "How can we avoid spills at the painting centre?"
  - "What can we do with our gerbil over the long weekend?"
- Set special problems and have the children suggest various solutions and plans (e.g., "How can we convert the house to a restaurant?" "What shall we do at our Halloween party?")
- Treat naturally arising social conflicts as problems to be solved. Have the children articulate the problem from their point of view, and try to arrive at a mutually agreeable solution.

Suggested Activities for Enhancing the Development of Physical Knowledge

- Make butter and have children describe the experience as they proceed. Discuss changes as they occur. Think of all the places butter is used.
- Explore the changes of state associated with water. Boil it. Freeze it. Melt ice. Gather and melt snow. Describe activities and discuss observations.
- Grow plants and observe and describe changes. Keep charts and records. Predict what will happen under various growing conditions. Experiment. Compare predictions with actual findings.
- Observe ants, spiders, or bees. Keep pets such as gerbils, hampsters, fish, or guinea pigs in the classroom. Discuss observations and the care of animals. Make charts or booklets, and share the information with others.
- Dehydrate fruits such as bananas, grapes, or apples. Note the changes in size, texture, shape, and taste.

Suggested Activities for Enhancing the Development of Social Knowledge

- Invite parents or grandparents to visit the kindergarten to share a variety of holiday customs.
- Set up a store, hospital, post office, or restaurant in the dramatic play centre. Use field trips, first-hand experiences at school, the child's experiences apart from school, books, media, and dialogue to extend knowledge and enrich dramatic play.
- Discuss appropriate ways to eat snacks, to share, and to care for books and toys as situations arise.
- Interview the principal and other school personnel. Use this information to extend knowledge about the school and those who work in it. Represent this knowledge in a variety of ways (e.g., talk, paint, draw, dramatize, construct, etc.).

Suggested Activities for Enhancing the Development of Logical Knowledge

Everyday experiences and activities can be used in a variety of ways to develop logical knowledge (e.g., classifications, patterning, seriation, number, time, and space). The children themselves can provide a basis for extending logical knowledge. Activities such as the following might be used.

- Classify by hair color, footwear, clothing, eye color, etc. Graph the results.
- Create patterns using various attributes (e.g., big/little, tall/short, sitting/standing, arms up/arms down).
- Seriate by height, size of shoes, or length of hair.
- Count attributes (e.g., those in the class, small groups at a centre, boys, girls, etc.). Compare the groups and graph.
- Move through space in response to directions (e.g., up/down, over/under, between, spread out/scrunched up).

Use objects of all kinds to enhance development of logical knowledge (e.g., keys, buttons, rocks, blocks, apples, leaves, tiles, cut-out shapes of paper, beads, bottlecaps, beans, toys, etc.). Activities such as the following might be used.

- Classify by color, shape, size, texture, thickness, and function. Graph the results.
- Create patterns using various attributes (e.g., color, shape, size, texture).
- Seriate by size (smallest to largest) and color (lightest to darkest).
- Count objects by fours, or arrange two groups of objects in one-to-one correspondence.
- Place items in different locations to make patterns (e.g., up on a block, down on the floor, etc.).
- Play a game. Establish a number of possible locations for hiding some things. Have one child hide them. Others can guess where they are by describing where they think the objects are located.

Use themes to enhance the development of logical knowledge. Activities such as the following might be used.

- Classify blue things in the room, blue things in the school, or blue things in the school grounds. Graph the results.
- Make patterns using shades of blue paint for prints.
- Seriate gradations of blue (e.g., jars of colored water).
- Count blue things; match blue things; put blue things into groups of four.
- Collect blue things from around the room and describe the location where each item was found.

Special experiences can be planned in order to enhance the development of logical knowledge. Activities such as the following might be used.

Classifying Activities

- Use sorting boxes to sort objects according to various attributes.
- Sort children, or name cards into groups according to various criteria (e.g., "What kind of pet do you have?").
- Take a sorting walk to find round things. Draw them and put them on a chart.
- Have the children count objects for a color table. Ask children to sort the objects into groups while describing the basis on which they decide to put certain objects into the certain groups.
- Put objects (or children with a common characteristic) into groups and have the children try to guess what the common characteristic of the group is. Then have them try to add the next object to the group.

Patterning Activities

- Create patterns by printing with natural items (e.g., leaves, nutshells, feathers).
- Make patterns using sounds, words, or phrases to create chants or songs.
- Explore patterns by creating sequences of simple movements or dance steps.
- Note patterns on pineapples, flowers, cloth, or butterfly wings.
- Note patterns of events in the kindergarten session, on the calendar, etc.

Seriation Activities

- Order the height of children in the class from shortest to tallest.
- Order pumpkins from smallest to largest.
- Order the steps in the preparation of snacks.
- Order the steps in the planting and growing of seeds.
- Bring teddy bears from home and order them from smallest to largest. Trace the bears on paper and add detail and color. Cut out the bears and place them on the wall in the determined order.

Numbering Activities

- Match bottle tops to bottles, locks to keys, clothes to a doll, or napkins to each child during snack time, thereby exposing children to the notion of one-to-one correspondence.
- Have the children learn to recognize and say their telephone numbers and addresses.
- Use snack time as an opportunity to incorporate a variety of counting and graphing activities.
- Use the calendar and daily attendance as the basis for a variety of counting and graphing activities.

Time Activities

- Discuss the concept of time with the children, and keep records on the calendar about such events as hatching chicks, the birth of a gerbil, and planting seeds or bulbs.
- Read stories such as *The Little House, Chicken Soup With Rice, A Book of Months,* and *One Monday Morning.*
- Help children keep track of time as they wait for jello to set, corn to pop, muffins to bake, or clay models to harden.
- Talk with the children about what they did first, next, and last when creating models, patterns, etc.
- Make picture cards of activities in the day, and arrange them in the order of the day's activities at the beginning of the day so that children know what will happen. This could also be done at the end of the day to review what was done.
- Count the number of days to an event, marking a number, an "X," or a color on the calendar.
- Talk about something that happened yesterday, what's happening today, and what will happen tomorrow. Make a time line recalling the past, observing the present, and predicting the future.
- Sort pictures into a temporal sequence (e.g., what happens first, second, third, etc.).

Space Activities

- Take walks in the neighborhood and locate the children's houses. Help the children give directions and draw maps for how to get to their homes.
- Map children's homes and neighborhoods; map children's bodies; or map block, Lego, or other construction projects.

Fostering Intellectual Development

- Notice and talk about things that are wide/narrow, high/low, above/below, etc., as children participate in various activities.
- Notice and comment upon classroom pets or fish moving backwards, across, into, between, rising, or burrowing. Imitate these movements.
- Help children make direction signs for sand, block, and construction play. Talk about relative position by using references such as "around the bend," "through the tunnel," "a turn to the right," "outside," etc.

Suggested Activities for Encouraging Representation of Knowledge

- After a nature walk, discuss the topic of frogs. Discuss their habitat and food; compare them to toads. Use pictures, slides, and books to illustrate the discussion and to foster interest.
- Dramatize traditional stories such as *Goldilocks and the Three Bears* or *The Little Fir Tree*.
- Play the xylophone; clap to music; move to the rhythm of a story or a record.
- Place blocks on paper to make a map in three-dimensional form that represents an airport, the way to school, or the kindergarten classroom. Once all the blocks are in place, trace around the outline of the blocks to create a two-dimensional map. Label.
- Model letters or items for the "toy shop" or the "bakery" from clay, Plasticine, or play dough.
- Paint a picture after listening to a story. Encourage children to share their pictoral representations and to discuss the difference between individual interpretations.

Fostering Intellectual Development

Fostering Language Development

There is a strong link between the development of language and the development of the intellect. Through language, thinking is complemented, clarified, and extended. The factors that affect the acquisition of language, the kindergarten child's learning stage, and the purposes of language are presented in the Curriculum Guide section of this book. Teachers are encouraged to provide opportunities for dialogue and for the development of a "set" for literacy, and also to facilitate representation of knowledge through language. The nature of emergent reading and writing behavior is discussed within the context of total language development. In this section, suggestions are provided to assist the teacher with the planning and preparation of experiences intended to foster language development.

Suggested Activities for Appreciating, Exploring, and Developing Language

Reading to Children

- Read from a wide variety of books. Children need to be exposed to all forms of print and to a broad range of good literature.
- Select a particular author or genre of literature for concentrated exploration. Encourage the children to identify which selections they prefer and to state reasons for their opinions.
- Develop key words.
- Make language-experience charts.
- Make booklets.
- Use enlarged print (i.e., big books for shared book experience).
- Point exactly to words or phrases on occasion while reading.
- Choose literature that has repeated rhythms, patterns, phrases, and words.
- Encourage children to look at the print and to chime in, anticipate, and predict lines, phrases, and words.
- Use pocket-chart observations about letters, their associated sounds, how words are spelled, etc., *always* and *only* within the context of enjoying good literature (or reading something meaningful).
- Arrange cross-age tutoring or buddy reading to simulate the experience of the bedtime-story.

Suggested Activities for Exposing Children to the Functional Uses of Reading and Writing

- Record children's talk to increase their understanding of the functions and value of written language.
  Descriptions, thoughts, comments, ideas, plans, and captions that children compose should be written down verbatim whenever possible. These statements serve as an accompaniment to the child's activity, drawing, or painting or as enhancement to the display of children's work.
- Write lists, plans, directions, recipes, and remembered steps or sequences, whenever possible.
- Make a written record of experiences (e.g., classroom news, field trips, descriptions of projects or creations, comparisons, individual scrapbooks, diaries, reasons for classification categories, observations, things to remember, word-storming activities).

By reading to children and familiarizing them with the characteristics of the medium, children learn the following:
- cover and title page of the text;
- title, author, and illustrator;
- how a book opens; the front and back;
- beginning, middle, and end;
- left to right; top to bottom;
- how to turn pages.

Reading with Children

- Reading with children increases their awareness of the conventions of printed language and enables them to acquire knowledge of literacy. They learn that
- writing is talk written down;
- print carries a message;
- the same print carries the same message every time it is read;
- words that look the same say the same thing;
- print moves from top to bottom and from left to right across the page;
- spaces separate words;
- there is a"match" (one-to-one correspondence) between spoken and written words;
- phrases or sentences are made up of discrete words;
- words are composed of letters;
- the same word contains the same letters, which can be recognized and named;
- often letters have a consistently associated sound.

Providing a print-saturated environment enables children to become familiar with the functions of reading and writing as well as the characteristics of the print itself. The teacher acts as scribe, creating written materials of all kinds, using *enlarged print* whenever possible. Engaging students in any of the following activities would constitute suitable experiences for children:
- making charts of songs, poems, or recipes;
- making signs for displays or centres;
- making big books;
- printing labels or sentences on large paper strips;
- making graphs or charts;
- brainstorming list of words for reference.

Fostering Language Development

- Make labels for displays, collections, activities, things brought from home, classification categories, storing equipment, centres, creations, construction and dramatic play projects. Print simple sentences rather than single words on large paper strips using enlarged print.

Communicating Messages

Providing experiences where children are involved in giving and receiving messages builds up the notion in the mind of the child that writing carries a message that can be read and responded to.
- Write thank you notes to field-trip hosts or in-class resource people.
- Make a classroom post office.
- Make cards for birthdays, Valentine's Day, Christmas, Hanukkah, and Chinese New Year.
- Write letters to parents about activities at school.
- Make notes and letters to children from teacher, parents, and others in the school community.

Communicating Observations and Ideas

In relation to any subject matter, writing can be used to record observations, ideas, and ways of thinking about or organizing experience. Involving children in these kinds of experiences helps to build up the notion that writing can be used to communicate and organize meaningful intellectual experience. Such activities focus on allowing the child to express and clarify various aspects of his or her social knowledge, physical knowledge, and logical knowledge.

Social Knowledge
- Provide opportunities for children to write books about their family, homes and neighborhoods, or about babies.
- Keep journals, diaries, and scrapbooks.
- Create class-authored big books about field trips, special days, and events to be remembered.

Physical Knowledge
- Provide opportunities for children to prepare child-authored books about colors, shapes, and natural phenomena.
- Label pictures for wall charts and bulletin boards to accompany or follow observation and exploration activities.

Logical Knowledge
- Sort objects, pictures, or photos. Identify groups with common attributes and write labels to accompany these collections.
- Trace objects; add details, and color. Arrange from largest to smallest and write captions for each object.
- Record and label measurements of various kinds (e.g., circumference of pumpkins, children's heights). Graph and make comparisons in relative terms. Write a summary to describe results.
- Use a large picture with caption to challenge the children (e.g., "How many eggs can you see?"). Children count and tell the answer and then write their response.
- Illustrate pages for number songs and rhymes and make them into class big books.
- Record experiences that involve counting, comparing, estimating, and sharing.

- Experiment with the writing of numbers (e.g., phone number, address, birthdays, etc.).
- Provide opportunities to identify and copy numerals in conjunction with counting activities.
- Use phrase cards to denote locations in space or time. Use them in conjunction with other class activities.
- Use a calendar and develop related activities that involve recording of information. Record and graph information over time. For example, an "On-going Observations" chart could provide a record of changes in the weather for a month.
- Use charts with big print in conjunction with action songs. Make words that denote special concepts and that stand out graphically (e.g., UP! UP! UP! the stairs I go!). Use interesting and varied kinds of print.
- Develop concepts such as "little," "middle-sized", and "big" within the context of enjoying good literature (e.g., *Goldilocks and the Three Bears*).

Self-Expression

Appropriate experiences develop the child's understanding that expressing oneself verbally and capturing that self-expression in print can be a creative and personally satisfying experience. Reading your own writing or the writing of others is equally pleasurable.
- Create captions for pictures.
- Record the child's idea or story and encourage the child to create an illustration to accompany it.
- Imitate language patterns in favorite stories and incorporate your own ideas, making up verses.
- Create your own page (picture and print for a class book).
- Record ideas for group plans. Follow through the plans to develop the event.
- Create imaginative books (e.g., first it was a pickle and then it was . . .).

Suggested Activities for Encouraging Representation

The kindergarten program provides a range of experiences designed to foster all aspects of development. Children, in turn, represent what they know (their understanding of their personal experience) in a variety of ways. Given the opportunity, children become increasingly adept at letting one thing stand for or represent another. Avenues for representation include
- rhythmic response to language or music;
- drawing, painting, and picture making;
- dramatic play;
- construction with wood, found materials, boxes, blocks, Lego, etc.;
- modelling with sand, dough, Plasticine, and clay.

Writing is a form of representation that is twice removed from reality. *Words* can be written down or read in place of *talk*, just as *talk* (like movement, pictures, dramatizations, and constructions) can take the place of actual *experience*. Using writing as an accompaniment to other forms of representation acquaints the child with the notion that symbols, like words or pictures, can stand for or represent experience. It is important to support the child's effort at representing his or her knowledge in various ways.
- Use charts and big books for songs, poems, and literature that illustrates a lyrical use of language. Children will gradually become aware of the "match" (correspondence) between movement, language, and print.

- Use writing to accompany, enhance, and extend dramatic play (e.g., make signs and sort boxes; write letters and address envelopes; draw pictures of homes and label street names, family names, and address numbers).
- Help children to reproduce the text of a familiar story, poem, or song in big book format by dramatizing or using puppets.
- Encourage children to incorporate forms of representation through the following kinds of activities into their play.

> Map, trace, paint, or draw the construction on a piece of paper. This creates a kind of a record of the activity; captions can then be composed and written down.
>
> Plan and prepare an underlay to accompany building ventures. For example, runways for planes, outer space terrain, and landing pads for rockets, roadways, bridges, buildings, or water masses can be drawn on a large piece of paper to serve as a "play mat."
>
> Compose labels or descriptions written on signs and incorporated into the construction itself. For example, make signs for a town, ocean and country scene (e.g., "Fire," "The New Town," "This is the farm," "This is all the water," etc.).
>
> Discuss and record group plans in relation to the making of models or construction projects (e.g., "Let's make a model of the Richmond Nature Park! What do we need to do?").

- Involve children in the creation of their own class big books to increase awareness of the characteristics of books and print and to provide an opportunity to practise emergent reading behaviors.
- Illustrate the text of a familiar song or story (smaller photocopied versions of these can be illustrated by individual children).
- Create verses or lines patterned on the language of familiar favorites. These can be written down, illustrated, and bound into class books.
- Develop original verses for songs.
- Encourage children to see themselves as illustrators and authors, and eventually as editors and publishers, of their own books. This can happen when

> drawings, paintings, pictures, and illustrations are valued and discussed;
>
> ideas are written down and recorded in book format;
>
> children are recorded as authors and encouraged to sign their own names on their own work (i.e., "by Kevin");
>
> children are given the opportunity to make their own books;
>
> the child's attempts at self-expression are encouraged and supported;
>
> scribes (parents, older students, aides) are available to engage the child in talk and to record the child's thoughts and comments;
>
> child-authored books are shared with large groups and included in the class library.

Suggested Activities for Facilitating Emergent Reading and Writing

Facilitating Emergent Reading

Emergent reading refers to the child's attempts to represent what he or she knows about reading. These attempts are less than perfect but should be encouraged at every stage as they follow an orderly sequence that leads to the actual ability to read. When children are looking at books, one can observe this pattern of behavior:

- retelling of parts of the story in own language;
- accurate retelling of entire text (memorizing is a postitive accomplishment as it frees the child to concentrate on particular features of the print associated with the spoken word);
- pointing to words, but not necessarily the words being said;
- pointing exactly to the words;
- making observations and asking questions about print;
- actually recognizing repeated words or phrases;
- recognizing some words in varying contexts;
- predicting words based on recognition of the first letter and its associated sound;
- perceiving whole words;
- actually reading.

Emergent reading develops in an environment where copious printed material is available and where the atmosphere is positive, non-competitive, and minimally corrective. Children need to be read to on a daily basis and need also to read along. Individual and group responses are to be encouraged and familiar favorites should be available for reading and rereading to facilitate responding.

In addition, teachers need to provide information about both books and print in order to increase an awareness of the process of reading. The teacher is encouraged to provide whole, meaningful stories and poems. Language should not be presented in a fragmented way. Teachers can expose children to copious book language that illustrates the use of a wide variety of literary structures.

A separate time and place for reading should be provided during each school day for all children to explore favorite stories independently. Materials that enable the child to transcend everyday experience and that encourage imaginative play and fantasy should be provided. It is important to accept and encourage approximations when the child begins to demonstrate emergent reading behavior. Self-selection of materials, self-motivation, and self-correction of interpretation leads to self-confidence.

Facilitating Emergent Writing

Emergent writing refers to the child's attempts to represent what he or she knows about writing. The child's first attempts at writing are only approximate but should be encouraged at every stage as they follow a sequence that leads to the actual ability to write. When children are encouraged to write by themselves, one can observe the following behavior:
- writing lines of zigzags or partial circles and sticks;
- writing strings of actual letters (in both cases, children can usually tell you what their writing says);
- copying words or simple sentences, but words are placed randomly on the page;
- copying words but leaving no spaces between them;
- writing known words (names, names of others in the family, teacher's name, "I love you," etc.);
- writing lists of words;
- inventing own spellings by listening to words and writing down the letters associated with the sounds based on phonetic knowledge to date ("kr" for "car"; "ILSDATOU" for "I lost a tooth");

Fostering Language Development

- copying sentences with left to right direction and spaces between words;
- expressing ideas in own writing.

Emergent writing develops in an environment where literature is enjoyed thoroughly and where print is used in many functional ways. Places for experimentation with drawing and writing must be provided, and children are encouraged to write as much as they can by copying if they want to or by inventing their own spellings.

ORGANIZING, ASSESSING, AND COMMUNICATING

Planning

Successful management of a kindergarten program is largely a function of successful planning and requires both a knowledge of the curriculum goals and a plan for organizing and implementing them. This section of the resource book provides you with sample overviews and plans that can assist you with your planning on a yearly, monthly, and daily basis.

Sample Yearly Overview

Month	Themes	Special Events Celebrations	Field Trips Resource People	Things to Collect for Learning Centres (Additions/Changes)
September........	"Me" "Change"	School Starts Fall Fair	Around School Principal Secretary Fall Fair	art centre mirror leaves paper leaves
October............	"Apples"	Halloween Thanksgiving	Visit Farm See Turkeys Pumpkins Apple Orchard	pumpkin, gourds, corn turkey feathers apple slicer/corer apple cutter dehydrator washable make up
November........	"Space"	Remembrance Day	Observatory	space capes space music plaster of paris large cartons landscape for Lego small blocks
December........	"Christmas"	Christmas Hanukkah	Shopping Centre Tree Lot	Christmas stories Christmas decorations Christmas records glitter
January	"Fairy Tales"		Library	Fisher Price Castle magic wand Delly Boppers crowns capes shampoo caps for Block Centre
February............	"Chinese New Year" "Fairy Tales"	Chinese New Year Valentines Day	Librarian Chinese Restaurant Author	pink, red, purple, and white items Valentine decorations fairy tale books paper doilies
March.................	"Bakery"	St. Patrick's Day	Bakery Kitchen Flour Mill Farm	kitchen tools green items wheat
April....................	"Collections" "Unique"	Easter	Museum Homes Chicken Farm Rabbit Hutch	Easter decorations tables to display collections personal collection
May	"Whales"	Victoria Day	Oceanographer	whale teeth photographs
June	"Hoedown"	School Closing	Farm Ranch Picnic Farmer Rodeo Rider	square dance records hay farm animals hats bandanas

Sample Yearly Overview

Month	Themes	Special Events Celebrations	Field Trips Resource People	Things to Collect for Learning Centres (Additions/Changes)
September				
October				
November				
December				
January				
February				
March				
April				
May				
June				

Sample Monthly Plans

NOVEMBER	
Week	Activities
1–3	"Space" theme
4	"Collections" theme

JANUARY	
Week	Activities
1	Back to school. Review safety co-operation strategies. Allow children to get comfortable with group routines.
2	Ukrainian Christmas New Year
3–4	"Fairy Tales" theme

MARCH	
Week	Activities
1	"Change" theme
2	St. Patrick's Day
3	"Bakery" theme
4	Easter

THEME _____

EMOTIONAL DEVELOPMENT AND WELL-BEING	SOCIAL DEVELOPMENT	SOCIAL RESPONSIBILITY IN A CHANGING WORLD

Note: The goals of providing experiences to foster growth in emotional and social development are inherent in and intrinsic to all other goals. Therefore, it is understood that much related activity and concept development occurs at all times.

PHYSICAL DEVELOPMENT AND WELL-BEING	AESTHETIC AND ARTISTIC DEVELOPMENT
Health and Safety	Art
Nutrition and Snack	Music
Movement Education	Drama

INTELLECTUAL DEVELOPMENT

Social Knowledge

Physical Knowledge

Logical Knowledge

Representation

LANGUAGE DEVELOPMENT

Listening

Language

Emergent Reading and Writing

SAMPLE WEBBING CHART

Making a webbing chart with the class is an excellent way to begin a unit. It involves and excites the children, indicates resources, and shows what the children know.

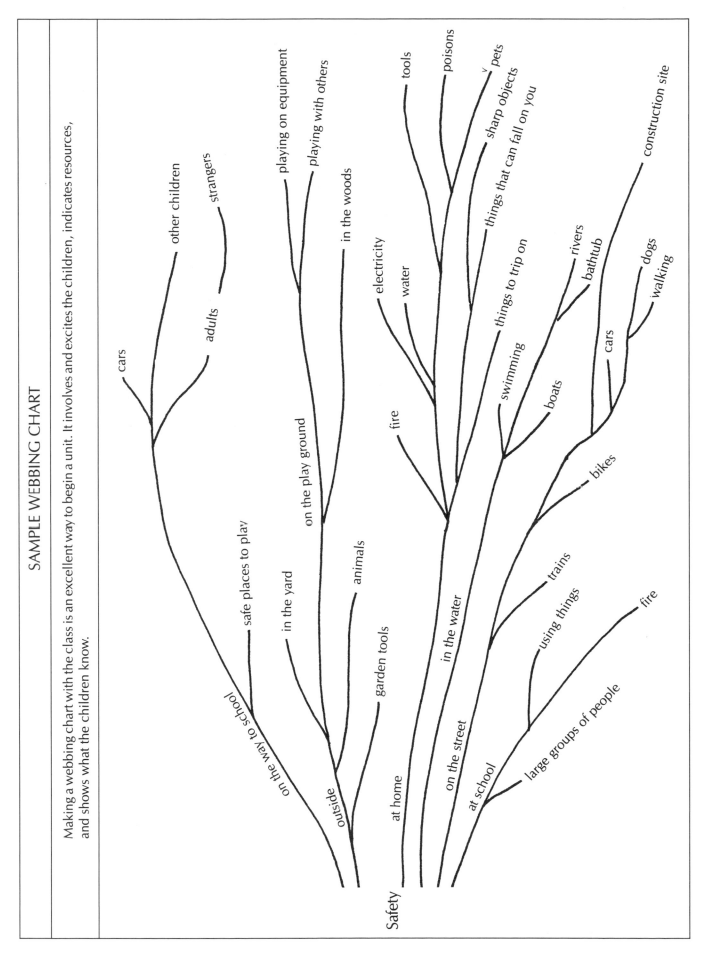

Sample Weekly Plan

Week of _____   Theme _____

	MONDAY	TUESDAY	WEDNESDAY	THURSDAY	FRIDAY
Opening: (9:00 a.m./12:45 p.m.) • greeting • attendance • calendar • routines • introduction • discussion of theme-related or featured activities					
Activities/learning centres: (9:30 a.m./1:15 p.m.)					
Booktime: (10:20 a.m./1:55 p.m.)					
Snack: (10:30 a.m./2:15 p.m.)					
Movement Education: (10:45 a.m./2:30 p.m.)					
Group Session: (11:00 a.m./2:45 p.m.) • literature • music • movement • featured activities					
Closing: (11:20 a.m./3:05 p.m.) • sharing and evaluation of days activities • reminders					

Date _____

Opening	song, weather, calendar, attendance, news, share and show, poem, oral work, plans for today
Activity and Learning Centres	books and library, listening, quiet place, construction, modelling, sand, water, woodworking, painting, drawing and writing, exploration, numbers, tabletoys and puzzles, blocks, dramatic play, music, beauty spot, special interests, art, cooking "Must" Jobs: Introduce New Activities
Writing	Keywords—language experience
Books	big books, books from home, library, class books, child/scribe-authored books
Snack	cooking two times a week
Washroom/Record	
Movement Education	gym/class/outside, games. Mary Helen Richards, Orff, dance or drama, fitness, space, equipment, gymnastics, trampoline
Meeting Group	storytime, music, drama, language development, number concepts, emergent reading and writing, discussion, group projects and plans
Closing	clean-up, recap of day, song, plans for tomorrow, discussion

Sample Day Plans

9:00 (12:30)	**Opening** • greeting/kindergarten news/general discussion • calendar/attendance/graphs/number activities • special thoughts/poems/songs/stories
9:30 (1:00)	**Movement Education** • music/drama/movement/dance/appreciation • adventure playground/gym • games/gymnastics/skill development
	Snack • food groups/cooking/ethnic dishes
10:00 (1:30)	**Learning Centres** introduction/discussion/participation in a variety of theme-related and special activities: • art (experimentation, expression, and representation using a variety of media) • experiments (manipulation of materials in order to discover their properties) • dramatic play (opportunity to recreate and better understand experiences) • writing table (opportunity to use literacy materials) • number activities (manipulation of objects in order to understand number and emergent math concepts)
	Books • daily opportunity to work on reading and rereading favorite stories, poems, songs, charts, etc.
11:00 (2:30)	**Group** • discussion/development of language and thinking • activities leading to the development of literacy • literature (wide variety of stories/songs/poems) • music (instruments/appreciation/rhythmic activities/chants/games)
	Closing • sharing/evaluation/reminders/notices

Time	Activity
9:00 (12:30)	Opening
9:30 (1:00)	Movement Education
	Snack
10:00 (1:30)	Learning Centres
	Books
11:00 (2:30)	Group
	Closing

Planning for Substitute Teachers

Teachers must also plan to accommodate changes in schedule and routine and for expected and unexpected absences from the classroom. When a situation arises in which the teacher must be away from the classroom, it is helpful to the substitute teacher, and comforting to the children, to maintain as much as possible of the existing routine. A general letter that provides "tips," and a "Daily Plan Outline for Substitutes," have been provided as suggestions.

SAMPLE INFORMATION FOR SUBSTITUTE TEACHERS

Sept. 1982

Dear Sub,

I have attempted to tell you about some routines that may be helpful to you. These are just a guide and for information. Please do not feel you must adhere rigidly to everything stated. I feel that it is good for the children to have a new person leading them and hope you will share your particular talents with our class. (For example, I am not musical so if you have the good fortune to be, please supplement planned activities with songs you know.) I ask that you make note of any activities you initiate so I know what has happened and can include the information in my Friday letter to parents.

Thank you.

★　　★　　★

HELPERS

There is a parent helper most days. The schedule is posted by my desk. If you would rather not have a helper, please let me know.

I usually have a job for the helper while the opening meeting is conducted. The helper circulates during centre time, interacts with the children, pours milk, does dishes, wipes tables. During closing, I usually plan a job for the helper so he or she is not left feeling unproductive. Jobs range from tidying up to preparing materials. I will attempt to leave some preplanned "Helper Jobs" if I know I will be absent. If not, use your discretion.

DISCIPLINE

Our all-encompassing rule is to be considerate of others. It is expected that no child will hurt or interfere with others. If someone forgets or makes a "poor" judgement, we talk about what happened and work on finding a mutually agreeable solution.

OUTSIDE TIME

If weather permits, the children go outdoors (9:00–9:20) (2:55–3:15).

Rules for Outside Time
Children must stay where I can see them, let me know if they are going to the washroom, and come quickly when I call "TIME."

COMING IN

Children hang up coats, put lunch kits in row under hooks, change shoes.

When children have changed shoes, they go to the rug, get a book or "Back of Bookshelf Activity" (a collection of classification games and small puzzles and toys that can be used briefly and put away quickly) until I call them together.

OPENING

(1) Calendar

We cover up one day each day on a large calendar, cross off day on small calendar.
We name number of day/name of day/name of month.
We count days gone/days remaining in the month or to a special event.

(2) News

Everyone who wishes to has a brief opportunity to talk.

(3) Show & Tell

Each child has been assigned a "Show & Tell" day. On his or her day, a child may bring an item to show. The item is to be brought in a bag or lunch kit. The child tells about the item without naming it, and then may choose two people to try and guess what has been described.

Following Show & Tell, I introduce new activities or go over rules we have agreed on for using equipment.

CENTRES

Circulate and talk with the children, assisting as requested.

During activity time, children may change activities as long as they clean up before changing.

If a person complains about others doing an activity, my standard replies include:

"What do you want to do about the problem?"
"You settle the problem or change activities."
"Try talking it over—if that doesn't work, let me know."

Some centres are limited to a number of people at one time. These are

Dramatic Play	4	Fisher Price Toys (each)	3
Water Table	3	Chalkboard	3
Blocks	4	Sand	4
Painting	4	Puppets	3
Modelling	6	Easels	4

CLEAN-UP

Five minutes prior to clean-up, the children are warned that the activity period is almost over. When I call "clean-up," the children keep talking very quietly and do the tidying. A person who finishes may help someone else. I help, too. At completion the children choose a book for "Booktime."

BOOKTIME

Each child gets a book to read or look at and may use any unused space. I read (as a model) or circulate to comment on concentration, choice of book, etc.

WASHROOMS

The children may go to the washrooms as they need to, as long as they tell me when they are going.

After clean-up, I take the whole class down to wash hands and use the bathroom, if necessary. When children are finished, they meet in the hall. We walk back to class together. The children get their snack and sit at a table.

SNACK

Our children bring their own snacks three days a week. When we have made a snack at school, the children set it out during clean-up. They sit at tables. We make sure everyone has a snack before we begin.

MILK

Parent helpers handle pouring milk and doing dishes. I ask the helper to pour the milk and set it out while the class is doing clean-up. To wash the glasses, I ask the helper to take the glasses to the staffroom in the yellow dishpan. It's brighter there, and there is hot water. If I don't have a helper, I wash the glasses after school.

MOVEMENT EDUCATION

Singing, singing games or exercises, and movement activities to music are part of our daily activities. Good choices for exercises are

"Waddlyatcha"—Sharon, Lois & Bram—Singin' and Swingin', and "Robin in the Rain"—Raffi—Singable Songs.

The plan for activity is indicated in the daybook.

GROUP MEETING

This block of time usually includes story time, discussion, films, and teacher-directed activities. The subject for the day is noted on daybook page.

CLOSING

The children get shoes, bring them to central floor area, change, put runners in bag, put bag in cubbyhole, get coat and lunch kit, sit down ready for home. The children comment on the day or provide information about activities to be done. I take the children out to meet their rides and make sure everyone makes their connections.

(a.m.: leaves by back door).
(p.m.: On fine days we play outdoors (3:00–3:15)).

GYM, LIBRARY, BUDDIES

Schedules indicating times are posted above my desk.

SIGNALS

"STOP AND LISTEN" and "TIME" are the verbal signals the children are accustomed to.

MEDICAL INFORMATION

Medical information is on record in the office. Please note:

a.m. class: Alan is violently allergic to fish.
p.m. class: Kindree is diabetic.
Sam and Joan are allergic to milk.

Planning

TIME	ACTIVITY	COMMENTS
9:00–9:25 12:45–12:55	P.M. Children: Enter room, hang up coats, change shoes, get a book, sit on rug. A.M. Children: If it is not raining, use playground 9:00–9:15, then follow routine as for p.m.	
9:25–9:35 12:55–1:10	Group meeting on rug. Attendance, calendar, news, sharing time. Each child has a "showing day" as shown on list posted beside chesterfield. Introduce new activities.	
9:35–10:15 1:10–1:45	Children work at activities and centres. Teacher circulates and talks with children, giving assistance if needed. Five minute warning for clean-up.	
10:15–10:25 1:45–2:05	Children clean up centres and then get a book on the rug.	Booktime allows everyone a chance to look at or read a book.
10:25–10:30 2:05–2:10	Children use washrooms. When finished, they wait in the hall.	
10:30–10:45 2:10–2:45	Snack Time: Milk is poured and set out by Grade Sevens. When everyone is ready, the children eat and have conversations. If we have prepared the snack at school, we talk about the preparations, discuss reactions, and so on.	Some days I give a sentence for each child to finish (e.g., "The vegetable I like is . . . . Today's Sentence: . . .).
10:45–11:05 2:25–2:40	Movement Education: We use this time for singing games and movement activities. Our actual turns to go to the gym are Monday, Wednesday, and Friday. Times are posted above my desk.	New Songs: _____ _____ _____
10:45–11:00 + 5 2:40–3:00 + 5		
11:05–11:25 2:40–3:00	Group Meeting: Group meets on rug for stories, discussions, planning activities.	
11:25–11:30 3:00–3:05	Children change shoes, get ready to go home. Check clean-up. Give out notices, projects. P.M. Class: Outdoors to playground 3:05–3:15. Teacher walks out with children.	
11:30 and 3:15	Dismissal	

SUPPLIES NEEDED	APPOINTMENTS	REMINDERS

Planning a Weekly Newsletter

To facilitate the writing of a weekly newsletter, it is useful to prepare a form for recording information about the events and activities that have taken place.

	MONDAY	TUESDAY	WEDNESDAY	THURSDAY	FRIDAY
Stories					
Songs					
Snacks					
Movement					
"Happenings"					
New Equipment					
Field Trips			<u>Birthdays</u>		
Visitors			<u>Notes</u>		

Multi-Age Grouping

Whether the formation of a combined class (multi-age or family grouping) is due to small enrolment at a particular school or catchment area or to district philosophy, such groupings exist in a variety of arrangements in school districts in B.C.

Combined classes can provide benefits and challenges for the children and the teacher. Most research shows that there are no noticeable cognitive differences between children in multi-age classrooms and children in graded classrooms. It does indicate, however, that there are benefits derived from multi-age grouping with respect to social development. Positive influences appear through self-concept, self-esteem, aspirations, feelings of success, perceptions of parental approval (support), and a lengthened teacher-child relationship.

Of the benefits inherent in the multi-age program, the concept of a learning continuum is highly significant. The information gained through experiences is explored, tested, and represented in a variety of ways and levels. Although the same experiences are presented to all, what each child learns depends on individual levels of development. Thus, the acquisition of knowledge is different for each child. As children become more mature, socially independent, and responsible, the types of activities they can undertake will range from open-ended learning experiences to more sophisticated assignments with differing levels of expectation.

Within the multi-age classroom, attempts are made to develop the whole child, taking into account those inconsistencies in individual learning that can be easily obscured by grade levels. While there are different age levels within a K-1, K-1-2, or K-1-2-3- class, (often as wide a range as four to seven years), we know that chronological age and mental age do not necessarily correspond. The teacher of a multi-age group is knowledgeable of early childhood development and thus can recognize and meet the needs of children at a variety of stages of development.

The kindergarten child gains the opportunity to interact with other children, and consequently to develop his or her language skills through large and small group discussions, interaction at centres, and activity and play. Children tell each other things in the form best suited for them. Thus they provide each other with a focus on one of the most important aspects of the situation. For example, a teacher giving complicated directions to a multi-age group of children might finish speaking and then turn to one of the children and say, "Would you tell Jennifer what she should do?" The child will likely translate the teacher's words into an entirely different form and yet retain the content. Much peer group teaching takes place in this way.

Other benefits to kindergarten children grouped in this way might include the following.
- A sharing and helping atmosphere develops as the children learn routines from each other.
- A teacher has the opportunity to teach the same child for two or more years. This permits the teacher to get to know the child and family thoroughly, thus eliminating wasted time and allowing the teacher to meet the child's needs more effectively.
- Materials can be combined for the greater benefit of all.
- Small groups of each age of children may be enrolled. This encourages greater teacher-child interaction. For example, while the kindergarten is in session, the teacher attempts to spend more time with the kindergarten children while delegating more independent activities to the older children.

Additional Resources

- *Resource Book for K-1 Teachers,* School District #43 (Coquitlam)

Multi-Age Grouping

- Parent-teacher communication and understanding can be improved because the teacher has the opportunity to interact with one child and his or her family over a longer period of time.
- The opportunity exists for a smooth transition and continuous progress for more capable children while those children who require more time to develop are given the opportunity to do so. Less mature children have the opportunity to feel successful and to use materials or engage in activities appropriate to their ability without the constraints of time and grade.
- Smaller, "ungraded" classes can help to prevent early "failure."
- The role-model provided by the older children for the kindergarten children is a positive one. Specific activities such as "buddy reading," sharing and labelling of drawings or other representations such as oral language development through discussions, group planning, the activities at the dramatic play centre, storytime, class news, music, movement, and mural making can occur. In fact, all the experiences that offer children the opportunity for social interaction result in benefits for all.

Considerations in multi-age grouping include the following.
- The teacher must select books carefully to ensure the interest of children with varying attention spans and levels of ability.
- Conscious effort must be made to preserve the quality of the play environment. Teachers should be cautioned against a desire to "structure" the activities of the younger children too soon.
- Careful planning of time is required in order to meet the Ministry of Education requirements for minutes of instruction for graded programs. However, with the flexible nature of the kindergarten program as it relates to the goals, the teacher will be able to integrate the programs for both groups of children.

The physical organization and learning environment in the classroom should be well-planned and thoughtfully arranged so as to provide accessibility to all resources for all children. Creating different spaces in the room and carefully including movement patterns will allow for both quiet and active participation and total involvement with materials. An integrated approach to the curriculum as well as the use of centres will ensure that many levels of understanding and types of activities can be ongoing. Thus, the needs of all the children can be met.

The teacher organizes the day plan to utilize equipment, activities, and open-ended experiences that challenge. A balance between teacher-directed, child-directed, and spontaneously arising events should be maintained.

When the kindergarten children leave at the end of a session, the small group of older children remaining will function in a more formal kind of setting.

A Sample Activity

Paying particular attention to what has been written in this curriculum guide about the language goal (specifically oral language and emergent reading and writing behavior), the kindergarten children will be exposed to the activities of the older children and will absorb and acquire knowledge in this regard at an individual rate. The kindergarten child will be developing a *set for literacy* through exposure to

- language experience
- big books
- story books
- journals and diaries
- writing centre
- alphabet and word games
- key vocabulary
- chart stories, choral speaking, poems, songs
- concept books and pattern books
- sentence makers
- library

The representation of a thought exists for the kindergarten child within a wealth of activities such as art media, Lego, Plasticine, blocks, etc. By saying, "Tell me about what you doing," the child shares orally and then is guided toward choosing one word, phrase, or sentence to label or represent the thought. This is read back to the child, shared with the others in the class, and recorded for reference at a later time. As the child observes this process repeatedly, he or she can become increasingly independent either in what can be done personally or in turning to the other children for assistance. Eventually, the kindergarten child will attempt to label and represent his or her expression of thought in a form that others can read.

Children are asked to choose some form to represent their thoughts. All centres, materials, and resources, as well as oral vocabulary and discussion, are available to them throughout this process. One child may build with Lego or blocks while others are coloring or drawing; another may be working at the construction centre; someone may paint, while others may choose to speak to a friend or to discuss ideas with the teacher.

Having completed a representation, a child may decide to share with a friend or the teacher, thereby translating the non-verbal to the verbal mode. When the teacher says, "Let's look at these thoughts written down," the following process may result.
- one word (key vocabulary);
- going to an older child or a dictionary;
- looking to other resources such as labels around the room or on other children's work;
- expanding the key word to sentences using known sentence stems or service words;
- exploration of sentence patterns.

Further, the activity can be expanded to include other activities such as
- typing the word in the typing centre;
- copying the word onto the chalkboard or paper;
- tracing or copying the word into a storybook or journal;
- cutting the letters of the word out of a magazine;
- painting the word at the painting centre;
- drawing the word in a sand or salt dish;
- using Lego blocks to recreate the word;
- sharing the word with a friend or a small group of children.

All or part of this process is applicable to different children in different ways at different times. It is the teacher's role to support, encourage, guide, and, where appropriate, teach each child throughout this task.

Orientation to Kindergarten

Orientation to kindergarten is so important that preparations are made each spring, prior to the September entry, to ensure that each child makes a successful adjustment to school and thus acquires a positive attitude. Without this, the transition from home to school can cause personal conflict, and a child in conflict has difficulty learning. The objective of kindergarten orientation is to ensure that each child within the total school situation is confident that he or she is valued on an individual and personal level. This confidence is based on the assurance that kindergarten offers to each child emotional security, social companionship, and intellectual stimulation. While the focus of successful orientation is the child, such success is only achieved through home and school co-operation. Organization for parent communication and understanding is initiated and planned in the spring in order to facilitate a successful transition (see Parent/Guardian-Teacher Partnership). Certain procedures help parents, children, and teachers establish positive relationships and attitudes conducive to learning. The procedures outlined for Spring, August, and September may be adapted to suit the needs of the children and school community in order to provide the necessary orientation in the most effective manner.

Orientation Procedures	
Spring................	• Registration • Parent/Guardian–Child Orientation • Organization of classes and preparation of information to be sent in August.
August	• Information sent to parents/guardians and children • Teacher planning of program • Teacher preparation of the kindergarten environment • Teacher organization for parent/guardian involvement
September	• Gradual entry and shortened sessions • Orientation of children to learning activities and class routines • Interviews with parents/guardians and children at school • Home visits, if applicable • Teacher adjustment in planning • Full time sessions
October–June ..	• Parent/Guardian communication • Ongoing letters to parents/guardians concerning learning activities • Reporting to parents/guardians

Spring

Public notification for kindergarten registration (co-ordinated by the school district central offices) organizes and clarifies an efficient registration in the specific time allotted.

The actual registration involves a parent or guardian completing the school district forms. Proof of the child's age is required at this registration.

Additional Resources

• *Kindergarten Parents' Handbook*, School District No. 24 (Kamloops)
• *Making the Most of Your Child's Skills and Abilities*, School District No. 31 (Merritt)
• *. . . And Soon I'll Go to School*, School District No. 38 (Richmond)

Orientation to Kindergarten

Orientation activities (planned by individual schools) supplement the formal registration and can help to establish positive parent/guardian–child–teacher relationships. Such activities may include the following.

- Parent/guardian and child make a short visit to see the kindergarten classroom and meet the teacher on the day of registration.
- Parent/guardian and child attend a May or June session planned by the teacher.
- An interview with parent/guardian and child may follow or be arranged separately.
- Parents/guardians and children attend a special one hour Parent/Guardian–Child Orientation Day. While the children are participating in this experience, it is beneficial to simultaneously provide parents/guardians with an adult orientation so that their questions may be answered and the philosophy and goals of the kindergarten program can be explained in a practical way. In order for the kindergarten teacher to provide a successful orientation experience for the incoming kindergarten class, the parent/guardian meeting could be conducted by the school principal or by district personnel knowledgeable of kindergarten. Such a meeting focusses on general issues and ensures that parents/guardians understand the philosophy. When teachers interview individual parents/guardians at a later date, discussion is focussed specifically on each child.

  Depending on numbers, the present kindergarten class may not attend on this Parent/Guardian–Child Orientation Day so that the kindergarten teacher may also have time to interview certain parents/guardians personally. A successful alternate practice has been to orient the present kindergarten class into the grade one classroom at this time. This co-operative venture is shared with the grade one teacher who introduces the kindergarten children to the grade one class for a combined experience and for introduction to the coming year.
- Informal small group meetings with parents/guardians that focus generally on the kindergarten philosophy and program may be held.
- A booklet or a pamphlet outlining the philosophy and program and including details such as snack fees may be provided. Such a booklet is a comprehensive reference but is not a substitute for group and individual communication between parent/guardian and teacher.
- A Parent/Guardian Information Sheet may be prepared. Inclusion of this reassures parents/guardians that their involvement is welcome and beneficial. In addition, it helps the teacher to include new resources into the program.

Organization of classes and notices to be sent in August are often completed by June. School staffs organize the composition of each kindergarten class to provide the best learning situation for each child. Considerations are given to the age of each child, to the ratio of girls and boys, and to those children with special needs.

Notices may include the following details:
- gradual entry (exact dates and times);
- general information including school procedures for absenteeism, supplies, arrival and departure times, and learning activities planned for September;
- class lists including home addresses and telephone numbers;
- a friendly letter of welcome to each child from the teacher.

- *Now I Am In Kindergarten,* School District No. 43 (Coquitlam)
- *Kindergarten Handbook for Parents,* School District No. 45 (West Vancouver)
- *Stepping into Kindergarten,* School District No. 68 (Nanaimo)

Sample Parent/Guardian Information Sheet

NAME: _____

To enrich the kindergarten program we would like to utilize the skills, interests, and talents of parents/guardians. Throughout the year we should like to call upon you to participate in the experiences in the kindergarten.

Please fill in the area or areas of interest to you.

1. Kindergarten children are interested in learning about occupations. Would you be willing to visit our class and tell us about your work?

   Occupation: _____

2. Children appreciate the opportunity to see an artist "in action." Would you be willing to come and demonstrate:
   (a) Painting_____   (e) Playing a musical instrument____
   (b) Sculpture_____   (f) Singing_____
   (c) Pottery_____   (g) Dancing_____
   (d) Acting_____   (h) Others_____

3. Children show an early interest in collections. If you have a collection you think the children would be interested in, please describe it:

   _____

4. Would you be willing to come and demonstrate how you:
   (a) Cook a special dish_____
   (b) Do needlework, sewing, or knitting_____
   (c) Bath a baby_____

5. Are you able to assist the teacher with:
   (a) Gardening_____   (c) Preparation of classroom
   (b) Woodwork_____   materials_____
                                     (d) Classroom routines_____

6. Field Trips:
   (a) Can you provide transportation? _____
   (b) Would you be willing to accompany us? _____

7. We would be pleased if you would come and share your holiday trips with us. Children like to see articles and slides of other places.

   _____

8. Other: _____

9. When are you available to assist in the above?

   Day: _____   Time: _____

Should your home or work situation prevent you from the above participation, it is important to remember that you are welcome to visit the classroom if you find available time in the future.

Sample Letter for Spring Parent/Guardian-Child Orientation

Dear _____

Your child, _____ , has been

registered for kindergarten at _____

School for the _____ class.

To ensure a successful beginning for each child, we are asking parents/

guardians to bring their children to kindergarten on _____

at _____ . While your child is being introduced to the
teacher and kindergarten activities for one hour, we invite you to meet the
other parents/guardians and join us for a coffee and an informal talk about the
kindergarten program for the coming year.

Sincerely,

_____

Teacher

_____

Principal

August

In August, the teacher plans the program, including information acquired from the
Spring orientation activities. Information is sent to parents/guardians. Teachers may
personally contact parents/guardians to schedule classroom assistance time.

Classroom preparation includes the selection of only those learning materials that
will stimulate learning without confusing the child. It is recommended that children
are involved in a gradual introduction to the varied materials available so that
maximum learning is facilitated.

Labelling specified spaces for children's personal belongings and activities with
names and identifying pictures helps give children a sense of belonging in the
classroom.

Sample Letter of Welcome to Children

_____ School

Dear _____

I hope that you and your family have had a nice summer. I have been thinking about you because kindergarten will be starting soon.

There will be many interesting things to do and talk about when you come to

school on _____ . You will make many new friends, too.

If you have a photograph of yourself, please bring it to school to share with us and to put on the Bulletin Board. Thanks!

If you would like to bring a painting or drawing to school to share with us, we would be pleased to see it.

These children will also be in your class and live close to you.

_____   _____   _____   _____

See you soon.

From,

_____
Your Kindergarten Teacher

Sample Letter for September Parent/Guardian-Orientation Day

Dear _____

Your child, _____ , has been

registered for kindergarten at _____

School for the _____ class.

The entrance of your child into a kindergarten class is most important. To ensure a successful beginning for each child, we are inviting parents/guardians and children in small groups to visit the kindergarten classroom for a 45-minute period during the week of September 7th.

You will become acquainted with the teacher, the classroom, a few of the basic procedures, and some of the materials.

We have scheduled your visit with your child for _____ .

It is important that you bring your child to visit the school so that when he or she joins the class your child will know the teacher and a few children. This should facilitate a positive transition from parents or guardians and home to school.

We hope that you will come to the school on many occasions so that we can work together to make school a happy, successful experience for your child.

Most sincerely,

_____
Teacher

_____
Principal

Please Note:
Each day the class has a snack time. There will be a nominal fee for snacks. The total amount may be paid at the time of your visit, or one half for the first term and the other half in February. (In the event of a transfer, the unused portion is refundable).

September Gradual Entry

The first weeks in September are directed towards ensuring that each child experiences the positive orientation that is essential for school success. In order to achieve this objective, the plan for gradual entry includes both the phasing-in of small groups and also shortened attendance time. The use of one of the models for gradual entry presented here, or a district-designed model that is flexible and designed to meet the varied needs of the children, the school, and the community, is recommended.

Gradual entry allows for each child's personal introduction to the new learning environment and simultaneously provides the teacher with opportunities essential to establishing positive relationships with each child and family. Guided by observations of the child in the small group and by information gained from parent/guardian interviews, the teacher reviews and adapts the program plans to meet each child's needs effectively.

Gradual entry helps each child understand the classroom routines necessary for safety and also facilitates optimum use of the learning environment. Establishment of consistent routines minimizes conflict by the provision of a safe, predictable climate wherein children not only understand the teacher expectations but also learn to accept and share responsibility for their own contribution towards maintenance of the environment.

Experience has shown that gradual entry focusses on appropriate learning experiences. These ensure a positive orientation for each child, and this is crucial as a foundation for school success.

Parent/Guardian—Child—Teacher Interviews

Individual initial interviews that focus specifically on each child are invaluable for establishing mutual positive relationships and also for the teacher to acquire understanding of the child's interests, social and emotional behavior, physical development, and individual personality. By discussion and observation, the teacher gathers necessary information to adapt the program to meet the needs of each child. Such interviews are usually held in the classroom so that all children may become accustomed to the school setting. Later, the child may demonstrate acquired skills or the teacher can refer to materials and activities for the parents'/guardians' information.

Further interviews during the school year continue to provide both parent/guardian and teacher with information on the child's general development. In addition to formal interviews, ongoing informal communication throughout the year helps to keep parents/guardians informed and the degree of participation at maximum levels.

Home visits, both during the orientation period and throughout the year, provide an alternative to the school setting, wherein both parent/guardian and child may feel more comfortable with the teacher. Parental/guardian agreement and co-operation are necessary to ensure that the additional time involved is beneficial to the child. School personnel should give parents/guardians the option of selecting home or school visits.

Routines

- daily timetable
- transition between activities
- large and small group behavior
- washroom
- fire drill
- gym safety procedures
- independence in care of personal belongings
- independence in care and use of class equipment
- movement around school
- recognition and obedience to class "attention" signal

To ensure a successful beginning for the children entering school, parent/guardian–child–teacher interviews are conducted prior to the formal introduction of a day at school. The following steps for arranging the interview take place prior to September.

- In the Spring, a pre-registration of kindergarten children is carried out.
- Three sets of parents/guardians and children are invited to attend as a group.
- The interviews are held in the kindergarten classroom and should be approximately forty-five minutes in length.
- The teacher should schedule fifteen minutes between interviews to write informal observation notes.

The purposes of the interview are
- to observe the parent/guardian–child relationship;
- to note the child's reaction to a new adult, (the teacher) and to other children;
- to introduce the child to a new environment in a personal way;
- to show the child where he or she is to place personal belongings;
- to show the child the washroom facilities and to ensure the parent/guardian that the child may use these facilities when necessary;
- to gain knowledge of the child and his or her home;
- to assure the parent/guardian that the school is interested in his or her child as an individual.

The interview may include the following.
- A welcome and brief introduction to both children and parents/guardians can be given.
- A general comment about the room and learning centres and the program in general can be made.
- The children can be shown where their personal belongings are to be placed. The children could watch the teacher print their names on cards and place them on their own niches.
- The washroom facilities can be located and procedures discussed.
- The children can be given time to explore the classroom. Some toys, a few blocks, puzzles, paper, and crayons should be available.
- While the children are occupied, the parents/guardians can speak with the teacher and fill out the "Getting Acquainted" information sheet and the Parents/Guardians Information Sheet.

This meeting of parents/guardians, children, and teacher provides the opportunity to become acquainted in a quiet, pleasant atmosphere. The teacher has the opportunity to express his or her warmth and understanding of children. The parents/guardians can see that school personnel care about their child and can be encouraged to participate in the kindergarten program during the year.

The children will make friends and have the opportunity to adjust gradually to this new environment. Their concerns have been allayed, and now they can come to school with more confidence, knowing their teachers, knowing some other children, and knowing that there are interesting things to do at school.

Orientation to Kindergarten

Sample "Getting Acquainted" Information Sheet

Please help us get acquainted with your child by completing the following items and writing in additional information:

Name of Child _____

Age on September 1st _____ Date of Birth _____
                     (years)   (months)

Address _____ Phone _____

Name(s) of Parent(s) or Guardian(s) _____

_____

Employer(s) _____ Phone _____

Language other than English spoken in the home _____

Convenient time for phone calls to parent/guardian _____

Person to call in case of accident _____ Phone _____

Family Physician _____ Phone _____

HEALTH—Any handicap or serious illness _____

FAMILY—Adults at home _____

    Names of brother(s) and sister(s)

    _____ Age _____ Grade _____

    _____ Age _____ Grade _____

    _____ Age _____ Grade _____

Usually my child likes to play with:

    _____ his/her brother(s)   _____ his/her sister(s)

    _____ himself/herself   _____ a friend

    _____ neighborhood children

When alone my child likes to play with _____

My child likes to pretend _____

When I am with my child we usually _____

Playschool or Day Care (if attended) _____

Any further information that will help the teacher in getting to know your child:

_____

_____

                 Signed _____

Sample Newsletter for Parents/Guardians at September Gradual
Entry Interviews

Dear _____

The following is intended to provide you with information to facilitate smooth operation of the kindergarten.

Slippers: Children will have use of the gym for physical education. Could you provide a pair of rubber-soled or non-skid slippers for your child? We would like these to remain at school so that they can be worn in the classroom during rainy weather.

Labelling: Please mark, with your child's name, all items of clothing and footwear. (Slippers, boots, coats, hats, sweaters, mittens, etc.).

Clothing: Smocks will be provided for your child for painting activities. However, it is advisable that he or she wears washable play clothes.

Absences: Would you please notify us if your child is going to be absent from kindergarten for several days.

Transfers: If you are moving and your child will be leaving the kindergarten, please notify the school in advance.

Arrival Time: In order to give the kindergarten teachers time to prepare for the day's program, could you please help by seeing that the children arrive shortly before or at the following times:

> 9:00 a.m. for the morning class
> 12:30 p.m. for the afternoon class

In September, emphasis will be placed on
- —emotional and social adjustment to school;
- —establishing routines for effective learning such as
  - listening to and following directions,
  - being responsibly independent,
  - participation in lessons, and
  - completing learning tasks;
- —stimulating intellectual development.

If you have any questions, please call me at _____.

Thank you,

_____

October — June Orientation Activities

Home Visits

Visiting the child's home enables the teacher to get to know the children and the parents/guardians in a setting where they feel comfortable and relaxed.

The teacher will find it helpful and useful to bring some concrete things on a home visit. These can provide a source of conversation. For example:
- puzzles or Lego for the child to play with;
- a booklet describing a child's day in kindergarten (This should be simple and specific with attractive illustrations. It can be used as a discussion topic with the parents/guardians and child);

- photographs of last year's kindergarten class (These should be action shots. Once again, they will provide a discussion topic.).

During a home visit, a child may want to show the teacher his or her favorite books, toys, pets, or room. Later, in kindergarten, the teacher will be able to chat to the child about the visit, thus helping establish the teacher-child relationship.

Sample Information Newsletters to Parents/Guardians

School _____

Street _____

Date _____

Dear Parents/Guardians:

What a busy week we've had at kindergarten! In addition to the regular activities, the following may be of special interest to you.

Monday   Mr. Freeman the Fire Chief came to visit the class. He spoke to the children about fire safety at home and school and helped the children practise emergency procedures.

Tuesday   We walked to the firehall to have a tour of the fire station, meet the firefighters, and see the trucks and equipment used in firefighting.

Wednesday We celebrated two birthdays, Tami's and Jesse's. Thanks for sending special snacks!

Thursday   The class built a fire station using boxes and the blocks from the construction centre. The children made instrument panels, labels, trucks, and equipment boxes. They had great fun taking turns re-enacting what would happen if the alarm was sounded.

Friday   Today, we made a large mural of the firehall. It will be displayed in the main entry to the school. Please take a moment to have a look at the children's work.

Reminder:

Next Thursday, the 27th, we are walking to the new Shopping Centre construction site. You're welcome to join us if you like. We'll leave the school at 1:30 and return at 2:30.

_____

Thanks to those who contributed fabric, yarn, and paper for our "scrap corner" -- we now have a great collection!

251

HAPPY NEW YEAR!

It was nice to welcome everyone back to school. We spent this week re-establishing routines, getting re-acquainted, and sharing news from the holidays. So that we can get back in operation, please ensure that your child has

- a gym bag
- a paint shirt
- some runners
- library books returned
- a "Show and Tell" item for assigned day

We couldn't go to the library this week because the Librarian was re-shelving holiday books. We will get books next Wednesday (our regular library day).

We went to the gym and enjoyed using the equipment. You might want to note that Monday p.m., Wednesday a.m., Thursday a.m., and Thursday p.m. are our days to go to the gym.

We have a new foam puzzle, a new kaleidoscope, and lovely play dough. Special thanks to Laura Parker for preparing this batch of modelling dough.

Our new theme will be Fairy Tales. We will be spending the rest of this month with this theme as our focus. Some of the activities planned are

- dramatizing stories
- making pictures to go with stories
- using a variety of art media to illustrate stories. (e.g., bean collages for Jack and the Beanstalk)
- cooking experiences (e.g., gingerbread baking)
- retelling stories
- contrasting real and make-believe
- mathematics activities related to stories. (e.g., counting characters, doing verbal problems: "How many pigs built houses?" "How many houses blew down?")

Any materials or ideas you can share will enrich our activities.

Have a good weekend!

Our last two stories in Fairy Tale theme were "The Runaway Pancake" and "The Gingerbread Man." We had cooking experiences to accompany both. The Pancake Day and gingerbread-making were certainly popular activities. The children asked me to share the recipe for cookies.

MRS. GREEN'S GREAT GINGERBREAD

Cream	Sift
118 mL margarine	10 mL soda
118 mL sugar	10 mL baking powder
	10 mL cloves
Add	15 mL cinnamon
	1.25 mL nutmeg
1 egg	10 mL ginger
125 mL molasses	625 mL flour

Combine wet and dry ingredients.
Refrigerate 4 + hours. Roll out. Cut out.
Bake at 350°F for 10 minutes.

For the next two weeks we are having "Unique Weeks." Thanks to Mrs. Stone for sharing her original idea. We will be doing a number of activities that are weird, wonderful, special, and different.

For "Show and Tell" for these two weeks I would like the children to try to bring an item they think is unique. Rather than doing the guessing game, I would like each child to come prepared to tell three or more things about their item. We will do these presentations in the form of oral reports. You could help your child by doing a rehearsal at home.

Our school is having open house on Tuesday. If you care to drop in, the best times for kindergarten would be 9:30–11:00 a.m. and 1:00–2:00 p.m.

The children made excellent sequence pictures of the "Runaway Pancake" story. The sequence is: Pancake/seven boys/man/cat/rooster/duck/cow/pig/what happened next? See how many your child can list.

The buddies acted as scribes so the children could tell how to make pancakes or gingerbread. We want to display these "recipes." Then they will be sent home.

Thanks to Lance's dad for the plastic bottles and to the parents who helped make them into the "Smell Game." Each bottle is covered in Mactac; the top is perforated, and it contains some spice. There are two bottles of each spice. The object of the game is to match pairs by using the sense of smell.

Button Day was fun. We classified the buttons by shape, color, size, kind, or decoration.

Next Thursday, children from both classes will attend from 10:00 a.m. to 12:00. We will be going on the bus to see the Axis Mime Theatre. There is no charge for our admission. Please fill out the form below and send it back to school.

DATES TO MARK:

March 2 — Visiting Day
March 4 — Axis Mime Theatre
March 5 — Professional Day — no school for children.

Thank you,

_____

My child, _____ may attend on Thursday,

Parent's/Guardian's Signature _____

Dear Parents/Guardians:

The kindergarten curriculum is concerned with seven major goal areas and consists of experiences designed to foster each of the goals. It is useful to organize these experiences around THEMES. Our first theme will be APPLES.

Over the next couple of weeks, we will be doing a wide variety of activities with APPLES. As part of the study, I would like each child to bring one apple from home on Monday. We will be doing a variety of things with the apple collection: observing; noting characteristics, similarities, and differences; counting; graphing; weighing; measuring; comparing; etc. Eventually we will use the apples for making apple sauce and apple pie. I hope that you will come to the "Meet the Teachers" evening. The room will be set out so that you can see the range and variety of activities that we will be doing in connection with this and all the other THEMES we take up during the year. I will keep you informed as to our current THEMES and upcoming field trips (which are usually related to the themes under study).

In connection with APPLES, we will be focussing on nutrition and learning about the first of the four major food groups, fruits and vegetables. We will also focus on the color RED, and children will be invited to bring items for the RED TABLE. (The color table will change every few weeks.)

We are going to take a walking trip to the Shopping Centre, where we do most of our snack shopping. The children will be looking at the varieties of apples and apple products. We will try to name as many of the fruits and vegetables as we can and notice which ones are red, so that when the children help me to plan future snacks they will have plenty of ideas. We usually get a "behind-the-scenes" tour, so the children learn a bit about the work that various people do in the store. After the trip we will be making a big book about our experience. We will also convert the dramatic play centre into a store, so that the children can re-enact their experiences. These are just a few of our plans. Busy times ahead!

Sincerely,

_____

Parent/Guardian–Teacher Partnership

It is generally accepted that family attitudes and home environment are factors that influence adjustment to school and that adjustment at the early stages can have a tremendous impact on the progress of students in later years. We know that when parents or guardians demonstrate a positive attitude toward education, their children have more successful school experiences. It then becomes apparent that we must search for ways to ensure the development of positive attitudes toward education and adjustment to the school environment. We must seek ways to break through the artificial divisions of home and school, recognizing that a single child travels between these two different settings. Through open communication with each other, parents/guardians and professional educators can co-operate to support the growth and learning of the children in our care. Understanding between parents/guardians and teachers cannot come through talk and letters alone. By involving parents and guardians in the education of their children, the distance between us will decrease and the likelihood of developing real understanding and mutual goals will increase.

Parents and guardians must be recognized as full and equal partners. They are, after all, the first and most important teachers the child has. Learning takes place and can be reinforced in both the home and the school. Mutual understanding between parents/guardians and teachers results in benefits to the child. The ultimate responsibility for initiating a partnership with parents/guardians rests with the teacher. The teacher who truly believes that parents/guardians are also educators communicates this attitude in both words and actions. Parents/guardians feel they are treated with dignity and will consider themselves a resource to the professional—they have a contribution to make to the total process of education. In order for a partnership to be effective, there must be benefits for both partners. Parents/guardians need to be aware of the advantages that involvement offers them and their children. They must know also that the teacher wishes to build a partnership based on mutual trust and understanding, thereby enhancing the possibility of successful school experiences for all children.

The greatest benefit of the parent/guardian–teacher partnership is to the child(ren). Individual help, warmth, and support are gained from a number of adults, and the curriculum can be enriched by volunteer involvement. In addition, parents/guardians gain personal satisfaction in that the partnership allows them to observe the children working with people and materials. They are making a real contribution to the educational program. Teachers gain satisfaction, too, when they see that communication is opened with parents/guardians, that experiences for all children are enhanced within an atmosphere of mutual co-operation, and that goals are effectively achieved.

Initial Contacts

Procedures may vary from school to school, but it is likely that the teacher's first contact with parents/guardians will be at registration time in the spring. Soon after, the teacher may wish to invite parents/guardians to bring the children to visit the kindergarten. This provides a good opportunity to familiarize both parents/guardians and children with the kindergarten environment. It is important to remember that first impressions have a high impact and are often long-lasting. It is therefore crucial that parents/guardians and children are made to feel welcome and comfortable.

Additional Resources

- *Kindergarten Parents' Handbook,* School District No. 24 (Kamloops)
- *Making the Most of Your Child's Skills and Abilities,* School District No. 31 (Merritt)
- *. . . And Soon I'll Go to School,* School District No. 38 (Richmond)
- *Kindergarten Handbook for Parents,* School District No. 45 (West Vancouver)
- *Stepping into Kindergarten,* School District No. 68 (Nanaimo)

When school begins in September, teachers can establish contact on a more personal level. Gradual entry (meeting for short periods of time) gives teachers, parents/guardians, and children an opportunity to become acquainted, ask and answer questions, and discuss mutual concerns. Some teachers find that home visits provide a means by which to accomplish this same end.

After a few weeks of kindergarten, the teacher may arrange a group meeting for parents/guardians. The teacher may decide to discuss child growth and development, present an overview of the goals for kindergarten, prepare a slide presentation such as "A Day in _____ Kindergarten," or answer questions about kindergarten and the curriculum. Meetings of this kind provide valuable information to parents/guardians, can help to establish the groundwork for communication, and encourage parents/guardians to participate as partners in their child's formal education.

Levels of Involvement of Parents/Guardians

Children come from a wide variety of backgrounds, bringing different interests, experiences, and levels of ability. This is true also of parents/guardians and teachers. Some parents/guardians have children in the school already and may already be well acquainted with the teacher. For others, this may be the first experience with public education. Some parents/guardians may feel they have particular interests, talents, and skills they would like to share with the teacher and children. Some parents/guardians have time available to commit to the school and school activities. Others may have less time available due to young children or the demands placed on their time because they work outside the home. Whatever the situation, the teacher acts as a facilitator and provides a *variety of opportunities at different levels* for parents/guardians to become involved in the child's education.

For an extensive list of references regarding parent involvement, see Alice S. Honig, *Parent Involvement in Early Childhood Education*

Parents/Guardians as Direct and Active Teachers of Their Own Children at Home

Parents/guardians are always teaching their children, either directly or indirectly. Informed and committed parents/guardians can do much to facilitate successful school experiences for their children and once they have access to information about child development, the goals of kindergarten and resources available, they are in a position to effectively reinforce and enhance the experiences provided in kindergarten.

Some parents/guardians and teachers find that establishing an ongoing discussion group provides them with a direct communication link. Meetings where common concerns can be aired, demonstrations can be given, information can be shared, or materials and resources can be discussed enable teachers, parents/guardians, and children to benefit from such co-operation.

Parents/Guardians as Observers and Learners

Parents/guardians have a right to basic information about child development. They can benefit from learning how to observe a young child. Often, they need strategies for problem prevention and knowledge of how to utilize resources available to them, and they often require information that enables them to utilize new skills effectively. The teacher can make this information available through newsletters, conferences, group meetings, a variety of media, workshops, and speakers invited to make presentations.

Parents/Guardians as Reference

Parents/guardians have a relationship with their child that exceeds that of any other adult in that it is longer-lasting and encompasses a greater variety of experiences. No other person knows about the child as the parent/guardian does. That parent/guardian–teacher conference then should become a two-way exchange. Both partners should have the opportunity to provide information and gain insights about the child through this process.

During the year, every parent/guardian should be invited for the specific purpose of observing his or her child at work. The length of time, direction by the teacher, and nature of activities observed will vary from one situation to another. Following the observation time, there should be an opportunity for the parent/guardian(s) and the teacher to discuss the child's progress and development. In addition to *scheduled* observation times, the kindergarten teacher may welcome parents/guardians to visit informally at any time convenient to both.

Parents/Guardians as Volunteers

Some parents/guardians are willing to offer to assist in the classroom. When considering a volunteer aide program, it is important to establish guidelines and to ensure that volunteers recognize expectations. An informal meeting can be planned to review the program and discuss classroom routines and procedures as well as to delineate responsibilities.

There are a number of ways to organize volunteer assistance and to create avenues for parents'/guardians' contributions. Some teachers send out a list of suggestions specifying how parents/guardians can become involved. It is important to offer them options for the times, number of visits, and level of commitment they wish to make. There should also be the opportunity for parents/guardians to visit the school informally at a time convenient to the teacher. No one should be made to feel excluded.

Sample Letter to Volunteer Parents/Guardians

School _____

Street _____

Date _____

Dear Parents/Guardians:

There are many ways your assistance can be put to good use in our classroom. To help with the organization of the volunteer aide program and to facilitate its smooth operation, I need information indicating whether you wish to become involved and what times are convenient for you.

Please return this questionnaire by _____. Thank you for your help. I'll be looking forward to meeting and working with you.

Sincerely,

_____

Name _____ Phone _____

1. I am able to assist in the classroom on:
   ___ Monday ___ Tuesday ___ Wednesday ___ Thursday ___ Friday.

2. The time that is best for me is
   ___ morning ___ lunchtime ___ afternoon ___ outside of school hours.

3. I am able to volunteer my services: ___ each day,   ___ twice a week,
   ___ once a week,   ___ twice a month,   ___ once a month,
   ___ at some time during the year, or _____.

4. I am unable to volunteer my services but would like to visit the classroom on
   _____ at _____.
          (day)   (time)

The following is a list of suggested areas you might consider as possible ways to volunteer your assistance. Please indicate which activities appeal to you most.
- assist children to follow directions
- share special skills, talents, hobby, or job information
- make learning aids or name tags
- assist students who have been absent
- organize games and activities
- read or tell stories to children
- sew puppets, doll clothes, costumes
- assist with field trips, drive on trips
- wash items from the dramatic play centre
- act as a support person to provide help and to talk with children
- interpret for a parent or guardian who speaks another language
- file children's work
- organize student paperwork for taking home
- collect and record money (tickets, special days, field trips, etc.)
- telephoning reminders
- prepare library cards, check out books
- set up bulletin boards and displays
- inventory supplies and books
- type children's stories
- photograph students
- prepare paint, play dough, etc.
- obtain supplies
- repair toys
- help with outdoor clothing
- food preparation
- clean-up
- babysit for other parents or guardians visiting the classroom
- other (please specify) _____.

Parents/Guardians as Decision-Makers

Parents/guardians make decisions that affect the way children grow and learn. They have made and will continue to make decisions daily that will influence all aspects of the child's development. As the child enters school, many new situations will become part of the child's experience and corresponding decisions will be made with regard to development and learning. Parents/guardians and teachers have the opportunity to assume joint responsibility for decision-making in this regard.

There will be many situations that will warrant parent/guardian–teacher collaboration at the classroom level. Both partners need to confer about individual children and how to best meet their needs. At the school level, parents/guardians have the opportunity to become involved in making decisions that will affect not only their own children but other children as well. For example, parents'/guardians' groups can provide considerable support in deciding what supplementary materials to purchase, what activities to promote, or what long-term goals to set for the school. Many school districts provide parents/guardians with the opportunity to serve on advisory committees or boards. These groups discuss issues and concerns, address policies, develop procedures for implementation, and so on. The key to involving parents/guardians at this level is to be mindful of the fact that sound and effective activity will result when parents/guardians *understand* and *support* the goals and objectives of professional educators.

Meetings with Parents/Guardians

There are many opportunities for parents/guardians and teachers to meet regarding the education of the children in their care. Meetings may be formal or informal. The format and purpose for meetings will differ, depending on the needs of the group and expertise available. The "expert(s)" may be a parent or guardian, the teacher, a special interest group, or a visiting professional. Parents/guardians or teachers may perceive the need to organize meetings that
- address specific objectives and activities (e.g., overview);
- familiarize parents/guardians with school experiences (e.g., "A Day . . .");
- provide information about a specific *aspect* of the curriculum (for example, the teacher may wish to focus on one of the goals);
- provide general information (e.g., guest speakers);
- are intended to be planning get-togethers (e.g., preparing for special events);
- are workshop-oriented (e.g., following initial presentation, parents/guardians "make and take" games to play at home with their children);
- offer a forum for discussion (e.g., talking about a particular educational movie, toys, games, books, or other resources).

As with conferences and interviews, the teacher participates by setting the purpose, contacting individuals, overseeing arrangements, facilitating the meeting, and providing the follow-up when necessary.

Parent/Guardian–Teacher Partnership

Evaluation and Communication

Early, systematic, ongoing evaluation is an integral part of teaching. In order to evaluate effectively, the teacher considers the purposes for evaluation and the goals of the curriculum. As specified in the curriculum guide, evaluation is intended to provide

- a developmental profile for each child;
- a basis for diagnosis;
- a means to assess the effectiveness of teaching and the program;
- information for parents/guardians and other professionals.

The Planning-Teaching-Evaluation Cycle

The teaching-evaluation cycle begins with the child — what is known about the child's background, experiences, and needs. This information, together with the goals for kindergarten, provides the basis for appropriate program planning. As the activities are carried out, the teacher collects and records information about the students' participation and response to the activities. Specific and isolated skills and bits of information are combined to form generalizations and tentative conclusions. This enables the teacher to plan experiences for the children based on the information collected. Once the teacher has had the opportunity to observe the students in the program systematically, it is then possible to provide meaningful information to parents/guardians and other professionals through formal and informal reporting procedures.

THE CHILD

Goals for kindergarten

Planning for teaching

Carrying out plans

Collecting and recording information

Organizing, analysing, and interpreting information

Ongoing program planning

Reporting to parents/guardians

Re-evaluation

Collecting and Recording Data

Knowledge of child development is necessary for planning a curriculum.	Observing children's responses to curriculum helps us learn more about child development.

Sample Questions to Guide Teacher Observation

The questions that follow serve as reminders to investigate the relationship between child development and the curriculum and also provide a framework to guide the teacher's observations. It is important to remember that observation provides a wealth of information to teachers. The questions are designed to reflect the philosophy of the kindergarten program — that the year is one of continuous growth and development in all areas. The list consists of sample questions developed from each of the goal statements. Observations can be used to convey information to parents about their child's response to experiences.

1. *Social Development*
   - How does the child play with others?
   - Is the child able to share and co-operate?
   - Can the child anticipate the consequences of action?

2. *Social Responsibility*
   - Does the child show sensitivity to others?
   - How does the child participate in a group?
   - Can the child make choices and decisions and accept responsibility for his or her own action?
   - Is there evidence to indicate that the child is gaining an awareness of and appreciation for the environment?

3. *Emotional Development and Well-Being*
   - What evidence is there that the child is developing confidence and feelings of self-worth?
   - How does the child "deal with" problems?
   - In what ways does the child express emotions?

4. *Physical Development and Well-Being*
   - Does the child show interest and enjoyment in physical activity and movement?
   - How does the child control physical movements?
   - Does the child show evidence of awareness of nutrition habits and safety procedures, and evidence of respect for his or her body?

5. *Intellectual Development*
   - How does the child indicate the development of his or her ability to link ideas together?
   - Does the child seek answers to satisfy curiosity?
   - What does the child do with materials?
   - Can the child identify, solve, and anticipate problems?

6. *Language Development*
   - Does the child listen for a variety of purposes and use language in a variety of ways?
   - Can the child represent what is known through language?
   - Is the child showing evidence of understanding the processes of reading and writing?
   - Does the child demonstrate emergent reading and writing behavior?

7. *Aesthetic and Artistic Development*
   - Does the child explore and participate in a wide variety of arts experiences (music, drama, art)?
   - What does the child's representation reveal about intellectual development?
   - How long does the child sustain interest?

Methods for Recording Data

The process of learning about children through observation will require a considerable amount of organization at the initial stages. The teacher must first decide how observations are to be recorded and filed. Some teachers find it useful to prepare a notebook with separate sections. Others may find that using index cards is most useful. Having slips of paper at individual centres will allow the teacher to record "on the spot" observations. The paper slips can be color-coded and collected in a storage box at the centre for sorting and analysis later.

It is important to remember that while the task may seem difficult at first, an efficient method for recording and systematic observation will yield a wealth of useful information. There is no substitute for direct observation and recording.

Purposes for Observation

The following list is intended to provide teachers with a variety of purposes for observation. Teachers can observe and record
- which learning centres the child selects;
- the amount of time spent at each centre;
- the child's interests and attitudes;
- who the child interacts with, and the nature of the interactions;
- what emotions are expressed;
- instances of a particular behavior;
- how the child solves problems or makes decisions;
- ways in which the child functions as part of the group;
- verbatim samples of the child's language.

A word of caution is necessary with respect to recording or charting development. While it may be reinforcing for the child who is progressing rapidly to see his or her name on the "These People Can Tie Their Shoes" chart; or to see a long row of stars beside his or her name on a graph, it may have the effect of discouraging the child who needs more time to develop. Private record-keeping is most useful; public announcements are not.

This list provides examples only. Each teacher may set additional *purposes* for observing the children in the class. Recording observations in this way gives the teacher a concise picture of the participation and progress of individual children or the class as a whole.

Sample Recording Forms

Jackie	
September 11	Jackie alternated left/right using scissors, became frustrated, asked Sarah to do the cutting for him.
	Left the construction centre after six minutes to play with blocks.
September 29	Jackie chose left-handed scissors for cutting — created collage at construction centre, — played at construction centre twenty minutes.

Jackie — September — Use of Centres						
Centre	Mon.	Tues.	Wed.	Thurs.	Fri.	No. of times
Dramatic Play						—
Block	III		I	I	I	6
Modelling	I	I				2
Water			I	I	I	3
Construction		II		I	II	5
Music	I	I	III	I		6
Puppet						—
Library						—

This following tally sheet provides information similar to the individual sheet, but for the whole class. Sheets with the children's names and spaces for learning centre titles can be prepared and completed on a weekly basis. The teacher gains information about the use of the centres and the participation of individual children.

	Block	Dramatic Play	Painting	Water	Sand	Construction	Library
Jackie	I	I			I	I	I
Ann		I	I	I		I	I
Beth	I	I	I		I	I	
Sarah		I	I		I	I	I
Bill	I		I	I	I	I	
Vanessa		I	I		I	I	I
Harvey	I	I		I		I	I

Dialogue with Children

As the teacher and the child engage in dialogue, the teacher has an opportunity to note the ways in which a child is able to use language. This can assist the teacher in planning experiences that will help children extend their language development. As the conversation progresses, the teacher enables the child to use language as fully as possible. The teacher's observations of language use constitute an ongoing record of the child's language development.

Collecting Samples of Children's Work

Another way to build a profile of the child's development is to maintain a file of each child's work. At regular intervals (weekly, biweekly, monthly), the teacher collects samples of the child's work and dates and files them. The purpose of this is to collect work samples and add them to the file on a regular basis so that the contents of the file are truly representative of the students' efforts. Work that cannot be kept in a file can be photographed, videotaped, or recorded in descriptive form by the teacher.

Collecting Information from Parents/Guardians

The teacher can collect a great deal of information from parents/guardians through home visits, conferences, questionnaires, and forms. This information, together with teacher observation, anecdotal comments, and samples of children's work serves to help create a more complete picture of the development of individual children.

Organizing, Analysing, and Interpreting Data

Information collected and recorded serves little purpose unless the teacher plans to organize, analyse, and interpret the data. The nature of the evaluation proposed requires that the teacher takes into account all the specific information obtained and seeks to find patterns and to analyse content. This information is formulated into generalizations from which specific examples can be extracted, using recorded data for confirmation. Thus specific observations, generalized and analysed, can be used to produce specific examples. The interpreted data becomes the general statements regarding the child's development and progress as reported to others (educators and parents/guardians). During the interview or conference, the teacher restates the generalization and uses the data to provide specific illustration.

Communication with Others

Indications of growth and development are communicated through interviews, home visits, phone conversations, letters, and reports. These contacts need to be frequent and built on mutual understanding and trust for optimum benefit to the child.

Writing Anecdotal Reports

Reporting is integral to the philosophy expressed for kindergarten.

Kindergarten contributes to the continuing growth of young children's knowledge and understanding of themselves and their world.

When reporting to parents/guardians, the teacher conveys information regarding the child's continuing progress and development. It is important that the anecdotal comments reflect the ongoing nature of growth and development. Teachers should state how the child is doing in relation to the goals for kindergarten. It is important that the teacher prepares accurate, specific, and non-judgemental comments. Reports are also official records. They must be meaningful and useful to those who have access to them.

The process of formal reporting can be threatening to parents/guardians. It may be the first time they have had to view their child through the subjective "eyes" of another. The teacher alleviates fears by objectively stating experiences presented (e.g., how the child responded) and outlining a plan for action. All comments should be stated concisely and be free of educational jargon. By reviewing the "Evaluation" sections in the curriculum guide, the teacher can reflect on the suggestions provided and begin to formulate a procedure for writing anecdotal reports. Samples have been prepared for your reference.

Sample Report Card Comments (November)

_____ has shown an increasing interest in the themes developed. She has particularly benefited from discussions about the calendar, weather, special occasions, weights, and sizes. _____ shows particular interest in stories and poems.

Dictated thoughts as a part of emergent writing have been stressed. _____ speaks quietly in sentences. She has good ideas but needs encouragement to express herself.

Social growth and responsibility have been encouraged. _____ has shown satisfactory development throughout our daily routines. She is now more willing to share in group discussion. _____ is easily distracted and needs assistance in learning to attend and participate actively in discussion to make optimum progress. _____ is more willing to do a good clean-up. She needs reminding to follow through on her responsibilities.

In physical and emotional areas, _____ has made satisfactory progress over the term. _____ has shown particular growth in her development of self-confidence by being a member of the group. She can speak to the whole group with increasing poise. _____ enjoys making and serving snacks.

Artistic and aesthetic development has been fostered through color themes, the beauty centre, picture making, and painting experiences. Crafts and class-made stories have provided group experiences in this area. She particularly enjoys art materials, puzzles, and role-playing activities.

In intellectual and language development, _____ has shown a growing interest in the themes such as plants, colors, and season and has particularly benefited from group discussion about our plants and cuttings, numbers, counting, and seasonal changes.

Dictated thoughts as a part of emergent writing have been stressed. _____ has interesting ideas to express about his cars and roads and our recent trip to the pumpkin patch.

Social growth and responsibility have been encouraged throughout the kindergarten day. _____ has shown satisfactory development through group, shared, and one-to-one activities. He is thoughtful of others at play. He shares his ideas enthusiastically. _____ is showing responsibility for his behavior and his belongings at school.

In physical and emotional areas, _____ has made satisfactory progress over the term. He has particularly developed in self-concept areas, showing increased confidence in speaking to the group and in giving responses to direct questioning.

Artistic and aesthetic development has been fostered through color themes, the beauty centre, picture making, and painting experiences. Crafts and class-made stories have provided group experiences in this area. _____ is making satisfactory progress in this area. He knows his colors and participates in group art activities.

Sample Report Card Comments (March)

_____ is more confident and secure at school now. He is no longer shy. He now bounds into the room full of smiles and immediately starts talking to the others. _____ plays with _____ almost exclusively. I am going to encourage him to play with some of the others as well.

_____ likes building constructions with blocks, Lego, or other materials. He likes to make tall towers and rockets. I have been encouraging him to print or draw pictures of his projects.

_____ needs encouragement to do art projects, make books, and collect key words. He recognizes numbers and letters and can read many words. The activities you and he are sharing at home are really showing in what he can do at school.

_____ is improving in his ability to listen and follow directions. He has progressed in his ability to express himself, and communicate his ideas. He enjoyed telling us about the "Lion Dance" he saw recently.

He is gaining in physical skill, both large muscle and small muscle control, and really enjoys our activities at gym time.

_____ still needs reminders to use equipment appropriately and to keep his activities purposeful and constructive, but generally I am pleased with his progress.

_____'s command of the English language has shown dramatic improvement this term. He is more able to express himself and communicate his ideas both in group discussion and while engaged in activities with his friends.

_____ enjoys dramatic play. He likes to pretend he is a postal worker in our Post Office. He has been busy collecting "key words" (favorite words he wants to learn to read and write), and he knows quite a few. He continues to make the most interesting books. His latest is a Valentine book patterned on the story "Just For You," which he liked very much. He sustained a theme throughout the book (six pages). This is quite an accomplishment for a kindergarten child, particularly in view of the fact that he received no assistance from me.

_____ is learning to take turns and share willingly, and to lead or follow as appropriate in group play. He enjoys playing with many of the children in his group.

Sample Report Card Comments (June)

_____ continued to progress this term. Although he found it tiring, he looked forward to sports day with great anticipation and participated well. He has also enjoyed doing "jazzmatazz" in the gym with the grade fives.

_____ can now choose his activities, see them through, and tidy-up without my assistance. He has begun to show an interest in letters and writing. He makes letter-like forms and signs his name. A few weeks back, he copied his first sentence. This shows that he is now able to clearly discriminate letter forms.

It will be important to read to _____ daily this summer and to provide him with the materials for drawing, cutting, and making things. In addition to the usual favorites, he needs to read ABC books and storybooks that refer to numbers and colors. Don't be afraid to repeat the same books time and time again—this allows children to build their familiarity with numbers, letters, colors, and the conventions of written English in an informal and enjoyable way.

_____ has gained in confidence and become more independent. Although he can become frustrated when tired, he is usually willing to co-operate when playing with others, and he tries to resolve conflicts himself. He can pay attention and contribute to discussions during teacher-directed activities when reminded to do so.

The following will appear on the Permanent Record Card: _____ made satisfactory progress in all aspects of the program and improved his social skills.

_____ continues to progress this term. She has a good understanding of numbers, mathematical concepts, and vocabulary. She now chooses the more difficult books for reading. She is able to express her own ideas in writing, and I have encouraged her to try to spell words she does not know as well as she can, using her own phonetic knowledge. If she is given the opportunity to compare her spellings with ours, (either through her reading; or by showing her how we spell the word, then comparing hers and ours; or by making a dictionary that contains the words she chooses to write), she will gradually self-correct the inaccuracies in her own writing in much the same way that she self-corrects when reading.

_____ enjoys socializing with her friends, and her leadership ability has been showing itself as she organizes others for dramatic play. She excelled on sports day and is very good at doing exercise routines to music. She is an eager and enthusiastic learner, and at the same time is helpful and tolerant of those who don't learn as easily as she does.

The following will appear on _____ permanent record: _____ made excellent progress in language arts and number activities as well as in all other aspects of the program. Her social skills are excellent. She is reading and writing.

Sample Letter to Accompany Report to Parents/Guardians

Many teachers find it useful to prepare a letter to accompany the report card(s). The letter may contain information such as
- goals emphasized in the term;
- expectations for students;
- activities provided.

This allows the teacher to focus on individual students' progress and should eliminate repetitious comments. The following is an example.

School_____

Street_____

Date_____

Dear Parents/Guardians:

This letter has been prepared to accompany your child's first report in order to familiarize you with the goals for the program, our expectations for students, and some of the activities provided. A letter of this kind allows me to comment specifically on the progress of your child in relation to the experiences provided at school.

During the first term, the children have been introduced to the routines of the classroom. They know where to put their belongings and are familiar with procedures for using and cleaning up materials and the activity centres. In addition to small group or individual activities, we have a number of large group sessions throughout the day when the children have music, use the gym, listen and react to stories, and participate in games and other teacher-directed activities. Most children are now able to assemble in the group quickly and with a minimum of disruption. Many recognize the need to listen attentively, to take turns speaking, and to participate within the large group.

When planning experiences for the children, evaluating individual progress, and preparing comments for this report, I have focussed my attention on the following goals for kindergarten:
- providing a variety of experiences that foster the child's social development;
- providing a variety of experiences that foster the child's emotional development and well-being;
- providing a variety of experiences that foster the child's intellectual development.

I have kept the following questions uppermost in my mind.
- How does the child play with others?
- Is the child able to share and co-operate?
- Can the child anticipate the consequences of action?
- What evidence is there that the child is developing confidence and feelings of self-worth?
- How does the child "deal with" problems?
- In what ways does the child express emotions?
- How does the child indicate his or her development of the ability to link ideas together?
- Does the child seek answers to satisfy curiosity?
- What does the child do with materials?
- Can the child identify, solve, and anticipate problems?

The comments in this report card reflect my interpretation of your child's progress based on observations of him or her in many situations. I hope the information provided will be of interest to you. If you have questions, concerns, or information to add, please feel free to discuss these matters.

Sincerely,

"Happygrams"

These letters are short messages sent to parents/guardians to comment positively on a child's behavior, performance, or accomplishments. These notes of encouragement can help to build feeling of positive self-image in the child and to improve communication between parent/guardian and teacher, parent/guardian and child, and teacher and child. The notes should be short and to the point; they should share with the parent/guardian your sense of excitement, and they should focus specifically on the child's progress. The following is an example. (Samples follow.)

September 29

Dear Ms. J.,

Jason has shown great improvement this week in his ability to work with others. He and Sandi played together at the Sand Centre, and he helped Jerry build a Lego spaceship and assisted with clean-up after using centre equipment. Thanks, Jason!

Mrs. M.

October 15

Dear Mr. and Mrs. B.,

Jenny has responded well to encouragement to try new activities. This week she tended the hampster, assisted a new child with school routines, and joined in all the games sessions during physical education lessons. With continued support and encouragement, Jenny can begin to experience successes more frequently. Well done, Jenny!

Mrs. M.

November 10

Dear Mrs. B.,

Alex has shown great fascination in the Exploration Centre this week. As a result of his investigation, he has collected and classified shells, read "The Seashell" book to a number of his friends, and made a booklet about animals that live in shells, complete with intricate illustrations. Good for you, Alex!

Mrs. M.

Interviews and Conferences

Initial contacts with parents/guardians, and professionals will likely include face-to-face discussions. Throughout the school year, there will be opportunities (or the need will arise) to discuss the progress of individual children. The purpose of such meetings is to create the opportunity to exchange information about the child's progress and development and thereby develop a better understanding of the needs of the child.

In preparation for the conference, the teacher
- notifies the people involved and arranges a suitable time and place for the meeting;
- prepares a reference file including observation sheets, checklists, and samples of the child's work;
- outlines the points to be discussed;
- prepares for questions parents/guardians may ask.

In a successful conference or interview, all are made to feel relaxed and to understand that the conference promotes two-way communication—the teacher stands to learn as much about the child from others as the parents/guardians and professionals can learn about the child from the teacher. The teacher will have compiled information in preparation for the conference. The others may have done so, also. It is important for both parties to listen carefully, to ask questions, and to make statements that are objective and honest and are conveyed with sensitivity. At the end of a conference, it is important to summarize the points discussed, set some mutual objectives, and, often, plan to meet again.

After the conference, it is important for the teacher to interpret the discussion and make notes regarding the outcome and follow-up.

General Information Newsletters

In addition to information presented at parent/guardian meetings and that exchanged during interviews and conferences, it is important that teachers make an effort to convey information to parents, guardians, and others through regular newsletters. Keeping people informed of the ongoing aspects of the program or special events in the kindergarten increases the likelihood of common understanding and provides information necessary for planning.

The following sample newsletters provide an expanded statement regarding goals. The letters state goals in general terms and then outline some of the specific experiences provided for the children. The letters are intended to encourage parents/guardians to become involved through discussion and by expanding on the experiences provided at school.

These letters are samples only. There are many other possibilities. Some teachers like to include black and white photographs taken of the children in kindergarten. Others like to include drawings or decoration done by the children. Some may wish to develop a different format or vary the rates of frequency. These are considerations of personal style and preference. What is important to remember is that this kind of information is useful and necessary if meaningful communication is to take place.

Sample Information Newsletter

School _____

Street _____

Date _____

Dear Parents/Guardians:

There are a number of goals for kindergarten. One of the goals is to provide a variety of experiences that foster the child's physical development and well-being. It is known that physical well-being is a factor in effective living and learning. In kindergarten, each child is encouraged to
- take care of and respect his or her body;
- learn and practise safety procedures;
- be aware of and practise good nutrition habits;
- develop physical fitness;
- develop muscle control and co-ordination.

Through daily activities, the kindergarten program addresses the children's need for physical activity and physical education. Children need information and the opportunity to develop personal habits and attitudes required for healthful living.

This month, attention has been focussed on safety in the classroom and school. We have discussed and practised emergency procedures, made picture booklets about playing safely, studied the school grounds to determine the safest place to play, had the crossing guard and a policeman discuss crosswalk and traffic safety with the children, made safety signs for around the school, and read the following books:
- *Dinosaurs Beware! A Safety Guide,* by Marc Brown and Stephen Krensky;
- *The Climb,* by Carrol Carrick;
- *The Bear's Bicycle,* by Emilie Warren McLeod;
- *Try It Again Sam. Safety When You Walk,* by Judith Viorst.

I hope you will take time to discuss this with your child, help to increase his or her awareness of it, and help reinforce the importance of being responsible for personal safety and that of others.

Sincerely,

_____

Visits to the Classroom by Parents/Guardians

Scheduling visits to the classroom provides parents/guardians with the opportunity to observe their child in the company of peers and the classroom setting. This allows them to make more realistic and objective judgements about the child's development, and it can form the basis for more meaningful communication through reports or conferences.

There are some general guidelines that may facilitate these visits.
- Invite parents/guardians and make clear the purpose of the visit.
- Limit the time and the number of parents/guardians who will visit at any one time.
- Make parents/guardians feel welcome and comfortable.
- Ask parents/guardians to observe classroom routines and to
  walk around, speak to children or ask questions while they are engaged in activities;
  remain seated when the teacher is giving directions or instructing students;
  please refrain from talking to fellow visitors since this distracts students;
  make a note of anything they wish to discuss with the teacher.
- Provide time for the visitor(s) to discuss their child(ren)'s progress privately following the observation.

Sample Invitation and Observation Guide for Class Visits

Some teachers find it useful to provide parents/guardians with invitation letters and a guide for observing children. This can provide a focus for discussion later. The following are examples.

School _____

Street _____

Date _____

Dear _____:

You are invited to come to visit our classroom. The purpose of this visit will be to give you an opportunity to observe your child at school.

Attached is a guide for observation. Please bring it with you when you visit. After the children have been dismissed, we can discuss your observations and any questions you may have.

Please send me a note indicating days and times convenient for you.

Thank you,

_____

SAMPLE OBSERVATION GUIDE

1. What kinds of activities was my child involved in? _____
   _____
   _____

2. What kinds of things did I see my child learning? _____
   _____
   _____

3. Who did my child play with? _____
   _____
   _____

4. What signs of sharing, co-operation, or interaction did I notice? _____
   _____
   _____

5. Questions?/Comments _____
   _____
   _____
   _____

Expanded Evaluation

From time to time, it will be necessary to arrange for more extensive evaluation of the development of individual children. Once the teacher has exhausted all personal resources in this regard, it is important that contact, information, and services can be accessed through other professionals.

The methods and procedures for involving other professionals will vary from district to district. At the school level, the learning assistance teacher, special class teacher or resource room teacher may be able to provide valuable suggestions or work with you to test, observe, or gather more information. In some school districts, personnel in the central office have been assigned to provide this kind of support to teachers. In addition, the Special Education Division of the Ministry of Education and independent societies or agencies can provide you with information, materials, names of people to contact, or consultative services.

Refer to the "Children with Special Needs" section of the curriculum guide for a more detailed discussion of the nature of special needs and for suggested procedures for providing suitable experiences for all children. Teachers are encouraged to consider the unique and individual needs of all the children, to include the parents/guardians in all aspects of the child's school experiences, and to request assistance from other professionals.

RESOURCE MATERIALS

Equipment, Materials, and Supplies

In choosing equipment, materials, and supplies, variety is a key concept. Items should meet the needs, interests, and abilities of young children. The selection must take into consideration both the goals of the kindergarten and the funds available for both essential and desirable acoutrements. When making selections, several basic questions can guide the choices.

- Does it comply with C.S.A. and Canadian Consumer Protection Standards?
- Is it suitable and safe for the ages of the children who are to use it?
- Will it stimulate and be of lasting interest to the children?
- Can it be used in a variety of ways?
- Can it be used individually and (or) by several children at the same time?
- Is it the appropriate size?
- Is it durable?
- Can it be kept clean?
- Is the paint or finish non-poisonous and non-flammable?
- Are the edges rounded rather than pointed and sharp?
- Will it significantly aid children in their physical, intellectual, emotional, or social development?
- Will it stimulate curiosity and imagination?
- Will its use bring pleasure and/or satisfaction?

The Canadian Toy Testing Council publishes guidelines for toy selection in both pamphlet form and in Canadian Consumer publications, 100 Gloucester Street, Ottawa, Ontario K2P 0A4.

Outdoors

A good portion of each day at kindergarten is, whenever possible, spent outdoors. This outdoor period offers practice of motor skills, release for feelings and energies, mental challenge in imaginative play, stimuli for the natural flow of language, development of sharing, and other social skills.

The outdoor setting should provide open space for exuberant play and quiet nooks for resting and reflecting. The ideal layout encourages a variety of activities with places for wheeled toys, sand and water play, gardening, climbing experiences, carpentry, dramatic play, and games. The children have the opportunity and space to romp and run vigorously, to ride tricycles, to push and pull wagons, to balance on boards, to climb and swing, to lift and carry, to dig and plant, and to experiment and observe.

The playground should be planned so that it is usuable in all seasons. To this end, it should have both sunny and shady areas, be well drained, and kept free from hazards. Provision of a protected area ensures that the benefits of outdoors can be enjoyed on wet or wintry days. Movable equipment and activity areas may be regrouped from time to time both to meet weather conditions and to stimulate new and imaginative uses. The play area should be located conveniently near the indoor rooms and toilet facilities. Outdoor equipment should be stored in readily accessible areas.

Outdoor Equipment

Information on the types of outdoor equipment available, indications of play and learning experiences encouraged by specific pieces of equipment, and the courtesy and safety rules that should apply to their use can be adapted from Clare Cherry, Barbara Harkness, and Kay Kuzuma, *Nursery School Day Care Centre Management Guide*, (n.p.: Pitman Learning, 1978). pp. 60–62.

Indoors

The kindergarten room should be on the main floor with its own outside entrance so that the children can enter and leave directly and have easy access to their outdoor play area. The room layout should be uncluttered and flexible in usage.

To maintain the flexibility of floor space, furniture should be kept to a minimum, thus leaving as much area as possible for the movement of the whole class and for floor activities. The ideal floor covering is carpet, with provision made for a tiled "wet" area for activities such as painting, clay modelling, and water play. Carpet is as reasonable in cost as other floor coverings and offers the advantage of warmth, comfort, safety, noise abatement, and minimum upkeep.

A sufficient number of cubicles or compartments for storage of children's personal belongings is important. Attached benches for the children to sit on while removing boots or shoes, and recessed hooks for increased safety, are desireable features. Provision of ample tackboards and chalkboards at a convenient height for children is also desirable.

Indoor Equipment, Materials, and Supplies

The following lists represent the compilation of items suggested for use in early childhood education classrooms. The lists are by no means inclusive. Rather, they are intended to provide guidance in the selection of items for kindergartens. Reference to specific needs is also made in the "Learning Centres," "Themes," and "Media Resources in the Classroom" sections of this resource book.

For organizational purposes, items have been classified as "equipment," "materials," and "supplies." In most instances, the use of product names has been avoided to facilitate preferences regarding the choice of products and suppliers.

Equipment, Materials, and
Supplies

Equipment

- built-in storage cupboards
- bulletin boards
- coat racks or hooks
- chalkboard
- wall-mounted, full-length mirror
- moveable storage cupboards
- balance beam
- room divider
- book stand
- puzzle storage case
- chart storage unit
- chart stand
- benches
- teacher's desk and chair
- clock
- filing cabinet
- kindergarten tables and chairs
- cooking facilities
- flannel board
- magnetic board
- painting easels (with trays)
- drying rack for paintings
- sand table
- water table
- puppet theatre
- aquarium and/or terrarium
- pet cage
- workbench

- Child-sized Furniture:
  —stove unit
  —fridge
  —table and chairs
  —dish cupboards
  —chest of drawers
  —doll bed, small crib
- Wheeled Toys
  —wheelbarrow
  —trucks
  —tricycle
  —tractor
  —train set

It is suggested that teachers have access to the following.

- piano
- cassette tape recorder
- listening post and earphones
- record player
- television set
- videotape recorder and player
- movie projector
- filmstrip projector

Equipment, Materials, and Supplies

Materials

- Blocks
  —hollow blocks
  —unit blocks
  —cardboard bricks
  —Froebel blocks (including houses, trees, animals)
  —pattern blocks
  —toy people
  —cars, trucks, playmobile sets, etc.
- Construction Toys
  —Beaufix
  —Connector Set
  —Multifit
  —Lego
  —Canadian Logs
  —Unifix
  —Multilink
  —Tinker Toys
- Exploration
  —magnets
  —individual magnifiers
  —magnifying stool
  —bucket balance and beam balance
  —scale (metric)
  —spring scale
  —thermometer
  —prism
  —kaleidoscope
  —measuring beakers
  —eye droppers
  —globe
  —teaching clock
  —abacus
  —calendar

- Books
  —teacher reference books
  —picture books
  —easy-to-read story books (fiction and non-fiction)
  —big books for shared reading
  —tapes and records of books and stories
- Dramatic Play and Puppets
  —dress-up clothes and costumes
  —clothes rack and hangers
  —props (jewellery, hats, shoes, wigs, glasses)
  —toy telephones
  —ironing board and iron
  —dolls (male and female, caucasian, oriental and black)
  —doll clothes
  —buggy
  —blanket sets
  —toy cooking sets and utensils
  —toy dishes and cutlery
  —house cleaning set
  —toy cash register
  —play money (Canadian coins and bills)
  —shopping cart
  —food models
  —puppets
- Movement Education
  —bean bags
  —skipping ropes
  —utility balls
  —sponge balls
  —hoops
  —plastic bats and balls

Equipment, Materials, and
Supplies

- Manipulative Materials
  —Parquetry blocks and pattern cards
  —colored wooden cubes and pattern cards
  —multivariant wooden beads and pattern cards
  —wooden pegboards and pegs
  —wooden puzzles
  —rubber inset puzzles
  —lacing boards or cards, shoelaces
  —lacing shoe
  —large attribute locks
  —geoboards and colored rubber bands
  —dominoes
  —picture dominoes
  —lotto games
  —bingo games
  —sorting boxes or trays
  —stacking toys
  —tactile letters (upper and lower case) and numerals
  —magnetic letters (upper and lower case) and numerals
  —magnetic shapes
  —flannelboard cutout sets
  —wipe-off cards
  —sequencing cards and puzzles
  —nursery rhyme pictures
  —bulletin board cutouts
  —rubber stamps
  —tracing forms and templates
  —cuisinaire rods
- Sand and Water Play
  —variety of containers and spoons
  —plastic funnels
  —sieve
  —sponges
  —plastic toys
  —plastic aprons
  —scoops
  —strainers
  —corks
  —egg beaters
- Music
  —records and tapes
  —rhythm band instruments (cymbals, drum, bells, maracas, rhythm sticks, castinets, xylophone, sand blocks, tambourine, tom-tom, tone blocks, triangles and beaters, baton)
  —autoharp
- Tools (woodworking and gardening)
  —clamps
  —nails
  —sandpaper
  —wooden dowel rods
  —wood container for wood
  —files
  —hammers
  —saw
  —drill
  —tape measure
  —screw drivers
  —paint brushes
  —tool box or holder
  —pliers
  —shovel
  —rake
  —hoe
  —watering can
  —trowel
  —cultivator
  —pails
- Small Toys
  —train and track set
  —assorted trucks and cars
  —large plastic zoo animals
  —large plastic domestic animals
  —tug boats and barges

Supplies

- General
  - chalkboard brushes and chamois
  - single (conductor's) and three-hole punch
  - scissors (right and left-handed) with rack
  - stapler, staples, and staple remover
  - date stamp and stamp pads
  - paper clips (assorted sizes)
  - tacks or pins
  - masking tape
  - scotch tape and dispenser
  - Bondfast glue
  - rubber cement
  - glue sticks
  - wall paper paste
- Drawing and Painting
  - white or yellow and colored chalk
  - primary pencils
  - felt pens
  - primary crayons (jumbo and regular)
  - pastels
  - powdered tempura paint
  - fingerpaint
  - starch
  - paint brushes (assorted sizes)
- Modelling
  - containers (with lids) for storage
  - Plasticine
  - clay and glazes
  - play dough
  - flour and salt
  - clay boards
  - Plasticine boards

- Arts and Crafts
  - nails, nuts, and bolts
  - popsicle sticks
  - cotton balls
  - Q-tips
  - glitter
  - straws
  - pipe cleaners
  - paper bags
  - doilies
  - parafin wax
  - string and yarn
  - sheets of felt
  - scraps of fabric
- Paper
  - newsprint
  - manilla tag
  - construction paper
  - fingerpainting paper
  - graph paper
  - chart paper
  - butcher paper rolls
  - tissue paper
  - crêpe paper
  - cellophane
  - self-stick colored paper
  - tracing paper
- Clean-up
  - plastic scrub pail
  - sponges
  - plastic pot scrubbers
  - soap and dish
  - liquid detergent
  - bleach
  - cleanser
  - broom, dust pan, and brush
  - first aid kit
  - paper towels

Equipment, Materials, and Supplies

Media Resources in the Classroom

Even very young children can be encouraged to use many kinds of references to gain information, broaden knowledge, and clarify concepts. Non-print materials—that is, picture sets, films, filmstrips, videotapes, audiotapes, and records—can be effective if carefully previewed and evaluated before either purchase or use. Accuracy of material, interpretation of theme, artistic and literary quality of presentation, as well as suitability of age and interest should be considered. There is a wide variety of media resources available for teacher use. Such tools are of particular value because they offer a means of bringing the outside world into the classroom. They also provide children with a common experience that can serve as an important point of reference for subsequent group discussions. Whether showing a filmstrip, film, or videotape, or listening to tapes and records, many teachers have found that following the four steps (outlined below), helps them make successful use of media in the classroom.

Preview the Program

It is important to preview any material you will be presenting to the children. As you watch or listen, make notes of discussion topics, new vocabulary, or questions that occur. Note, also, any points during the program where you might wish to stop for a discussion with the children. If you are using a videotape player or tape recorder, you can make note of and use the counter numbers on the machine to assist you in locating a particular segment.

Previewing enables you to become familiar with the equipment you will be using in the classroom. Sufficient practice beforehand can allow you to concentrate on the children and forget about the machinery while you are presenting the program.

Prepare the Audience

Because the children in the class have different characteristics and fields of experience, they might not respond to a program in the same way, see the same relationships, or come to the same conclusions. In fact, we may not want them to. Teachers may wish to encourage different viewpoints and experiences as a result of a shared viewing. While the intent and the outcomes of the experience may differ, preparation for viewing or listening should include the following steps:
- explaining the purpose to the children;
- discussing the relationship of the media presentation to the current theme;
- providing a brief overview of the content;
- providing students with a bridge to their own lives;
- introducing and explaining unfamiliar vocabulary;
- indicating those aspects of the program to which children should pay particular attention.

Present the Program

As suggested previously, the more familiar you are with the equipment you are using, the better. Before the presentation, position the equipment so that students will see and/or hear well; connect the power; and make sure the program is running smoothly, that the picture and sound quality are adjusted properly, and that the program is cued at the right place. If you are using video, be sure that distracting pictures or noises are not emanating from the T.V. set while you are preparing the audience for viewing.

Suggested Equipment
- record player
- filmstrip projector
- filmstrip viewers
- tape recorder
- tapes
- listening post and earphones
- screen
- sixteen mm movie projector
- slide projector
- television set
- video tape player and recorder

Use and Evaluate the Program

It is imperative for the successful use of media that the children's experiences do not stop after viewing or listening. The children should have an opportunity to respond immediately following the presentation to reinforce what has been learned and to reveal what knowledge has been acquired. Evaluation might initially take the form of teacher-initiated questions and general discussion. For example,

- have the children tell what was happening in the program (initial interpretation);
- have the children tell or list things they noticed (active observation);
- have the children pretend to be various people in the program and to tell what they would be doing or feeling (identifying problems to solve) and what they would be concerned about (identifying decisions to make).

As children discuss the program, their progress and skill development can be observed by noting their ability to

- acquire information through listening and observing;
- organize information;
- evaluate information;
- solve problems;
- make decisions;
- communicate orally;
- participate in group activities.

During subsequent lessons, children should engage in activities that allow each individual to use the information and explore the concepts contained in the program. Giving children an opportunity to respond in a variety of ways (e.g., talking, drawing, painting, modelling, building), will serve to further reinforce and reveal what has been learned.

Records and Tapes

Records and tapes can be used to enrich the music experiences of the children or to add variation to the literature program. If feasible, an area of the room may be furnished with equipment that the children are allowed to operate after training in use and care. Included among the records and tapes should be those for sheer listening enjoyment and those to which the children may wish to respond actively.

The wide range of recorded stories based upon children's literature makes it essential to be selective. The narrator should possess a pleasant, natural voice with clear enunciation and variation in tone; the record should be paced to the understanding and interest span of young children.

Teacher-made tapes can be useful in developing listening and viewing skills. The children, individually or in small groups, may listen to the tapes and follow directions that may include imitating sounds, making a picture, manipulating flannel board materials, or doing simple experiments.

Either the children or the teacher, or both together, may tape-record stories, poems, and songs, including original compositions for play-back and enjoyment.

Picture Sets

Particularly at the beginning of the year, the kindergarten teacher may find large pictures that reflect the children's interests useful for expanding vocabulary and concepts and for fostering verbal communication. There can be a sense of security in relating a discussion to a picture that encourages some children to join in the conversation.

Ordering Videotapes

The P.E.M.C. *video dubbing service* is available to all schools, registered independent schools, regional colleges, and universities in British Columbia. Videotapes are for sale and are not available on loan.

Videotapes must be ordered through a P.E.M.C. liaison person who is appointed by the school district to co-ordinate videotape purchases within the district. Check with your resource centre for the name of your current P.E.M.C. liaison person.

All orders must be submitted through a district P.E.M.C. liaison person on P.E.M.C. videotape order forms.

Ordering Films

The P.E.M.C. film library is open to all public schools, registered independent schools, colleges, and universities in British Columbia.

Films must be ordered through a P.E.M.C. representative—a person appointed by each school to be responsible for the ordering, receiving, and returning of P.E.M.C. films—so that orders from all teachers within the institution can be co-ordinated. To register for borrowing, the principal or head teacher must submit to P.E.M.C. the name of the person who will be responsible; this person will then be supplied with catalogues, requisition forms, and ordering instructions.

Teachers who wish to order films must submit a requisition form through their school P.E.M.C. representative. Teachers are asked to give a preferred date and alternative dates for each film—up to one month before the preferred date, up to one month after, or any time within the two-month period.

`Children's Books: Themes

The following bibliography provides a sample of the available books, organized according to themes.

"Apples"

Barrett, Judith. *An Apple A Day.* New York: Atheneum, 1973.
Bruna, Dick. *The Apple.* New York: Metheuen, 1965.
Greenaway, Kate. *An Apple Pie.* New York: Warne, 1886.
Hogrogian, Nonny. *Apples.* New York: MacMillan, 1972.
Le Seig, Theo. *Ten Apples Up On Top.* New York: Random House, 1961.
Martin, Dick. *The Apple Book.* New York: Golden Press, 1964.
Montgomery, Herbert. *Johnny Appleseed.* Minneapolis: Winston Press, 1979.
Orbach, Ruth. *Apple Pigs.* New York: Putnam, 1981.
Scheer, Julian. *Rain Makes Applesauce.* New York: Holiday House, 1964.
Silverstein, Shel. *The Giving Tree.* New York: Harper and Row, 1964.
Stobbs, William. *A is an Apple Pie.* Bridgeport, Conn.: Merrimack, 1980.
Watson, Clyde. *Apple Bet Story.* New York: Farrar, Strauss and Giroux, 1982.
Watson, Clyde. *Tom Fox and the Apple Pie.* New York: Harper and Row, 1972.
Wellington, Anne. *Apple Pie.* Englewood-Cliffs, N.J.: Prentice-Hall, 1978.

"Bears"

Alexander, Martha. *Blackboard Bear.* New York: Doubleday, 1969 (see also other titles by this author).
Craft, Ruth. *The Winter Bear.* Cleveland, Ohio: Collins, 1974.
Flack, Marjorie. *Ask Mr. Bear.* New York: MacMillan, 1971.
Freeman, Don. *Corduroy.* Harmondsworth: Penguin, 1976.
Galdone, Paul. *The Three Bears.* New York: Scholastic, 1973.
Gretz, Susanna. *Teddy Bear's Moving Day.* New York: Scholastic, 1981.
Guilfoile, Elizabeth. *Nobody Listens to Andrew.* New York: Scholastic, 1957.
Hazen, Barbara. *Where Do Bears Sleep?* Reading, Mass.: Addison-Wesley, 1970.
Krauss, Ruth. *Bears, Bears, Bears.* New York: Scholastic, 1968.
Kuskin, Karla. *The Bear Who Saw Spring.* New York: Harper and Row, 1961.
Lebrun, Claude. *Little Brown Bear Rides a Tricycle.* New York: Barron, Woodland, 1984.
Mack, Stanley. *Ten Bears in My Bed.* New York: Random House, 1974.
Martin, Bill Jr. *Brown Bear Brown Bear, What Do You See?* New York: Holt, Rinehart and Winston, 1970.
McCloskey, Robert. *Blueberries for Sal.* New York: Viking, 1948.
McPhail, David. *The Bear's Toothache.* Boston: Little, Brown, 1972.
Milne, A. A. *Winnie the Pooh.* New York: Dutton, 1926.
Milne, A. A. *The Pooh Story Book.* New York: Dutton, 1965.
Milne, A. A. *The House at Pooh Corner.* New York: Dutton, 1928.
Minarik, Elsie H. *Little Bear.* New York: Harper and Row, 1957.
Minarik, Elsie H. *Father Bear Comes Home.* New York: Harper and Row, 1959.
Minarik, Elsie H. *Little Bear's Friend.* New York: Harper and Row, 1960.
Minarik, Elsie H. *Little Bear's Visit.* New York: Harper and Row, 1961.
Minarik, Elsie H. *A Kiss for Little Bear.* New York: Harper and Row, 1968.
Turkle, Brinton. *Deep in the Forest.* New York: Dutton, 1976.
Waber, Bernard. *Ira Sleeps Over.* Boston: Houghton-Mifflin, 1972.
Ward, Lynn. *The Biggest Bear.* Boston: Houghton-Mifflin, 1952.
Wildsmith, Brian. *The Lazy Bear.* New York: Franklin Watts, 1974.

Children's Books: Themes

"Change"

Beskow, Elsa. *Pelle's New Suit*. New York: Harper and Row, 1929.
Brown, Margaret Wise. *The Runaway Bunny*. New York: Harper and Row, 1972.
Brown, Margaret Wise. *The Dead Bird*. Reading, Mass.: Addison-Wesley, 1958.
Cameron, Polly. *I Can't, Said the Ant*. New York: Putnam, 1961.
Carle, Eric. *The Very Hungry Caterpillar*. New York: Scholastic, 1974.
DePaola, Tomie. *Charlie Needs a Cloak*. Englewood Cliffs, N.J.: Prentice-Hall, 1974.
Hutchins, Pat. *The Wind Blew*. New York: MacMillan, 1974.
Hutchins, Pat. *Changes, Changes*. New York: MacMillan, 1973.
Keats, Ezra Jack. *The Snowy Day*. New York: Viking, 1962.
Krauss, Ruth. *The Carrot Seed*. New York: Harper and Row, 1945.
Lionni, Leo. *Little Blue and Little Yellow*. New York: Astee-Hanor, 1959.
Piatti, Clestino. *Happy Owls*. New York: Atheneum, 1964.
Rice, Eve. *Goodnight, Goodnight*. New York: Greenwillow, 1980.
Sendak, Maurice. *Chicken Soup with Rice: A Book of Months*. New York: Harper and Row, 1962.
Shaw, Charles. *It Looked Like Spilt Milk*. New York: Harper and Row, 1947.
Viorst, Judith. *The Tenth Good Thing About Barney*. New York: Atheneum, 1971.

"Chinese New Year"

Bishop, Claire. *The Five Chinese Brothers*. New York: Putnam, 1938.
Flack, Marjorie. *The Story of Ping*. New York: Viking, 1970.
Handforth, Thomas. *Mei Li*. New York: Doubleday, 1938.
Lattimore, Eleanor. *Little Pear*. New York: Harcourt Brace Jovanovich, 1968.
Moses, Arlene. *Ticki Ticki Tembo*. New York: Holt, Rinehart & Winston, 1968.
Nash, Ogden. *Custard the Dragon*. Boston: Little, Brown, 1961.
Politi, Leo. *Moy, Moy*. New York: Scribner's, 1960.
Weise, Kurt. *Fish in the Air*. New York: Viking, 1948.
Yoshiko, Samuel. *Twelve Years, Twelve Animals*. Nashville: Abingdon, 1972.

"Collections"

Ahlberg, Janet and Ahlberg, Allen. *Each Peach Pear Plum*. New York: Scholastic, 1981.
Ahlberg, Janet and Ahlberg, Allen. *The Baby's Catalogue*. Boston: Little, Brown, 1983.
Barrett, Judith. *Animals Should Definitely Not Wear Clothing*. New York: Atheneum, 1970.
Burmingham, John. *Mr. Gumpy's Outing*. New York: Holt, Rinehart & Winston, 1971.
Carle, Eric. *The Very Hungry Caterpillar*. Cleveland: Collins, 1970.
Emberley, Barbara. *Drummer Hoff*. Englewood Cliffs, N.J.: Prentice-Hall, 1967.
Gag, Wanda. *Millions of Cats?* New York: Coward, McCann & Geoghegan, 1928.
Hoberman, Mary Ann. *A House is a House for Me*. Harmondsworth: Penguin, 1982.
Krauss, Ruth. *A Hole is to Dig*. New York: Harper and Row, 1982.
Mayer, Mercer. *What Do You Do With A Kangaroo?* New York: Ashton Scholastic, 1973.

Quackenbush, R.   *Old MacDonald Had a Farm.* Washington Square: Lippincott, 1972.

Sandberg, Carl.   *The Wedding Procession of The Rag Doll and the Broom Handle and Who Was In It.* New York: Harcourt Brace Jovanovich, 1967.

Shulevitz, Uri.   *One Monday Morning.* New York: Scribner, 1967.

Wildsmith, Brian.   *Brian Wildsmith's Fishes.* New York: Franklin Watts, 1968.

Wildsmith, Brian.   *Birds by Brian Wildsmith.* London: Oxford Univ. Press, 1980.

(See also various alphabet and counting books.)

"Fairy Tales"

For fairy tale books, see "Children's Books: Curriculum Goals" under the heading "Language Development."

"Hoedown"

Barton, Byrom.   *Buzz Buzz Buzz.* New York: MacMillan, 1973.

Brown, Margaret Wise.   *Big Red Barn.* Reading, Mass.: Addison-Wesley, 1956.

Brown, Margaret Wise.   *Once Upon a Time in a Pig Pen.* Reading, Mass.: Addison-Wesley, 1980.

Burningham, John.   *Mr. Gumpy's Outing.* New York: Holt, Rinehart & Winston, 1971.

Duvoisin, R.   *Petunia.* New York: Alfred A. Knopf, 1950.

Einsel, Walter.   *Did You Ever See?* New York: Scholastic, 1962.

Ets, Marie Hall.   *Just Me.* New York: Viking, 1965.

Garelick, May.   *What's Inside?* New York: Scholastic, 1968.

Ginsberg, Mirra.   *The Chick and the Duckling.* New York: MacMillan, 197?

Greene, Carla.   *Cowboys: What Do They Do?* New York: Harper and Row, 1972.

Hutchins, Pat.   *Rosie's Walk.* New York: MacMillan, 1967.

Lobel, Arnold.   *How the Rooster Saved the Day.* New York: Greenwillow, 1977.

Pomerantz, Charlotte.   *Piggy in the Puddle.* New York: MacMillan, 1974.

Preston, Edna Mitchell.   *Popcorn and Ma Goodness.* New York: Viking, 1969.

Provenson, Alice and Provenson, Martin.   *Our Animal Friends at Maple Hill Farm.* New York: Random House, 1974.

Provenson, Alice and Provenson, Martin.   *The Year at Maple Hill Farm.* New York: Atheneum, 1978.

Quackenbush, Robert.   *Old MacDonald Had a Farm.* Washington Square: Lippincott, 1972.

Rojankovsky, Feodor.   *Animals on the Farm.* New York: Alfred A. Knopf, 1967.

Rojankovsky, Feodor.   *The Great Big Animal Book.* New York: Golden Press, 1976.

Steig, William.   *Farmer Palmer's Wagon Ride.* Harmondsworth: Penguin, 1978.

Tresselt, Alvin.   *Wake Up Farm.* New York: Lothrop, Lee & Shephard, 1955.

Williams, Garth.   *The Chicken Book.* New York: Delacorte Press, 1970.

"Machines"

Brown, Margaret Wise.   *The Steamroller.* New York: Walker, 1972.

Burningham, John.   *Mr. Gumpy's Motor Car.* New York: Thomas Y. Crowell, 1973.

Burton, Virginia Lee.   *Mike Mulligan and his Steam Shovel.* Boston: Houghton-Mifflin, 1939.

Burton, Virginia Lee. *Katy and the Big Snow*. Boston: Houghton-Mifflin, 1974.

Crews, Donald. *Truck*. New York: Greenwillow, 1980.

Crews, Donald. *Freight Train*. New York: Greenwillow, 1978.

Gergely, Tibor. *Tootle*. New York: Golden Press, 1974.

Gramatky, Hardie. *Little Toot*. New York: Putnam, 1939.

Hoban, Tana. *Dig, Drill, Dump, Fill*. New York: Greenwillow, 1975.

Hoban, Tana. *Over, Under and Through*. New York: MacMillan, 1973.

Hutchins, Pat. *Clocks and More Clocks*. New York: MacMillan, 1970.

Hutchins, Pat. *The Wind Blew*. New York: MacMillan, 1974.

Kaufman, Joe. *What Makes It Go, Work, Fly, Float*. New York: Golden Press, 1971.

Keats, Ezra Jack. *Skates*. New York: Franklin Watts, 1973.

McNaught, Harry. *The Truck Book*. New York: Random House, 1978.

Petersham, Maud and Petersham, Miska. *The Box with Red Wheels*. New York: MacMillan, 1973.

Piper, Watty. *The Little Engine That Could*. New York: Platt and Munk, 1930.

Rey, H. A. *Curious George Rides a Bike*. Boston: Houghton-Mifflin, 1973.

Rockwell, Anne F. *The Tool Box*. New York: MacMillan, 1971.

Rockwell, Anne F. and Rockwell, Harlow. *Machines*. New York: MacMillan, 1972.

Scarry, Richard. *Going Places*. New York: Golden Press, 1961 (see also other titles by this author).

Spier, Peter. *Crash Bang Boom*. New York: Doubleday, 1972.

Steig, William. *Farmer Palmer's Wagon Ride*. Harmondsworth: Penguin, 1978.

Swift, Hildegard. *The Little Red Light House* and *The Great Grey Bridge*. New York: Harcourt, Brace, Jovanovich, 1942.

Young, Miriam. *If I Drove a Car*. New York: Lothrop, Lee & Shephard, 1971 (see also other titles in the *If I Had a . . .* series).

"Me"

Brown, Margaret Wise. *The Runaway Bunny*. New York: Harper and Row, 1977.

Buckley, Helen E. *Grandfather and I*. New York: Lothrop, Lee & Shephard, 1959.

Buckley, Helen E. *Grandmother and I*. New York: Lothrop, Lee & Shephard, 1961.

Cohen, M. *Will I Have a Friend?* New York: MacMillan, 1967.

DePaola, Tomie. *Watch Out for the Chicken Feet in Your Soup*. Englewood Cliffs, N.J.: Prentice-Hall, 1974.

Ets, M. *Play With Me*. New York: Viking Press, 1955.

Guilfoile, E. *Nobody Listens to Andrew*. New York: Scholastic, 1973.

Hann, J. *Up Day, Down Day*. New York: Four Winds, 1978.

Hoban, Russell. *A Birthday for Frances*. New York: Harper and Row, 1968.

Hoban, Russell. *A Baby Sister for Frances*. New York: Harper and Row, 1964.

Hoban, Russell. *A Bargain for Frances*. New York: Harper and Row, 1970.

Hoban, Russell. *Bedtime for Frances*. New York: Harper and Row, 1960.

Hoban, Russell. *Bread and Jam for Frances*. New York: Harper and Row, 1964.

Kellogg, Steven. *Won't Somebody Play With Me?* New York: Dial Press, 1979.

Kraus, Robert. *Whose Mouse Are You?* New York: MacMillan, 1970.

Lexaw, Joan. *Me Day*. New York: Dial Press, 1971.

Mayer, Mercer. *Just for You*. New York: Golden Press, 1975.

Mayer, Mercer. *There's a Nightmare in My Closet*. New York: Dial Press, 1968.

Preston, Edna. *The Temper Tantrum Book*. Harmondsworth: Penguin, 1976.

Udry, Janice May. *Let's Be Enemies*. New York: Harper and Row, 1961.

Children's Books: Themes

Viorst, Judith. *Alexander and the Terrible, Horrible, No Good Very Bad Day*. New York: Atheneum, 1972.

Viorst, Judith. *Rosie and Michael*. New York: Atheneum, 1978.

Zolotow, Charlotte. *William's Doll*. New York: Harper and Row, 1972.

Zolotow, Charlotte. *My Grandson Lew*. New York: Harper and Row, 1974.

"Space"

Brown, Margaret Wise. *Goodnight Moon*. New York: Harper and Row, 1947.

Brown, W. W. *Wait Til the Moon Is Full*. New York: Harper and Row, 1948.

Freeman, Don. *Space Witch*. New York: Viking, 1949.

Freeman, Mae B. and Freeman, Ira. *You Will Go to the Moon*. New York: Random House, 1971.

Goudey, Alice. *The Day We Saw the Sun Come Up*. New York: Scribner's, 1961.

Keats, Ezra Jack. *Regards to the Man in the Moon*. New York: Scholastic, 1981.

Kotzwinkle, William. *E.T.* New York: Putnam, 1982.

Kraus, Robert. *See the Moon*. New York: Simon and Schuster, 1980.

Kuskin, Karla S. *A Space Story*. New York: Harper and Row, 1978.

Longden, Peter. *The Planet of the Elves*. Longburough, England: Wills and Hepworth, 1982.

Pienkowski, Jan. *Robot*. New York: Delacourt, 1981.

Ravielli, Anthony. *The World Is Round*. New York: Viking, 1963.

Rey, H. A. *Curious George Gets a Medal*. New York: Houghton-Mifflin, 1957.

Schulz, Charles. *Charlie Brown's 'Cyclopedia Space Travel*. New York: Funk & Wagnalls, 1980.

Shulevitz, Uri. *Dawn*. New York: Farrar, Strauss & Giroux, 1974.

Sonneborn, Ruth E. *Someone Is Eating the Sun*. New York: Random House, 1974.

Ungerer, Tomi. *Moon Man*. New York: Harper and Row, 1967.

Watson, Clyde. *Midnight Moon*. Cleveland: Collins, 1979.

Wildsmith, Brian. *What the Moon Saw*. London: Oxford Univ. Press, 1978.

Zaffo, George. *The Giant Book of Things In Space*. New York: Doubleday, 1969.

"Whales"

Ashlee, Ted. *Skana*. New York: Holt, Rinehart & Winston, 1971.

Duvoisin, Roger. *The Christmas Whale*. New York: Alfred A. Knopf, 1945.

Hurd, E. T. *The Mother Whale*. New York: Little, Brown, 1973.

McGovern, Ann. *Little Whale*. Bristol, Fl.: Four Winds, 1979.

Phleger, Fred. *The Whales Go By*. New York: Random House, 1959.

Pluckrose, Henry, ed. *Whales*. New York: Gloucester Press, 1979.

Steig, William. *Amos and Boris*. New York: Farrar, Strauss and Giroux, 1978.

Stevenson, John. *Whale Tale*. New York: Random House, 1981.

Vaughan, Jennifer. *Whales*. London: Macdonald Educational, 1974.

"Unique"

Adolf, Arnold. *Black Is Brown Is Tan*. New York: Harper and Row, 1973.

Alexander, Martha. *Nobody Asked Me If I Wanted A Baby Sister*. New York: Dial Press, 1971.

Bales, Lucy. *Little Rabbit's Loose Tooth*. New York, Crown, 1975.

Domanska, Janina. *What Do You See?* New York: MacMillan, 1974.

Eastman, P. D. *Are You My Mother?* trans. Jean Vallier. New York: Random House, 1967.

Freeman, Don. *Mop Top*. New York: Viking, 1955.

Freeman, Lydia and Freeman, Don. *Dandelion*. New York: Viking, 1964.

Hoff, Syd. *Lengthy*. New York: Putnam, 1979.

Hutchins, Pat. *Titch*. New York: MacMillan, 1971.

Keats, Ezra Jack. *A Letter to Amy*. New York: Harper and Row, 1968.

Keats, Ezra Jack. *Peter's Chair*. New York: Harper and Row, 1967.

Keats, Ezra Jack. *Whistle for Willie*. Harmondsworth: Penguin, 1977.

Kellogg, Steven. *Much Bigger Than Martin*. New York: Dial Press, 1976.

Kraus, Robert. *Leo the Late Bloomer*. New York: Windmill, 1971.

Kraus, Robert. *Milton the Early Riser*. New York: Windmill, 1972.

Kraus, Robert. *Owliver*. New York: Harper and Row, 1960.

Marshall, James. *George and Martha*. Boston: Houghton-Mifflin, 1972.

Peppe, Rodney. *Odd One Out*. New York: Viking, 1974.

Petuson, Jeanne W. *I Have a Sister, My Sister Is Deaf*. New York: Harper and Row, 1977.

Scott, Ann Herbert. *On Mother's Lap*. New York: McGraw-Hill, 1972.

Sendak, Maurice. *Pierre*. New York: Harper and Row, 1962.

Stein, Sarah, B. *About Handicaps*. New York: Walker's, 1974.

Ungerer, Tomi. *Crictor*. New York: Harper and Row, 1958.

Waber, Bernard. *Lyle, Lyle Crocodile*. Boston: Houghton-Mifflin, 1965.

Waber, Bernard. *Mice On My Mind*. Boston: Houghton-Mifflin, 1977.

Waxman, Marion. *What Is a Girl, What Is a Boy?* Culver City, Ca.: Peace Press, 1976.

Yashima, Taro. *Crow Boy*. Harmondsworth: Penguin, 1976.

Zolotow, Charlotte. *A Father Like That*. New York: Harper and Row, 1971.

Zolotow, Charlotte. *William's Doll*. New York: Harper and Row, 1972.

Children's Books: Curriculum Goals

The following bibliography provides a sample of the available books, organized according to goals.

Emotional Development, Social Development, and the Development of Social Responsibility

Alexander, Martha. *I'll Protect You from the Jungle Beasts*. New York: Dial Press, 1973.

Ancona, George. *I Feel: A Picture Book of Emotions*. New York: Dutton, 1977.

Barrett, Judi. *Peter's Pocket*. New York: Atheneum, 1974.

Birmingham, John. *Would You Rather . . .* New York: Harper and Row, 1978.

Borack, Barbara. *Grandpa*. New York: Harper and Row, 1967.

Brown, Margaret Wise. *The Runaway Bunny*. New York: Harper and Row, 1977.

Burningham, John. *Mr. Gumpy's Outing*. New York: Holt, Rinehart & Winston, 1971.

Carle, Eric. *Do You Want to Be My Friend?* New York: Harper and Row, 1971.

Clure, Beth and Rumsey, Helen. *Through the Day*. Glendale, Ca., Bowmar Publishing, 1968.

Clure, Beth and Rumsey, Helen. *Me!* Glendale Ca., Bowmar Publishing, 1968.

Cohen, M. *Will I Have a Friend*. New York: MacMillan, 1971.

De Paola, Tomie. *Nana Upstairs, Nana Downstairs*. New York: Putnam, 1973.

De Paola, Tomie. *The Quick Sand Book*. New York: Holiday House, 1977.

De Regniers, Beatrice S. *Little House of Your Own*. New York: Harcourt Brace Jovanovich, 1955.

De Regniers, Beatrices. *May I Bring a a Friend?* New York: Atheneum, 1964.

Eastman, P. D. *Are You My Mother?* New York: Random House, 1960.

Fassler, Joan. *The Boy With a Problem*. New York: Behavioral Publications, 1971.

Emberley, Ed. *A Birthday Wish*. Boston: Little, Brown, 1977.

Ets, Marie Hall. *Play With Me*. New York: Viking, 1955.

Fassler, Joan. *Don't Worry Dear*. New York: Behavioral Publications, 1971.

Flack, M. *Ask Mr. Bear*. New York: MacMillan, 1966.

Flack, Marjorie. *Angus Lost*. New York: Doubleday, 1941.

Flack, Marjorie. *Wait for William*. Boston: Houghton-Mifflin, 1935.

Freeman, Don. *Mop Top*. New York: Viking, 1955.

Fritz, Jean. *Growing Up*. Eau Claire, Wis.: E. M. Hale, 1956.

Grollman, Earl. *Talking About Death*. Boston: Beacon Press, 1970.

Hoban, Russell. *A Birthday for Frances*. New York: Harper and Row, 1968.

Hutchins, Pat. *Happy Birthday, Son*. New York: Greenwillow, 1978.

Hutchins, Pat. *Titch*. New York: MacMillan, 1971.

Keats, Ezra Jack. *The Snowy Day*. New York: Viking, 1962.

Keats, Ezra Jack. *Peter's Chair*. New York: Harper and Row, 1967.

Kraus, Robert. *Owliver*. New York: Windmill, 1974.

Krauss, Ruth. *A Very Special House*. New York: Harper and Row, 1953.

Lasker, Joe. *He's My Brother*. Chicago: Albert Whitman, 1974.

Lobel, Arnold. *Frog and Toad Are Friends*. New York: Harper and Row, 1970.

Pomerantz, Charlotte. *The Piggy in the Puddle*. New York: MacMillan, 1974.

Schick, Eleanor. *Peggy's New Brother*. New York: MacMillan, 1970.

Scott, Ann Herbert. *On Mother's Lap*. New York: Harper and Row, 1972.

Scheer, Julian. *Rain Makes Applesauce*. New York: Holiday House, 1964.

Segal, Lore. *Tell Me a Mitzi*. New York: Scholastic, 1978.

Sendak, Maurice. *In the Night Kitchen*. New York: Harper and Row, 1962.

Sendak, Maurice. *The Nutshell Library*. New York: Harper and Row, 1970.

Showers, Paul. *The Book of Scary Things*. New York: Doubleday, 1977.

Simon, Norma. *What Do I Do?* Chicago: Albert Whitman, 1969.
Sonneborn, Ruth. *I Love Gram.* New York: Viking, 1971.
Tove, William. *The Loon's Necklace.* London: Oxford Univ. Press, 1977.
Turkle, Brinton. *Deep in the Forest.* New York: Dutton, 1976.
Viorst, Judith. *Alexander and the Terrible, Horrible, No Good Very Bad Day.* New York: Atheneum, 1972.
Weber, Bernard. *Ira Sleeps Over.* Boston: Houghton-Mifflin, 1975.
Welber, Robert. *The Winter Picnic.* New York: Random House, 1970.
Wolff, Robert Jay. *Feeling Blue.* New York: Scribner's, 1968.
Zion, Gene. *Hide and Seek Day.* New York: Harper and Row, 1954.
Zola, Meguido. *Only the Best.* New York: Julia MacRae, 1981.
Zolotow, Charlotte. *A Father Like That.* New York: Harper and Row, 1971.
Zolotow, Charlotte. *My Grandson Lew.* New York: Harper and Row, 1974.

Physical Development and Well-Being

Carle, Eric. *The Very Hungry Caterpillar.* Cleveland: Collins, 1970.
Krauss, Ruth. *Carrot Seed.* New York: Harper and Row, 1945.
Krauss, Ruth. *The Growing Seed.* New York: Harper and Row, 1947.
McCloskey, Robert. *Blueberries for Sal.* New York: Viking, 1948.
Selsam, Millicent. *Seeds and More Seeds.* New York: Harper and Row, 1959.
Shaw, Charles, G. *It Looked Like Spilt Milk.* New York: Harper and Row, 1947.

Aesthetic and Artistic Development

Aliki. *My Five Senses.* New York: Thomas Y. Crowell, 1962.
Blue, Rose. *I Am Here, Yo Estoy Aqui.* New York: Franklin Watts, 1971.
Borten, Helen. *Do You Hear What I Hear?* New York: Abelard-Schuman, 1960.
Brown, Margaret Wise. *The Country Noisy Book.* New York: Harper and Row, 1942.
Brown, Margaret Wise. *The Indoor Noisy Book.* New York: Harper and Row, 1943.
Brown, Margaret Wise. *The Quiet Noisy Book.* New York: Harper and Row, 1950.
Brown, Margaret Wise. *The Seashore Noisy Book.* New York: Harper and Row, 1941.
Brown, Margaret Wise. *The Summer Noisy Book.* New York: Harper and Row, 1940.
Brown, Margaret Wise. *The Winter Noisy Book.* New York: Harper and Row, 1947.
Buckley, Helen. *Grandfather and I.* New York: Lothrop, Lee & Shephard, 1959.
Flack, Marjorie. *Ask Mr. Bear.* New York: MacMillan, 1971.
Freeman, Don. *Mop Top.* New York: Viking, 1955.
Hoban, Tana. *Look Again!* New York: MacMillan, 1971.
Johnson, Crocket. *Harold and the Purple Crayon.* New York: Harper and Row, 1955.
Keats, Ezra Jack. *Peter's Chair.* New York: Harper and Row, 1967.
Lionni, Leo. *Little Blue and Little Yellow.* New York: Pantheon Books, 1969.
Miles, Miska. *Apricot ABC.* Boston: Little, Brown, 1969.
Polland, Barbara Kay. *The Sensible Book: A Celebration of Your Five Senses.* Millbrae, Ca.: Celestial Arts Publishing, 1974.
Showers, Paul. *Find Out by Touching.* New York: Thomas Y. Crowell, 1961.

Showers, Paul. *Your Skin and Mine.* New York: Thomas Y. Crowell, 1965.

Showers, Paul. *Follow Your Nose.* New York: Thomas Y. Crowell, 1963.

Slobodkina, Esphyr. *Caps for Sale.* Reading, Mass.: Addison-Wesley, 1947.

Tudor, Tasha. *First Delights: A Book About the Five Senses.* New York: Platt & Munk, 1966.

Language Development

Aesop. *The Caldecott Aesop.* New York: Doubleday, 1978.

Aesop. *The Hare and the Tortoise.* New York: McGraw-Hill, 1962.

Alexander, Martha. *Maybe a Monster.* New York: Dial Press, 1968.

Ardizzone, Edward. *Little Tim and the Brave Sea Captain.* Harmondsworth: Penguin, 1983.

Aruego, Jose. *Look What I Can Do.* New York: Scribner's, 1971.

Bailey, Carolyn. *The Little Rabbit Who Wanted Red Wings.* New York: Platt & Munk, 1978.

Barrett, Judith. *Animals Should Definitely Not Wear Clothing.* New York: Atheneum, 1970.

Baum, Arline and Baum, Joseph. *One Bright Monday Morning.* New York: Random House, 1962.

Bishop, Claire. *The Five Chinese Brothers.* New York: Putnam, 1938.

Briggs, Raymond. *Jim and the Beanstalk.* New York: Putnam, 1980.

Bright, Robert. *Georgie.* New York: Doubleday, 1959.

Brown, Marcia. *The Three Billy Goats Gruff.* New York: Harcourt Brace Jovanovich, 1957.

Brown, Marcia. *Once a Mouse.* New York: Scribner's, 1962.

Brown, Margaret Wise. *The Important Book.* New York: Harper and Row, 1949.

Brown, Margaret Wise. *Goodnight Moon.* New York: Harper and Row, 1947.

Brown, Margaret Wise. *The Runaway Bunny.* New York: Harper and Row, 1972.

Brunhoff, Jean de. *The Story of Babar.* New York: Random House, 1937.

Buckley, Helen. *Grandfather and I.* New York: Lothrop, Lee & Shephard, 1959.

Burningham, John. *Mr. Gumpy's Motor Car.* New York: Harper and Row, 1976.

Burningham, John. *Mr. Gumpy's Outing.* New York: Harper and Row, 1971.

Byars, Betsy. *Go and Hush the Baby.* New York: Viking Press, 1971.

Cameron, Polly. *I Can't Said the Ant.* New York: Scholastic, 1961.

Carle, Eric. *The Very Hungry Caterpillar.* Cleveland: Collins, 1970.

Chaucer, Geoffrey. *Chanticleer and the Fox.* New York: Thomas Y. Crowell, 1958.

Daugherty, James. *Andy and the Lion.* New York: Viking, 1938.

De Paola, Tomie. *Strega Nona.* Englewood Cliffs, N.J.: Prentice-Hall, 1975.

De Regniers, Beatrice S. *May I Bring a Friend?* New York: Atheneum, 1964.

Duvoisin, Roger. *Petunia.* New York: Alfred A. Knopf, 1950.

Ehrlich, Amy. *Thumbelina.* New York: Dial Press, 1979.

Einsel, Walter. *Did You Ever See?* New York: Scholastic, 1969.

Emberley, Barbara. *Drummer Hoff.* Englewood Cliffs, N.J.: Prentice-Hall, 1967.

Ets, Marie Hall. *In the Forest.* Harmondsworth: Penguin, 1976.

Ets, Marie Hall. *Play With Me.* Harmondsworth: Penguin, 1976.

Ets, Marie Hall. *Just Me.* Harmondsworth: Penguin, 1978.

Ets, Marie Hall. *Gilberto and the Wind.* New York: Viking, 1963.

Flack, Marjorie. *Angus Lost.* New York: Doubleday, 1932.

Flack, Marjorie. *Angus and the Ducks.* New York: Doubleday, 1930.

Frasconi, Antonio *The House that Jack Built: A Picture Book in Two Languages.* New York: Harcourt Brace Jovanovich, 1958.

Galdone, Paul. *The Gingerbread Boy.* New York: Seabury Press, 1975.

Galdone, Paul. *Henny Penny.* New York: Seabury Press, 1968.

Galdone, Paul. *The History of Mother Twaddle and the Marvelous Achievements of Her Son Jack.* New York: Seabury Press, 1974.

Galdone, Paul. *The History of Simple Simon.* New York: McGraw-Hill, 1966.

Galdone, Paul. *House that Jack Built.* New York: McGraw-Hill, 1961.

Galdone, Paul. *The Little Red Hen.* New York: Seabury Press, 1973.

Galdone, Paul. *The Old Woman and Her Pig.* New York: McGraw-Hill, 1960.

Galdone, Paul. *The Three Bears.* New York: Seabury Press, 1972.

Galdone, Paul. *The Three Little Pigs.* New York: Seabury Press, 1970.

Ginsberg, Mirra. *The Chick and the Duckling.* New York: MacMillan, 1972.

Ginsberg, Mirra. *Mushroom in the Rain.* New York: MacMillan, 1974.

Gramatky, Hardie. *Little Toot.* New York: Putnam, 1939.

Hall, Donald. *Ox-Cart Man.* New York: Viking, 1979.

Hann, Jacquie. *Up Day, Down Day.* New York: Four Winds, 1978.

Hoban, Russell. *Bread and Jam for Frances.* New York: Harper and Row, 1964.

Hoberman, Mary Ann. *A House Is a House for Me.* New York: Viking, 1978.

Hogrogian, Nonny. *One Fine Day.* New York: MacMillan, 1971.

Iwasaki, Chihiro. *Brother for Momoko.* London: Bodley-Head, 1970.

Jacobs, Joseph. *Tom Tit Tot.* New York: Scribner's, 1965.

Jacobs, Leland. *Good Night, Mr. Beetle.* New York: Holt, Rinehart & Winston, 1963.

Joslin, Sesyle. *What Do You Say, Dear?* New York: Scholastic, 1958.

Kalan, Robert. *Rain.* New York: Greenwillow, 1978.

Keats, Ezra Jack. *Over in the Meadow.* New York: Four Winds, 1971.

Keats, Ezra Jack. *The Snowy Day.* New York: Viking, 1962.

Keats, Ezra Jack. *Goggles.* New York: MacMillan, 1969.

Keats, Ezra Jack. *Hi, Cat.* New York: MacMillan, 1970.

Keats, Ezra Jack. *Peter's Chair.* New York: Harper and Row, 1967.

Kellogg, Steven. *Pinkerton, Behave.* New York: Dial Press, 1979.

Kellogg, Steven. *Can I Keep Him?* New York: Dial Press, 1971.

Kellogg, Steven. *Won't Somebody Play with Me?* New York: Dial Press, 1972.

Kikaku, Issa and Kikaku, Baslio. *Don't Tell the Scarecrow.* New York: Scholastic, 1969.

Kraus, Robert. *Whose Mouse Are You?* New York: MacMillan, 1970.

Krauss, Ruth. *Bears.* New York: Scholastic, 1968.

Lee, Dennis. *Alligator Pie.* New York: MacMillan, 1974.

Lobel, Anita. *King Rooster, Queen Hen.* New York: Greenwillow, 1975.

Martin, Bill Jr. *Brown Bear.* New York: Holt, Rinehart & Winston, 1970.

Mayer, Mercer. *Just for You.* New York: Golden Press, 1975.

Mayer, Mercer. *There's a Nightmare in My Closet.* New York: Dial Press, 1968.

Merriam, Eve. *Do You Want to See Something?* New York: Scholastic, 1965.

Paterson, Diane. *If I Were a Toad.* New York: Dial Press, 1977.

Perrault, Charles. *Cinderella.* trans. David Walser. New York: Thomas Y. Crowell, 1978.

Petersham, Maud and Petersham, Miska. *The Box with Red Wheels.* New York: MacMillan, 1973.

Pomerantz, Charlotte. *The Piggy in the Puddle.* New York: MacMillan, 1974.

Preston, Edna. *The Temper Tantrum Book.* Harmondsworth: Penguin, 1976.

Raskin, Ellen. *Nothing Ever Happens On My Block.* New York: Scholastic, 1966.

Rockwell, Anne. *The Old Woman and Her Pig and Ten Other Stories.* New York: Thomas Y. Crowell, 1979.

Rockwell, Anne. *The Three Bears and Fifteen Other Stories.* New York: Thomas Y. Crowell, 1975.

*Children's Books:
Curriculum Goals*

Scheer, Julian. *Rain Makes Applesauce*. New York: Holiday House, 1964.

Sendak, Maurice. *Chicken Soup with Rice*. New York: Scholastic, 1962.

Sendak, Maurice. *Seven Little Monsters*. New York: Harper and Row, 1975.

Sendak, Maurice. *Where the Wild Things Are*. Harmondsworth: Penguin, 1970.

Slobodkina, Esphyr. *Caps for Sale*. New York: Scholastic, 1947.

Spier, Peter. *Noah's Ark*. New York: Doubleday, 1977.

Stevenson, James. *Could Be Worse*. Harmondsworth: Penguin, 1977.

Sullivan, Joan. *Round Is a Pancake*. New York: Holt, Rinehart & Winston, n.d.

Viorst, Judith. *My Mama Says*. New York: Atheneum, 1974.

Viorst, Judith. *Rosie and Michael*. New York: Atheneum, 1974.

Viorst, Judith. *The Tenth Good Thing About Barney*. New York: Atheneum, 1971.

Waber, Bernard. *Lyle, Lyle, Crocodile*. Boston: Houghton-Mifflin, 1965.

Wildsmith, Brian. *The Lazy Bear*. New York: Franklin Watts, 1974.

Wildsmith, Brian. *The Hare and the Tortoise*. London: Oxford Univ. Press, 1966.

Wright, H. R. *A Maker of Boxes*. New York: Holt, Rinehart & Winston, n.d.

Zemach, Harve and Zemach, Margot. *The Judge*. New York: Farrar, Strauss & Giroux, 1967.

Zolotow, Charlotte. *Mr. Rabbit and the Lovely Present*. New York: Harper and Row, 1962.

Zolotow, Charlotte. *Someday*. New York: Harper and Row, 1965.

Zolotow, Charlotte. *Do You Know What I'll Do?* New York: Harper and Row, 1958.

The following big books are also useful for language development.

- The following big books are available from Class Size Books Ltd., Box 366, Port Coquitlam, B.C., V3C 1Y6. The pages are provided, and children color and bind them.

  Five Little Frogs
  Five Little Pumpkins
  Must Be Santa
  Nuttin' for Christmas
  I Know an Old Lady
  Hush Little Baby
  Sing a Song of Sixpence
  Skip to My Lou
  Down by the Bay
  One Elephant, Two Elephants
  The Little Red Hen
  The Little Red Hen Song
  Comin' Round the Mountain

- The following are available in Scholastic Book's Read it Again series, 1983. A large book, a set of small books, and a tape for use in the listening centre are provided.

  Billy Ballroom
  Neat and Scruffy
  Trouble in the Ark
  What Do You Do?
  The Thing From Somewhere
  Hubert Hunts His Hum
  Grant the Ant
  Lester & Clyde
  What Do You Do with a Kangaroo?

*Children's Books:
Curriculum Goals*

There Are Trolls
I Know an Old Lady
Just in Time for the King's Birthday
The Magic Fish
The Adventures of the Three Blind Mice
The Gingerbread Man
The Three Billy Goats Gruff

- The following Bill Martin Jr. big books come with small books and tapes and are available in sets from Holt, Rinehart & Winston.

  SET A
  Brown Bear, Brown Bear, What do You See?
  The Longest Journey in the World
  Fire! Fire! Said Mrs. McGuin

  SET B
  Monday, Monday, I Like Monday
  How to Catch a Ghost
  The Happy Hippopotami

- The following big books are available separately from Ginn and Co. (The Story Box, 1983). Also included in the storybook are many small books of excellent quality.

  Hairy Bear
  The Hungry Giant
  Smarty Pants
  Lazy Mary
  Mrs. Wishy-Washy
  Sing a Song
  Yes Ma'am
  Granpa Granpa
  The Red Rose
  Will You Be My Mother
  Meanies
  The Monster's Party
  The Farm Concert
  To Town
  The Jigaree
  Dan the Flying Man

Intellectual Development

Logical Knowledge

De Regniers, Beatrice S. and Gordon, Isabel. *The Shadow Book.* New York: Harcourt Brace Jovanovich, 1962.
Fisher, Aileen. *In the Middle of the Night.* New York: Thomas Y. Crowell, 1965.
Françoise. *What Time Is It Jeanne-Marie.* New York: Scribner's, 1973.
Goudey, Alice E. *The Day We Saw the Sun Come Up.* New York: Scribner's, 1961.
Hoban, Russell. *A Birthday for Frances.* New York: Harper and Row, 1968.
Hutchins, Pat. *Clocks and More Clocks.* New York: MacMillan, 1970.
Hutchins, Pat. *Changes, Changes.* New York: MacMillan, 1971.
Kessler, Ethel. *Are You Square?* New York: Doubleday, 1969.

Schlein, Miriam. *Fast Is Not a Ladybug*. Reading, Mass.: Addison-Wesley, 1953.

Schlein, Miriam. *Heavy is a Hippopotamus*. Reading, Mass.: Addison-Wesley, 1954.

Schlein, Miriam. *Shapes*. Reading, Mass.: Addison-Wesley, 1952.

Shaw, Charles G. *It Looked Like Spilt Milk*. New York: Harper and Row, 1947.

Shulevitz, Uri. *Dawn*. New York: Farrar, Strauss & Giroux, 1974.

Spier, Peter. *Fast-Slow, High-Low*. New York: Doubleday, 1972.

Tresselt, Alvin. *The Hide and Seek Fog*. New York: Lothrop, Lee & Shephard, 1966.

Zolotow, Charlotte. *Over and Over, Big and Little, A Big Golden Book*. New York: Harper and Row, 1957.

Physical Knowledge

Alexander, Anne. *ABC of Cars and Trucks*. New York: Doubleday, 1971.

Alexander, Martha. *I'll Protect You From the Jungle Beasts*. New York: Dial Press, 1973.

Alexander, Martha. *No Ducks in Our Bathtub*. New York: Dial Press, 1973.

Brown, Margaret Wise. *Country Noisy Book*. New York: Harper and Row, 1940.

Brown, Margaret Wise. *The Dead Bird*. Reading, Mass.: Addison-Wesley, 1958.

Burningham, John. *Borka; The Adventures of a Goose With No Feathers*. New York: Random House, 1964.

Burningham, John. *Seasons*. New York: Bobbs-Merrill, 1970.

Burton, Virginia Lee. *Choo, Choo, the Runaway Engine*. New York: Scholastic, 1971.

Burton, Virginia Lee. *The Little House*. Boston: Houghton-Mifflin, 1969.

Carle, Eric. *The Very Hungry Caterpillar*. Cleveland: Collins, 1970.

De Paola, Tomie. *Charlie Needs a Cloak*. Englewood Cliffs, N.J.: Prentice-Hall, 1973.

De Regniers, Beatrice. *It Does Not Say Meow*. New York: Seabury Press, 1972.

Duvoisin, Roger. *Two Lonely Ducks*. New York: Alfred A. Knopf, 1955.

Ets, Marie Hall. *Gilberto and the Wind*. New York: Viking, 1963.

Ets, Marie Hall. *Play with Me*. New York: Viking, 1955.

Fisher, Aileen. *Listen Rabbit*. New York: Thomas Y. Crowell, 1964.

Flack, Marjorie. *Angus and the Cat*. New York: Doubleday, 1971.

Flack, Marjorie. *Ask Mr. Bear*. New York: MacMillan, 1971.

Flack, Marjorie. *Time Tadpole and the Great Bullfrog*. New York: Doubleday, 1959.

Francoise. *Springtime for Jeanne-Marie*. New York: Scribner's, 1965.

Freeman, Don. *Dandelion*. New York: Viking, 1964.

Freeman, Mae B. and Freeman, Ira M. *You Will Go to the Moon*. New York: Random House, 1971.

Freschet, Bernice. *The Web in the Grass*. New York: Scribner's, 1972.

Friskey, Margaret. *Seven Diving Ducks*. Chicago: Childrens' Press, 1965.

Gag, Wanda. *Millions of Cats*. New York: Coward, McCann & Geoghegan, 1938.

Galdone, Paul. *The Little Red Hen*. New York: Seabury Press, 1973.

Garelick, May. *Where Does the Butterfly Go When It Rains?* Reading, Mass.: Addison-Wesley, 1961.

Graham, Margaret Bloy. *Be Nice to Spiders*. New York: Harper and Row, 1967.

Gramatky, Hardy. *Little Toot*. New York: Putnam's, 1939.

Hazen, Barbara. *Where Do Bears Sleep?* Reading, Mass.: Addison-Wesley, 1970.

Hutchins, Pat. *The Wind Blew*. New York: MacMillan, 1974.

Hyman, Robin and Hyman, Inge. *Run Run Chase the Sun*. London: Evans Bros., 1969.

Keats, Ezra Jack. *Hi Cat!* New York: MacMillan, 1970.

Keats, Ezra Jack. *A Letter to Amy*. New York: Harper and Row, 1968.

Keats, Ezra Jack. *Over in the Meadow*. New York: Four Winds, 1971.

Keats, Erza Jack. *Skates*. New York: Franklin Watts, 1973.

Keats, Ezra Jack. *The Snowy Day*. New York: Viking, 1962.

Keats, Erza Jack. *Whistle for Willie*. Harmondsworth: Penguin, 1977.

Kellogg, Steven. *Can I Keep Him?* New York: Dial Press, 1971.

Krauss, Ruth. *Bears*. New York: Harper and Row, 1948.

Krauss, Ruth. *The Growing Story*. New York: Harper and Row, 1947.

Kuskin, Karla. *The Bear Who Saw the Spring*. New York: Harper and Row, 1961.

Langstaff, John. *Oh, A-Hunting We Will Go*. New York: Atheneum, 1974.

Lewis, Richard. *In a Spring Garden*. New York: Dial Press, 1976.

Lionni, Leo. *Inch by Inch*. New York: Astor-Honor, 1962.

Lionni, Leo. *Swimmy*. New York: Pantheon, 1963.

McCloskey, Robert. *Blueberries for Sal*. New York: Viking, 1948.

McCloskey, Robert. *Make Way for Ducklings*. New York: Viking, 1969.

McCloskey, Robert. *One Morning in Maine*. New York: Viking, 1952.

Miller, Edna. *Mousekin Finds a Friend*. Englewood Cliffs, N.J.: Prentice-Hall, 1967.

Miller, Edna. *Mousekin's Woodland Sleepers*. Englewood Cliffs, N.J.: Prentice-Hall, 1970.

Petersham, Maud and Petersham, Miska. *The Box with Red Wheels*. New York: MacMillan, 1973.

Provenson, Alice and Provenson, Martin. *Our Animal Friends at Maple Hill Farm*. New York: Random House, 1974.

Piper, Watty. *The Little Engine That Could*. New York: Platt & Munk, 1954.

Raskin, Ellen. *Who Said Sue, Said Whoo?* New York: Atheneum, 1973.

Rojankovsky, Feodor. *Animals in the Zoo*. New York: Alfred A. Knopf, 1962.

Rojankovsky, Feodor. *Animals on the Farm*. New York: Alfred A. Knopf, 1967.

Rojankovsky, Feodor. *The Great Big Animal Book*. New York: Golden Press, 1976.

Scheer, Julian. *Rain Makes Applesauce*. New York: Holiday House, 1964.

Schick, Eleanor. *City in the Summer*. New York: MacMillan, 1969.

Schlein, Miriam. *Heavy is a Hippopotamus*. Reading Mass.: Addison-Wesley, 1954.

Selsam, Millicent. *All About Eggs*. Reading Mass.: Addison-Wesley, 1952.

Selsam, Millicent. *How the Animals Eat*. New York: E. M. Yale, 1955.

Selsam, Millicent. *Seeds and More Seeds*. New York: Harper and Row, 1959.

Selsam, Millicent. *Terry and the Caterpillars*. New York: Harper and Row, 1962.

Shaw, Charles. G. *It Looked Like Spilt Milk*. New York: Harper and Row, 1947.

Shulevitz, Uri. *Rain Rain Rivers*. New York: Farrar, Strauss & Giroux, 1969.

Tresselt, Alvin. *Beaver Pond*. New York: Lothrop, Lee & Shephard, 1970.

Tresselt, Alvin. *Follow the Wind*. New York: Lothrop, Lee & Shephard, 1950.

Tresselt, Alvin. *The Frog in the Well*. New York: Lothrop, Lee & Shephard, 1958.

Tresselt, Alvin. *Hide and Seek Fog*. New York: Lothrop, Lee & Shephard, 1965.

Tresselt, Alvin. *I Saw the Sea Come In*. New York: Lothrop, Lee & Shephard, 1965.

Tresselt, Alvin. *It's Time Now*. New York: Lothrop, Lee & Shephard, 1969.

Tresselt, Alvin. *The Mitten*. New York: Lothrop, Lee & Shephard, 1964.

Tresselt, Alvin. *Rain, Drop, Splash*. New York: Lothrop, Lee & Shephard, 1965.

Tresselt, Alvin. *Sun Up!* New York: Lothrop, Lee & Shephard, 1949.

Children's Books:
Curriculum Goals

Tresselt, Alvin.   *Under the Trees and Through the Grass*. New York: Lothrop, Lee & Shephard, 1962.
Tresselt, Alvin.   *Wake Up Farm*. New York: Lothrop, Lee & Shephard, 1955.
Tresselt, Alvin.   *White Snow, Bright Snow*. New York: Lothrop, Lee & Shephard, 1947.
Udry, Janice.   *A Tree is Nice*. New York: Harper and Row, 1956.
Welber, Robert.   *The Winter Picnic*. New York: Pantheon Books, 1970.
Wildsmith, Brian.   *Birds by Brian Wildsmith*. London: Oxford Univ. Press, 1980.
Wildsmith, Brian.   *The Circus*. New York: Franklin Watts, 1980.
Wildsmith, Brian.   *Brian Wildsmith's Fishes*. New York: Franklin Watts, 1968.
Williams, Garth.   *The Chicken Book*. New York: Delacorte Press, 1970.
Yashima, Mitsu and Yashima, Taro.   *Momo's Kitten*. New York: Viking, 1961.
Yashimo, Taro.   *Umbrella*. New York: Viking, 1958.
Yolen, Jane.   *The Emperor and the Kite*. Cleveland: Collins, 1967.
Zaffo, George.   *Airplanes and Trucks and Trains, Fire Engines, Boats and Ships, and Buildings and Wrecking Machines*. New York: Grosset & Dunlap, 1968.
Zaffo, George.   *The Big Book of Airplanes*. New York: Grosset & Dunlap, 1966.
Zaffo, George.   *The Great Big Book of Real Fire Engines*. New York: Grosset & Dunlap, 1958.
Zion, Gene.   *All Falling Down*. New York: Harper and Row, 1951.
Zion, Gene.   *Harry by the Sea*. New York: E. M. Hale, 1965.

Social Knowledge

Tresselt, Alvin.   *Hide and Seek Fog*. New York: Lothrop, Lee & Shephard, 1965.

Symbols

Anno, Mitsumasa.   *Anno's Counting Book*. New York: Thomas Y. Crowell, 1977.
De Paola, Tomie.   *Any, That's My Name*. Spokane, Wa., Treehouse, 1973.
Feelings, Muriel.   *Moja Means One: A Swahili Counting Book*. New York: Dial Press, 1976.
Francoise.   *Jeanne-Marie Counts Her Sheep*. New York: Scribner's, 1957.
Hoban, Tana.   *Count and See*. New York: MacMillan, 1972.
Lionni, Leo.   *Inch by Inch*. New York: Astor-Honor, 1962.
Yolen, Jane.   *An Invitation to the Butterfly Ball*. New York: Putnam, 1983.

Thought Processes

De Paola, Tomie.   *Pancakes for Breakfast*. New York: Harcourt Bruce Jovanovich, 1978.
Flack, Marjorie.   *Ask Mr. Bear*. New York: MacMillan, 1971.
Galdone, Paul.   *The Little Red Hen*. New York: Seabury Press, 1973.
Ginsburg, Mirra.   *Mushroom in the Rain*. New York: MacMillan, 1974.
Hoban, Tana.   *Look Again*. New York: MacMillan, 1971.
Hoban, Tana.   *Take Another Look*. New York: Greenwillow, 1981.
Hutchins, Pat.   *Happy Birthday, Sam*. New York: Greenwillow, 1978.
Hutchins, Pat.   *Rosie's Walk*. New York: MacMillan, 1968.
Lionni, Leo.   *Frederick*. New York: Pantheon, 1967.
Wildsmith, Brian.   *The Lazy Bear*. New York: Franklin Watts, 1974.
Williams, Garth.   *The Chicken Book*. New York: Delacorte Press, 1946.
Zolotow, Charlotte.   *Mr. Rabbit and the Lovely Present*. New York: Harper and Row, 1962.

Bibliography

The following is a sample list of some of the available professional references.

Anderson, Valerie. *Field Tripping.* Toronto: O.I.S.E. Press, 1980

Andress, Barbara. *Music Experiences in Early Childhood.* New York: Holt, Rinehart & Winston, 1980.

Baretta, Lorton M. *Mathematics . . . Their Way.* Reading, Mass.: Addison-Wesley, 1976.

Beall, Pamela Conn and Nipp, Susan Hagen. *We Sing and Play.* Los Angeles: Price Stern Sloan, 1981.

Bettelheim, Bruno. *The Uses of Enchantment: The Meaning and Importance of Fairy Tales.* New York: Random House, 1976.

Brown, Sam, ed. *Bubbles, Rainbows and Worms: Science Experiments for Preschool Children.* Mt. Ranier, Md.: Gryphon House, 1981.

Brown, Sam, ed. *One, Two Buckle My Shoe: Math Activities for Young Children.* Mt. Ranier, Md.: Gryphon House, 1982.

Bullock, Allan. *A Language for Life.* London: H.M.S.O., 1975.

Burton, Leon and Hughes, William. *Music Play.* Reading, Mass.: Addison-Wesley, 1979.

Burton, Leon and Kuroda, Kathy. *Arts Play.* Reading, Mass.: Addison-Wesley, 1981.

Brittain, Lambert W. *Creativity, Art and the Young Child.* New York: MacMillan, 1979.

Carson, Rachael L. *The Sense of Wonder.* New York: Harper and Row, 1956.

Cazden, C. B. *Language in Early Childhood Education.* Washington: The National Association for the Education of Young Children. 1981.

Cherry, Clare; Harkness, Barbara and Kuzma, Kay. *Nursery School Day Care Centre Management Guide.* n.p.: Pitman Learning, 1978.

Clay, M. M. *What Did I Write?* Chelmsford, Mass.: Heienemann Educational, 1981.

Copple, C.; Sigel, I. E. and Saunders, R. *Educating the Young Thinker: Classroom Strategies for Cognitive Growth.* New York: Van Nostrand, 1979.

Cozden, C. *Child Language and Education.* New York: Holt, Rinehart & Winston, 1972.

Croft, Doreen J. and Hess, Robert D. *An Activities Handbook for Teachers of Young Children.* 2nd ed. Boston: Houghton-Mifflin, 1975.

Currie, M. and Foster, L. *Play's the Thing.* London: MacDonald Educational, 1975.

Debelak, Marianne. *Creating Innovative Classroom Materials for Teaching Young Children.* New York: Harcourt Brace Jovanovich, 1981.

DeBono, Edward. *Children Solve Problems.* Harmondsworth: Penguin Educational, 1972.

DeBono, Edward: "The Direct Teaching of Thinking As a Skill." *Phi Delta Kappan* (June 1983).

Deford, D. E. "Young Children and Their Writing." *Theory Into Practice* (Summer 1980).

Doake, D. "Book Experience and Emergent Reading Behavior." A Paper Presented at the International Reading Association's Annual Convention. Atlanta: Pre-Convention Institute. Part I — Research in Written Language Development, April 23–26, 1979.

Eden, Susanne. *Early Experiences.* Scarborough, Ont.: Nelson, 1983.

Elkins, Dove Peretz. *Glad to Be Me: Building Self-Esteem in Yourself and Others.* Englewood Cliffs, N.J.: Prentice-Hall, 1976.

Engstrom, G. *The Significance of the Young Child's Motor Development.* Washington: National Association for the Education of Young Children, 1971.

Engstrom, G. *Play: The Child Strives Toward Self-Realization.* Washington: The National Association for the Education of Young Children, 1971.

Ferriero, E. and Teberosky, A. *Literacy Before Schooling.* London: Heinemann Educational, 1983.

Flemming, B. M.; Hamilton, D. S. and Hicks, J. D. *Resources for Creative Teaching in Early Childhood Education.* New York: Harcourt Brace Jovanovich, 1977.

Fowler, John S. *Movement in Education.* Philidelphia: Saunders, 1981.

Frank, Marjorie. *I Can Make a Rainbow.* Nashville: Incentive Publications, 1976.

Gallahue, David. *Developmental Movement Experiences for Young Children.* New York: Wiley, 1982.

Garritson, Jane Schmalholz. *Child Arts: Integrating Curriculum Through the Arts.* Reading, Mass.: Addison-Wesley, 1979.

Gentile, Lance M. and Hoot, James L. "Kindergarten Play: The Foundation of Reading." *The Reading Teacher* (January 1983).

Goodwin, Mary T. and Pollen, Gerry. *Creative Food Experiences for Children.* Washington: Centre for Science in the Public Interest, 1974.

Hart, L. A. "Three Brain Concept and the Classroom." *Phi Delta Kappan* (March 1981).

Hart, N. W. M.; Walker, R, J, and Gray, B. *The Language of Children: A Key to Literacy.* Reading, Mass.: Addison-Wesley, 1977.

Hildebrand, Verna. *Guiding Young Children.* 2nd ed. New York: Collier-Mac-Millan, 1980.

Holdaway, D. *The Foundations of Literacy.* Auckland, N.Z.: Ashton Scholastic, 1979.

Holt, Bess and Holt, Gene. *Science with Young Children.* Washington: The National Association for the Education of Young Children, 1977.

Honig, Alice S. *Parent Involvement in Early Childhood Education.* 2nd ed. rev. Washington: National Association for the Education of Young Children, 1979.

Hum, Suzing. *Play and Recreation.* Ottawa: The Canadian Commission International Year of the Child, 1979.

Isenberg, J. and Jacob, E. "Literacy and Symbolic Play: A Review of the Literature." *Childhood Education* (March-April 1983).

Jeffries, D. "Focus On Childhood." *Access* (1977).

Kamii, Constance. "A Sketch of the Piaget — Derived Preschool Curriculum Developed by the Ypsilanti Early Education Program." In J. L. Frost, ed. *Revisiting Early Childhood Education.* New York: Holt, Rinehart & Winston, 1973.

Kamii, Constance. "One Intelligence Indivisible. *Young Children,* 30, 4 (May 1975), pp. 228-38.

Kamii, Constance. "Evaluation of Learning in Preschool Education: Socio-Emotional, Perceptual-Motor, Cognitive Development." In B. S. Bloom, J. T. Hastings, and G. F. Madaus, eds. *Handbook on Formative and Summative Evaluation of Student Learning.* New York: McGraw-Hill, 1971.

Kaplan, Boche. *The Munchy Crunchy Healthy Kid's Snack Book.* New York: Walker, 1976.

Kaplan, Sandra Nina *et al. A Young Child Experiences: Activities for Teaching and Learning.* Palisades, Ca.: Goodyear, 1975.

Kenworthy, L. S. "Accepting the Selves of Others: People Around the World." In *Learning to Live As Neighbors.* Washington: Association for Childhood Education International, 1972.

King, Joyce and Katzman, Carol. *Imagine That! Illustrated Poems & Creative Learning Experiences.* Glenview, Ill.: Scott, Foresman, 1976.

Kirk, S. A. *Educating Exceptional Children.* Boston: Houghton-Mifflin, 1972.

Klein, Marvin L. "Key Generalizations About Language and Children." *Educational Leadership,* 38, 6 (March 1981), pp. 446–48.

Labinowicz, E. *The Piaget Primer: Thinking, Learning, Teaching.* Reading, Mass.: Addison-Wesley, 1980.

Languis, M.; Sanders, T. and Tipps, S. *Brain and Learning: Directions in Early Childhood Education.* Washington: The National Association for the Education of Young Children, 1980.

Lasky, L. and Mukerji, R. *Art: Basic for Young Children.* Washington: The National Association for the Education of Young Children, 1980.

Lavatelli, C. S. *Piaget's Theory Applied to an Early Childhood Curriculum.* Cambridge, Mass.: American Science and Engineering, 1970.

Lay, M. and Dopyyera, T. *Becoming a Teacher of Young Children.* Toronto: D. C. Heath, 1977.

Lowenfeld, Victor and Brittain, W. Lambert. *Creative and Mental Growth.* New York: MacMillan, 1975.

Lucas, M. A. "One Way of Organizing a Centre for Young Children." *Insights,* 8, 3 (November 1975).

Luke, Moira. A presentation on *Movement* made to the Provincial Kindergarten Curriculum Committee In Richmond, February 23, 1982.

Luria, A., R. and la Yodovich, F. *Speech and the Developmental Process in the Child.* Harmondsworth: Penguin Educational, 1971.

Malloch, Jean. *Chime In: Teacher Resource Guide.* Toronto: Doubleday, 1981.

Matterson, Elizabeth. *This Little Puffin.* Harmondsworth: Penguin, 1969.

Melser, J. *The Story Box Teachers' Book.* Auckland, N.Z.: Shortland, 1983.

Meil, A. "The World House: Building a Qualitative Environment for all the World's Children." In *Learning to Live As Neighbors.* Washington: Association for Childhood Education International, 1972.

Milburn, D. "Children in Time and Space." In J. Parsons, G. Milburn, and M. Van Manen, eds. *A Canadian Social Studies.* Edmonton: Univ. of Alberta, 1983.

Moyer, J. E. *Bases for World Understanding and Co-operation.* Alexandria, Va.: Association for Supervision and Curriculum Development, 1970.

Norris, D. and Boucher, J. *Observing Children.* Toronto: Board of Education for the City of Toronto, 1980.

Olson, Willard C. *Child Development.* Toronto: D. C. Heath, 1959.

Orlick, Terry. *Winning Through Cooperation: Competitive Insanity, Cooperative Alternatives.* Washington: Acropolis, 1978.

Parten, M. and Newhall, S. "Social Behaviour of Preshool Children." *Genetic Psychology Monographs* 24 (1941).

Petrich, Patricia and Dalton, Rosemary. *The Kid's Cookbook.* Concord, Ca.: Nitty Gritty Productions, 1973.

Pflaum, S. W. *The Development of Language and Reading in the Young Child.* Columbus, Ohio: Charles E. Merrill, 1974.

Piaget, Jean. *The Psychology of Intelligence.* New York: Harcourt, Brace & World, 1950.

Piaget, Jean. *Play, Dreams and Imitation in Childhood.* New York: Norton, 1951.

Ramsay, P. G. "Multicultural Education in Early Childhood." *Young Children* (January 1982).

Redleaf, Rhoda. *Open the Door, Let's Explore Neighborhood: Field Trips for Children.* St. Paul, Mn.: Resources for Child Caring, 1983.

Richards, R. *Early Experiences.* London: MacDonald Educational, 1972.

Rockwell, Robert E. and Williams, Robert A. *Hug a Tree and Other Things to Do Outdoors with Young Children.* Mt. Rainier, Md.: Gryphon House, 1983.

Scarfe, N. V. "Play Is Education." Presentation given at the O.M.E.P. Congress, Prague, Czechoslovakia, 1956.

Schickendans, Judith. " 'You Be the Doctor and I'll Be Sick': Preschoolers Learn the Language Arts Through Play." *Language Arts* (Sept. 1978).

Sharon, Lois and Bram. *Elephant Jam.* Toronto: McGraw-Hill Ryerson, 1980.

Silvern, Steven B. "Play As an Avenue for Social Growth," *Journal of Research and Development in Education,* 14, 3 (1981).

Sime, M. *A Child's Eye View: Piaget for Young Parents and Teachers.* London: Thames and Hudson, 1973.

Smith, E. B.; Goodman, K. S. and Meredith, R. *Language and Thinking in School.* New York: Holt, Rinehart & Winston, 1970.

Smith, Frank. *Reading Without Nonsense.* New York: Teacher's College Press, 1980.

Spodek, Bernard. *Teaching in the Early Years.* Englewood Cliff, N.J.: Prentice-Hall, 1978.

Sponseller, D. ed. *Play As a Learning Medium.* Washington: The National Association for the Education of Young Children, 1974.

Sprinthall, Richard C. and Sprinthall, Norman A. *Educational Psychology: A Developmental Approach.* 2nd ed. Reading, Mass.: Addison-Wesley, 1977.

Stevens, J. H. "Everyday Experience and Intellectual Development." *Young Children* (November 1981).

Strother, B. D. "Play." *Phi Delta Kappan,* 5, 2 (December, 1982).

Sweeny, Fleurette and Wharram, Margaret. *Experience Games Through Music.* California: Richards Institute of Music, 1973.

Tipps, S. "Play and the Brain: Relations and Reciprocity." *Journal of Research and Development in Education.* 14, 3 (1981).

Thompson, David T. *Easy Woodstuff for Kids.* Mt. Rainier, Md.: Gryphon House, 1981.

Tough, Joan. *Talking and Learning: A Guide to Fostering Communications Skills in Nursery and Infant Schools.* London: Ward Lock Educational, 1977.

Tough, Joan. *Listening to Children Talking: A Guide to the Appraisal of Children's Use of Language.* London: Ward Lock Educational, 1976.

Veitch, Beverly and Harms, Thelma. *Cook and Learn.* Don Mills, Ont.: Addison-Wesley, 1981.

Weikart, D. P. et al. *The Cognitively Oriented Curriculum: A Framework for Pre-School Teachers.* Urbana, Ill.: University of Illinois, 1971.

Weininger, Otto. *Play and Education: The Basic Tool for Early Childhood Learning.* Springfield, Ill.: Thomas, 1979.

Weininger, Otto. "Play: Reality Versus Public Fantasy." *Courier* (April 1978).

Wells, G. *Learning Through Interaction: The Study of Language Development.* Cambridge, Mass.: Cambridge Univ. Press, 1981.

Wettlaufer, George. et al. *Children's World.* New York: Holt, Rinehart & Winston, 1968.

Widmer, E. L. *The Critical Years: Early Childhood Education at the Crossroads.* Toronto: Copp Clark, 1974.

Wolfgang, C. H. and Sanders, T. S. "Defending Young Children's Play as the Ladder to Literacy." *Theory Into Practice,* 20, 2 (Spring, 1981).

Wood, Lucille. *Rhythms to Reading Picture Song Book.* Glendale, Ca.: Bowman Publishing, 1972.

Queen's Printer for British Columbia ©
Victoria, 1985